ENDURING GRIEF

TRUE STORIES OF PERSONAL LOSS

Editors

Florence Selder, PhD, RN, FAAN

Mary Kachoyeanos, EdD, RN; Mary Jo Baisch, MS, RN
Mary Gissler, RN

The Charles Press, Publishers
Philadelphia

The Charles Press, Publishers
Post Office Box 15715
Philadelphia, PA 19103
(215) 545-8933

The publisher acknowledges the cooperation of The American Institute of Life-
Threatening Illness and Loss.

Library of Congress Cataloging-in-Publication Data

Enduring grief: true stories of personal loss / Florence Selder, editor.
        p.   cm.
    ISBN 0-914783-69-6
    1. Nursing — Psychological aspects. 2. Loss (Psychology) — Case
Studies. 3. Bereavement — Psychological aspects — Case Studies
4. Grief — Case Studies.   I. Selder, Florence.
RT86.E53 1995
155.9'37—dc20   95-38130
                                                                      CIP

Printed in the United States of America

ISBN 0-914783-69-6

The publisher would like to thank Jonathan Olsen for his assistance in editing this book.

Dedicated with
love and admiration
to
Lawrence E. Meltzer, MD

Editors

Florence Selder, PhD, RN, FAAN
Professor of Nursing
University of Wisconsin-Milwaukee
Director, Kalyx Counseling Center
Milwaukee, Wisconsin

Mary Kachoyeanos, EdD, RN
Nursing Research Coordinator
Children's Hospital of Wisconsin
Lecturer in Nursing
University of Wisconsin-Milwaukee
Milwaukee, Wisconsin

Mary Jo Baisch, MS, RN
Clinical Assistant Professor of Nursing
University of Wisconsin-Milwaukee
Milwaukee, Wisconsin

Mary Gissler, RN
AIDS Hospice Volunteer
St. Luke's-Roosevelt Hospital
New York, New York

Contents

Preface

Several years ago Bill Kutscher, President of The American Institute of Life-Threatening Illness and Loss in New York City, suggested that I consider writing a book about the loss that nurse clinicians experience as a result of their daily encounters with death and dying. Intrigued with his idea, I gathered together a group of people to discuss various approaches and formats for such a book. When we reviewed the existing literature on loss, we observed that it was primarily discussions of and theories on other people's losses, that there was a significant lack of personal and subjective reports. We therefore decided that our book should be a collection of *personal* stories — first-hand accounts of loss — written by nurses about their own experiences with death and dying. This unique approach, we felt, would offer to the literature a much-needed inside perspective on reactions to loss.

Our plans for the book changed as we compiled it. When we received stories from nurses that included losses *other* than those associated with death, we decided to expand the range of loss topics to include many types of loss. Also, when we observed that in their stories, the nurses not only described their own feelings of loss, but also the feelings and experiences of their co-workers, their patients and their patients' families, it inspired us to include stories by different kinds of people. We felt that this more comprehensive presentation of loss would be an invaluable tool for providing real insight into the many different ways that people react to and cope with loss.

We knew that we had hit upon a novel approach when saw how readers reacted to the stories. Several of the people who were typing the submissions asked if they too could write stories about their own experiences with loss. They told us that reading the stories had caused them to think about their own losses and they believed that through writing, they might be able to more fully understand their emotions. In addition, they hoped that by sharing their stories, they would be able to help others in the same way they had been helped. When we observed the process these typists had gone through, we began to see how truly helpful a book of this kind would be.

We ended up with a wonderful assortment of very moving stories about human loss, most of which are written by nurses, physicians, therapists, psychiatrists, social workers and other types of caregivers about the losses they experienced as a result of working in an environment where loss is an everyday experience, but we also included stories written by other people about other losses. Whether they wrote about personal experiences or about someone else's loss, we were always impressed with the depth of feeling and insight each storyteller offered. Each of us had our own favorite stories that were important to us in one way or another: stories that moved us, that we connected to or that made us think about issues in our own lives. The stories spoke to us on many different and personal levels. Sometimes they caused us to look at things in a new way or to change the way we approached issues in our personal lives or in our work. Sometimes they helped us expand our understanding of the nature of loss and how it affects different people. Every story gave us an inside view of loss and an understanding of how different people deal with it. Everyone who reads these stories will be affected, like we were, in their own way.

We grouped the stories into four general categories, the division of which was determined mainly by what we felt was most significant about the story. The first section concerns the overwhelming but inevitable losses that result from death and dying. Each storyteller writes from a different point of view that is affected by her relation to the deceased and each has her own reactions and methods of coping with her grief. While the stories in this first part are categorized by the event that *caused* the loss, in this case death and dying, the stories in the second section are categorized by how the storyteller *reacted*. These stories are written by people who have not yet or may never recover from the loss they experienced, people who were overcome by loss. Even with the passage of time, these storytellers have been unable to get their lives back on track after a terrible tragedy; their grief has not receded and their loss has become the main focus of their lives. In sharp contrast, the third part is composed of storytellers who were able to find meaning in their loss, who transformed adversity into a positive experience that empowered them both in terms of understanding themselves in a new light and understanding others. The storytellers in this section are survivors in the truest sense of the word and there is much to be learned from them. The fourth and last category concerns losses other than death, such as job termination, divorce, illness, sexual abuse and imprisonment, to name just a few.

Compiling this book has been an extremely daunting task. Not only was the subject of loss and the management of so many first-time storytellers a complex affair, but the issue of death and loss itself presented a special challenge. Sometimes the stories we received triggered our own unresolved losses and this would cause the project to stall. Some of the storytellers who had promised to send us submissions bowed out when they found that writing about their loss was too intense and they couldn't or didn't want to continue the task. Other storytellers reported that even though writing about their loss had been difficult and that it made them sad, they confessed that it had also been very therapeutic. Writing about the loss helped them "work through" their grief — grief that, until now, they had perhaps denied, hidden or had never been able to resolve.

While there is no magic cure for getting over loss, or at least adjusting to it, one surprisingly effective method that has helped many people is talking and listening to others who have experienced a similar incident — the people-help-ing-people dynamic known as the self-help method; in this sense, *Enduring Loss* is a self-help group in the form of a book. While of course there is not the verbal sharing that occurs when people are physically together, this book inspires a similar kind of interaction between reader and writer. The best advice often comes from those who have "been there" and by reading another person's story of loss, readers will be able to discover how others felt and reacted and how they solved their problems and coped — or didn't. In this case, because the storytellers are anonymous, they are completely honest about their feelings and readers can therefore benefit from an uncensored voice. Readers will be able to learn new or alternative ways to approach similar issues that will enable them to help themselves and to help others. Finally, with the companionship of the storytellers, readers will obtain a sense of belonging, reducing the alienation that is typical of severe loss and grief.

People have told stories from the beginning of time and it is through stories that history, legends and life experiences are passed from person to person, century to century. In an age that places emphasis on scientific methods and theories, in an age where people often forget the value of the individual human experience, we have rediscovered the power of storytelling.

Florence Selder, PhD, RN, FAAN

Acknowledgments

Many people have contributed to the completion of this book. Our original group was composed of Debra Mamura Belter, Marcia Van Riper, Joanna Briggs, Pam Schroeder, Connie Guist, Susan Westlake, Mary Gissler and Mary Kachoyeanos.

Dr. Catherine Norris helped us identify many aspects of loss that we had overlooked and we enjoyed her wit and astute comments about our group process. Mary Ann Filo read all of the stories to verify the correct placement within our classification scheme. She offered a unique perspective. Mary Jo Baisch came late to the project, but her efforts were so inspired that it seems as if she was with us from the beginning.

My partner, Dr. Mary Kachoyeanos, was involved in every aspect of this project. Not only was she very sensitive, but her organizational skills were able to propel the project forward when it had stalled. Mary Gissler showed an unfailing commitment to this project by encouraging the storytellers to continue writing until they had a finished piece. Because she works with people who are dying, she was able to keep us aware of the importance of this book at all times.

This book has gone through numerous rewrites. The excellent administrative and secretarial support we received was of enormous help. At times, the stories we received were handwritten and took patience and skill to decipher. First and foremost, Alice Pulka was responsible for managing the production of this manuscript over many hard months. Valerie Jines, Jackie Davidson and Joyce Lewin helped type the manuscript.

Special recognition is given to Dr. Debra Vest for her masterly final editing of the stories. As we found out, it is no easy task to keep the storyteller's voice and at the same time make the words understandable and clear to the reader. Debra untangled many of these problems.

Lastly, we would like to thank all the storytellers for being courageous enough to share their personal stories with us. We learned so much from them as we worked through the manuscript and we continue to learn from them every time we reread their stories.

Florence Selder, RN, PhD, FAAN

Storytellers

Unfortunately, space did not allow us to include all the stories we received, however we would like to thank everyone who shared their losses with us.

Richard Bauman
Connie Blomberg
Margaret Boynton
George R. Braunstein
Forrest Bright
Jeanne Browning
Constance Captain
Meg Christianson
Debbie Crane
Lisa Crook
Val Christell
Karen Davis
Joanna Deeken
Judy Diekmann
Susan Dietz
Cynthia Domer
Georgia Edwards
Mary Bernau Eigen
Cheryl Eskender
Gretchen Farrar-Foley
Emma Felder
William Finn
James Fonk
Susan Fuhrman
Barb Galvan
Gary Gissler
Mary Gissler
Melinda Gissler
Karen Green-Tarney

Cherie Greek
William Gribble
Connie Guist
Fredric Hartman
Joan Heimler
Mary Kay Jiricka
Mary Kachoyeanos
Karen Kaufmann-Rauen
Judy Kite
Janet Kraegel
Elizabeth Kraniak
Julee Kutil
Adrian Lomax
Madeline Kelly Lubar
Thomas Maclean
Eunice Madsen
Patti Marchant
Linda Marker
Roberta McCanse
Margaret Meagher
Bonnie Miller
David Neil
Lois Nelson
Susan Nuccio
Judyann Olson
Mary Puetzer
Patricia Quinn-Casper
Thomas J. Radlet
Ruth Redman

Pam Reynolds
Roxanne Reynolds-Lair
Thelma Riederer
Ronald Rizer
Rosemary Rizer
Chris Schaefer
Sandy Schmidt
Marilyn Schnettler
Robyn Shapiro
Raphella Sohier
Jean Speer
Vickie Stangel
Shebby Sueppie
Geraldine Talarczyk
Brenda Thigpen-Seals
Dot Trottier
Marcia Van Riper
Jane Wall
Rebecca Wassem
Lila Walters
Jackie White
Joan Wilk
Marcia Williams
Lindy Woodard
Lugene Wyland
Mary Ellen Yahle
Rachel Zachariah
Kenneth W. Ziebel
Cecelia Petrack Zorn

LOSS FROM DEATH

The Complexities of
Maintaining Hope

Rebecca was only 45 when she was diagnosed with melanoma of the right breast with axillary metastasis. She underwent a modified radical mastectomy and then radiation therapy. She did quite well for two years and then she developed a malignancy (fibrosarcoma) of the clavicle. She began radiation therapy and chemotherapy simultaneously. Rebecca had a particularly difficult time with the radiation therapy. Her skin broke down and she developed a severe and painful skin infection which markedly reduced her ability to use one of her arms. She also had bad side effects from the chemotherapy. The treatments did not help and within nine months she developed liver metastasis and died later that year. I was the social worker who counseled Rebecca during the terminal phase of her illness.

Rebecca was married and had two sons in their twenties and a daughter in college. At the time of her illness only the youngest son still lived at home. This family did not appear to have a good communication system, nor were they particularly supportive of Rebecca. The most support came from her youngest son. Even though it was difficult and painful for her, Rebecca would frequently drive herself to the hospital for treatment. Her family couldn't even be bothered to accompany her.

Rebecca's radiation therapist spent quite a lot of time with her during treatments and they became extremely fond of each other. When it became evident that Rebecca was entering a terminal phase, the radiation therapist referred her to the counseling department where I was assigned her case. The radiation therapist felt he had done a good job of counseling her until that point, but did not know how to proceed now that she was terminal.

Rebecca realized that she wasn't getting better but no one had told her directly how serious her illness was or that she was dying. Staff seemed to be giving her mixed messages about the severity and course of her disease. After completing the radiation therapy, the therapist continued to see her for regular check-ups, symptom management and pain control. By the time she was referred to me she could not get to her appointments without assistance, so her husband began to drive her. It was the first time he had done this. He appeared uneasy in a hospital setting and did not want to discuss her condition.

On one afternoon Rebecca seemed even more depressed than usual and asked the radiation therapist directly if there was really anything more he could do for her. The radiation therapist was afraid to dash her hopes and answered that the only possible way to help her condition might be radical surgery—the removal of her arm and shoulder. Rebecca was appalled by this suggestion and immediately rejected it. She said that she would rather die than live like that, that losing a breast had been bad enough. Her husband quickly interjected that Rebecca's father had had his leg amputated due to a diabetic problem and that he had lived for 10 years afterward without much trouble. Rebecca said that she was not the same as her father and would not consider this radical surgery.

After Rebecca left, I spoke with the radiation therapist and told him I was surprised that he had suggested the surgery to Rebecca. He said that she couldn't even have the surgery, that her disease was too far along for this procedure to even be considered, but that he had mentioned it to help her maintain hope. He wanted her to feel that there was an additional course of treatment open and that the staff hadn't given up on her. It was apparent that he was very fond of Rebecca and felt frustrated that nothing he could do would save her. Because she had been struggling with depression, he didn't want to tell her directly that they had exhausted all medical options. I thought that Rebecca realized the seriousness of her situation and was asking for clarification and continued support, not treatment. The radiation therapist disagreed with me.

At the next visit, I had the opportunity to see Rebecca alone. She said she was feeling more and more depressed because she wasn't improving. And she was getting weaker. Her family, especially her husband, had been pressuring her to have the radical surgery and when she refused, accused her of "not wanting to get better." She related that her husband was quite religious, and that he saw her illness as a "punishment." Rebecca told me that after her mastectomy, her husband had told her that he no longer found her physically desirable. Since then she said they had had very poor communication and that her husband was certainly unable to give her support. Her son did his best but it was very difficult for him. Rebecca was still confused about the status of her condition and indicated that she was willing to accept any treatment other than the surgery.

Despite her deteriorating condition, Rebecca continued to receive aggressive chemotherapy. The fact that doctors continued to order these treatments led her to believe that she still had a chance of getting better. Different doctors told her different things about the extent of her liver metastasis. Everyone seemed to be trying to help her maintain hope that she could get better when the real truth was that she was dying. No one was helping her come to terms with the illness and her impending death. Her husband continued to focus on Rebecca's refusal of the radical surgery and that caused further alienation. I asked the radiation therapist to speak with Rebecca's husband to tell him that that option was no longer viable, but the opportunity never presented itself.

Rebecca's son was to get married in two weeks and Rebecca planned to attend the wedding. When she appeared for a check-up in radiation therapy, she was very debilitated. The doctor suggested that she come into the hospital for several days for hyperalimentation (intravenous nutrition). During that time, radiation therapy for palliation purposes (to relieve symptoms) was started.

When I went to see her, she said, "Have you come to tell me something?" as if she knew she was dying and anticipated being told. When I replied that I had nothing to tell her, that I had just come to visit, she asked, "Is this the end of the line?" I said I didn't know for sure and asked her what she thought. She responded, "I think it is." I told her that made me very sad and that we would do all we could to make her comfortable. Her sisters (who had accompanied her to the hospital and were in the room) told her she shouldn't give up. But Rebecca said it was no use, that she couldn't go on. She died three days later.

Discussion

Many of the staff members liked Rebecca. She was younger than most of their other clients and she was a fighter. Because of this, it was very hard for the staff to stop trying to help her. As a result, aggressive therapy continued longer than normal and the staff tried to maintain Rebecca's hope and encouraged her to fight. Although the staff was only trying to help, Rebecca's best interest was not really served.

The problems between Rebecca and her husband were longstanding and had been exacerbated by her illness. He had difficulty supporting her through the treatment, and tended to give a religious interpretation to her problems. The suggestion of radical surgery contributed to, or at least became part of, the continuing difficulties for the family.

I believe that the suggestion of radical surgery and the continuation of aggressive chemotherapy until shortly before the end were strategies the staff used to avoid facing Rebecca's death. The physicians cared deeply for this patient and were unable to tell her directly that all avenues had been exhausted and that she was going to die. In the staff's attempt to maintain Rebecca's hope, they unknowingly contributed to the family's confusion and problems. A more honest approach would have been much more helpful for Rebecca and her family.

In retrospect, several things were apparent. First, a referral for counseling after Rebecca's mastectomy would have improved her self-image and decreased her feelings of rejection. While the radiation therapist felt his intervention was sufficient, many problems were not addressed. Better communication among team members about the management of Rebecca's case would have helped. The staff's efforts to maintain hope became part of the problem. A more honest response to Rebecca's questions and the assurance of continued support and care until her death might have been the kinder course.

Helping a Patient Die

I was sitting in my office late one afternoon talking with my colleagues—clinical nurse specialists—when I received a page from a coronary care unit staff nurse. The nurse on the telephone said, "We have a patient with ALS [amyotrophic lateral sclerosis] and he's on a respirator. He was admitted to our unit on Wednesday because the respiratory care unit was full."

I wondered what course of events had led to this patient's intubation and dependency on a respirator. The odds that he would ever be discharged from the hospital were not good. ALS (Lou Gehrig's disease) causes progressive loss of strength and muscle control. Muscles of the arms, legs and trunk become shrunken and thinned. When the muscles needed for chewing, swallowing, talking and breathing become affected, a patient's chance of survival is slim. The cause of ALS is unknown and there is still no specific treatment known to modify the course of the disease.

Mrs. Austin had cared for her husband at home over the previous eight months, during which time he had rapidly deteriorated. He was wheelchair-bound one month after he was diagnosed with ALS and at the time of his hospital admission, he was quadriplegic. His arm and leg muscles were limp, but he could turn his head and neck and had control of his facial muscles.

Just prior to his admission, Mr. Austin's breathing had become more and more labored. He was admitted to the hospital through the emergency room because his ability to breathe had become extremely difficult. In the emergency room, he became breathless and unresponsive. Because of these emergency conditions, Mr. Austin was intubated and placed on a respirator.

I introduced myself to Mrs. Austin. Because her husband was finally resting, she felt comfortable leaving his bedside. Mrs. Austin stated that her major concern was her husband's physical comfort. She also wanted to find some way to lessen the frustration he felt because of his inability to communicate effectively. She told me that he didn't want to come to the hospital because he was afraid that he'd never leave.

I can't really say why, but I did not explore with Mrs. Austin her statement about her husband not leaving the hospital. Instead, I asked her to tell me what she had done at home to make her husband more comfortable. I shared her comfort measures with the nurses so that these could be carried over while Mr. Austin was in the hospital.

Mr. Austin communicated by mouthing words and through eye contact. Of course, this system was only as efficient as was the recipient's ability to decipher it. Right away, I placed a phone call to a speech therapist to find a better communication technique. I had a feeling that Mr. Austin would soon need to communicate some major decisions about his treatment. I also left some professional literature about ALS for the nursing staff to read, because Mr. Austin was not a typical coronary intensive care patient. That night I thought a lot about Mr. Austin. He was young and he had a wife and children. I also thought about the downhill course of his disease and his inability to breathe without the respirator.

I began Friday morning by looking for Mrs. Austin. Her husband had been moved to the respiratory intensive care unit. "How soon before the doctor knows if my husband's respiratory infection will improve?" she asked. I thought to myself, surely she can't believe her husband's breathing problems are due to an infection!

"Have you considered the possibility that your husband's difficulty breathing may be due to a worsening of his ALS?" I asked her. I then asked Mr. Austin's physician to talk to Mrs. Austin.

By mid morning, the doctor had spoken with both Mr. and Mrs. Austin. The doctor confirmed that the past two days' unsuccessful attempts to wean Mr. Austin from the respirator had not been successful. The ALS had taken its toll on his respiratory muscles and Mr. Austin would be dependent on the respirator for the remainder of his life. Mr. and Mrs. Austin spent time alone to discuss this poor prognosis. Mr. Austin communicated with his wife by making eye movements to indicate on an alphabet board the letter of a word he wanted to spell. Letter by letter, Mr. Austin spelled key words to communicate his thoughts.

Mrs. Austin willingly accepted my invitation to have lunch. After we were seated she nervously raised the question of how to tell her 10-year-old daughter about her father's decision not to be kept alive by a respirator. I asked Mrs. Austin the extent of the children's knowledge about their father's illness and if she and her husband had talked with them about the decisions they would face if the ALS compromised his breathing.

Mrs. Austin said, "Our 18-year-old has had the most difficulty dealing with his dad's failing health. He sometimes cries himself to sleep at night. Yet he also has attempted to help with his little sister and be strong for me. He talks about dropping out of college and going to work full time to provide for us, but his dad and I want him to stay in school.

"And our daughter, well, she knows her dad is very ill, but neither my husband nor I have told her about the possibility of his death. She hasn't been showing any signs of worry; she's doing well in school and has no problems with us at home.

"As for me and my husband, the doctor who diagnosed the ALS told us from the beginning that my husband's chances were not good. My husband and I have discussed the possibility of his needing a respirator and he always said that he never wanted to live that way. The ALS has progressed so rapidly in just eight months...."

I encouraged Mrs. Austin to continue talking to me about her feelings, to discuss the impact of her husband's illness on herself, the children and her husband. We talked about her husband's impending death. Mrs. Austin reminisced about the years before her husband was ill and told me about his life. I did not ask her to tell me how the decision was made to put her husband on a respirator that last day in the emergency room. Maybe, I thought, she had given her consent to the procedure instinctively when her husband's life was threatened.

Early Friday afternoon Mr. Austin told his family that he wanted to be taken off the respirator and that he wanted to die at home. Then he requested to speak to a priest who was a long-time friend.

Mr. Austin's doctor made numerous phone calls to legal authorities as well as administrative and medical personnel about the legalities of granting Mr. Austin's wish to be taken off the respirator and go home to die. It was suggested that Mr. Austin's wishes regarding the use of life support be specified in a living will. Since Mr. Austin was not really dying, his case presented some ethical issues, so consultation was sought from the bioethics committee of the hospital. Mr. Austin's respiratory status was so compromised that there was no possibility of removing the respirator in the hospital and sending him home; he would not live long enough to get home. If Mr. Austin went home with the respirator, who would remove it? Throughout the afternoon, Mr. Austin's doctor continued to communicate with Mr. Austin about the legal dilemmas he was encountering. The final decision was that it would not be possible to help Mr. Austin return home to die.

Even though he could appreciate the legal complications of his desire to die at home, Mr. Austin was becoming frustrated. He then said that he would stay in the hospital to die, but that he also wanted the respirator stopped as soon as possible. Mr. Austin refused his nurse's offer to be moved to a different hospital room which would be more home-like.

Mr. Austin's doctor made him a "No Code 4" patient, meaning that he would receive no cardiopulmonary resuscitation or life support medications. Mr. Austin and his family were told which medications he would receive to keep him comfortable upon removal of the respirator and endotracheal tube. Mr. Austin kept mouthing the words "thank you."

Early Friday evening, Mr. Austin was surrounded by his wife, son, daughter, brother, sister-in-law and 10 other close relatives. His nurse, his doctor, the unit chaplain and I also gathered nearby. His elated mood indicated that he felt in control and at peace. The respirator and endotracheal tube were removed and he died quietly about half an hour later, in the arms of his wife, his son and his daughter.

I thought a lot about Mr. Austin and his family over the next several months. Every now and then memories of my short but intense interactions with the Austin family still re-enter my mind.

Discussion

Although Mr. Austin and his wife had previously discussed his desire not to be put on a respirator, this case illustrates how difficult it can be to follow through on such a decision. Mrs. Austin was required to make a decision about this on her own when her husband was initially admitted. That Mrs. Austin clung to a differential diagnosis of a respiratory infection implies that it was hard for her to face the reality that her husband had reached a terminal level.

Not all of the caregivers in the intensive care unit were in agreement with Mr. Austin's request to have the respiratory support discontinued and to die at home, but Mr. Austin was fortunate to have a caring doctor who bothered to find a way to carry out his request to die.

I personally supported Mr. Austin's decision to have respiratory support discontinued. Therefore I feel comfortable about having helped his family deal with his decision to die sooner than he may have had he stayed on the respirator. When I look back, however, I realize that at the time, I was not completely sure about the ethics of helping someone die. Perhaps this is why I continue to think about this case.

Knowing Helps:
Death in a Family Setting

Mac Coleman was a 56-year-old man who was dying of pancreatic cancer. He and his family were referred to a hospice for nursing care following the exacerbation of the disease and his hospitalization for pain control. The physician told Mac's family that because all curative medical therapy had failed he now had less than two months to live.

The hospice nurse visited Mac in the hospital the day he was discharged. She introduced herself to him, to his 71-year-old mother, Luanne, and to Mac's three younger brothers and began to explain the nature of hospice care. Luanne hurriedly whispered to the nurse that Mac did not know that he was dying and was not to be told. The nurse had been granted permission to care for Mac only if she would not discuss Mac's terminal illness with him. She agreed not to mention it again.

That evening, following Mac's discharge from the hospital, the nurse visited the family at home. She brought a wheelchair with her and Mac immediately wanted to be helped into it. Though it was a very warm summer night, he pushed himself around the neighborhood in that wheelchair, greeting neighbors and friends while the nurse and hospice social worker talked to Luanne and helped set up the "sick room." Luanne appeared to enjoy the visit by the nurse and the social worker and she was pleased to have Mac at home. It was never determined how many people actually lived in this small, two-bedroom home. While the nurse was there she was introduced to two more brothers and a teenaged nephew. Two of Mac's daughters had come to visit from out of town, and there were assorted grandchildren and great-grandchildren running about.

Luanne was clearly the head of the family and intended to care for Mac by herself: "I always care for them when they're sick. I make them well with God's help." She went on to relate that she had been through 21 pregnancies, "not counting miscarriages," and that God had healed her womb each

11

time. "The doctor is amazed because here I am at 70 and I'm just like I was when I was 30."

When the nurse visited two days later, Mac was bedfast with swollen arms and legs, the result of his excessive wheelchair activities. Luanne was cheerfully cooking huge quantities of beans and greens and pork chops, which Mac adamantly refused to eat. The nurse explained the effect of the tumor and pain on Mac's appetite and suggested to Luanne that she offer him smaller amounts of his favorite foods at frequent intervals. Luanne smiled and nodded and continued to cook. During subsequent visits the nurse again made these suggestions to no avail, and Mac eventually refused to eat or even speak to anyone in the family.

"All of my children like this food," said Luanne, and the nurse, having been invited to eat with the family during practically every visit, agreed that it was very good.

As Mac continued to withdraw, Luanne's energy began to wane. Mac required an increasing amount of personal care and Luanne became more and more discouraged. At last she was persuaded to allow other stronger and younger family members to lift Mac from the bed to his chair as well as bathe and dress him. A favorite grandchild was able to feed him small bites of food now and then.

Soon Luanne complained that Mac refused to sleep and that he kept her awake all night long. Forgetting the agreement that Mac not be told he was dying, the nurse said to Mac and Luanne, "Sometimes people who are dying are afraid to sleep because they think they might not wake up." Mac eagerly agreed that this was so. He said that many dying people he had known were afraid to go to sleep. Luanne then realized that Mac knew he was dying. She informed the family of Mac's awareness and they were at last able to grieve together and communicate their mutual sorrow. But despite all of the relief engendered by this new awareness and communication, Luanne continued to insist that God would heal her much-loved oldest son.

As Mac continued to fail, the previously busy and noisy house became still. Even the children whispered when they were in Mac's presence. He lay facing the wall and when sitting in his chair, he refused to look at anyone. Luanne began to administer his pain medication sporadically, saying that he "couldn't possibly be so sick that he needs all that morphine; prayer will serve him better." Later a daughter who had come from out of town to help with Mac's care admitted she had been giving him doses of pain medication "when Mama wasn't looking," and the nurse supported her in this.

The nurse suggested that the family sing together occasionally. This suggestion was greeted with enthusiasm and the nurse often joined the family for an evening of musical and spiritual revival led by a minister with a stirring bass voice. Mac never spoke but he would turn toward the family and on one occasion he smiled as the nurse struggled with an unfamiliar hymn. He also seemed to enjoy it when the nurse took Luanne's blood pressure or checked a grandchild's sore throat.

At last the day came for the nurse to explain the actual physical signs of dying that Mac was beginning to display. Mac had periods of apnea during which he did not breathe for 15 to 20 seconds while he was sleeping. He slept more and more. When awake he was sometimes very agitated, mumbling unusual demands and nonsense words. More often Mac seemed simply not to pay attention to noise, lights or movement, or to any stimulus at all. Following the nurse's frank explanations and her statement that Mac was approaching death, Luanne had begun to implore God to heal her son and she asked her prayer circle to join her in prayer.

Later that same evening the nurse received a phone call from the daughter. "You said to call if there were any changes. Well, Mac just passed."

When she arrived at the home, the nurse asked what had happened. "Jesus appeared to me in a vision and told me to let him go," said Luanne. "So we did and he gave up the ghost. Can't you still feel his presence, nurse?" And the nurse said she could. Mac's funeral was a graceful, music-filled event attended by hundreds of family members and friends including several members of the hospice staff.

Luanne occasionally attends bereavement group gatherings held at the hospice for families of patients who have died. The nurse continues to visit the family now and then to sing or to sit quietly on Luanne's front porch, especially on warm summer evenings.

Discussion

Because hospice care is family-based, hospice nurses must be able to assess and support family strengths. This usually begins, as it did with Mac, during the first visit. Abraham Maslow's premise that basic physiological needs must be met before social and emotional needs can be addressed is an intuitive given. Once the family felt confident that basic care could be rendered in the home and that Luanne would be periodically relieved from caring for Mac, then grieving patterns and coping skills were addressed.

Each individual's grief belongs to the family as a whole. Shared acknowledgment of pending and actual loss seems to encourage gradual acceptance by the patient of the inevitability of his own death, though the family's grief may become more and more acute. Sharing anticipatory grief frequently results in a less traumatic bereavement period for the family following the death. Luanne and her family did very well after Mac's death because of their ability to share their grief.

Families must be assured that they will not be abandoned or judged by health care personnel regardless of spiritual beliefs or personal or financial limitations. Luanne's spiritual strength served her and the family well despite her denial of Mac's mortality. Mac's last fling in the wheelchair was probably worth the physical price the nurse knew that he would pay. Had the nurse interfered or warned of dire consequences, she might not have been allowed to provide the support and care the family would need in the future. The nurse's respect for each family member's role helped maintain their congruency and allowed her to become a therapeutic and caring part of the family unit.

Giving Birth to Death

Karen, a 46-year-old housewife and mother of three, gave birth to a stillborn baby 16 years ago. Today she is still in the process of integrating this loss into her life. She called me one morning last week and tearfully recounted a dream she'd had that night about the birth: He didn't have a face, only eyebrows. I was struggling to make out his facial features but everything was blurred. I woke up feeling overwhelmed with sadness. I can't believe, after all this time, I'm still doing my grief work.

Is Karen's experience unusual? There is no definitive answer. Little is known, clinically or empirically, about the long-term effects of experiencing the terrible loss of having a stillborn child. The death of an infant is a special loss, especially right after a mother has spent nine months carrying the infant, feeling its life within her and fantasizing about her child and its future. A mother may feel that she herself has died when she loses her infant. For her, personal rebirth is only possible through successful resolution of the grieving process. However, if the mother fails to grieve (unresolved grieving) or does not grieve adequately (incomplete grieving), the journey to a healthful resolution may be lengthy, if it occurs at all. This is especially true for women who had stillborn infants prior to the death awareness movement in the 1970s—a time when professionals lacked the knowledge and skills to help these mothers with their grieving. These mothers, like Karen, are at higher risk for experiencing delayed grief responses.

This case study describes one woman's quest for resolution of a major loss in her life. The case illustrates several important factors necessary in the successful treatment of unresolved grief: identifying precondition factors, recognizing the problem, doing remedial grief work and, finally, helping the mother find meaning in her loss. If she is able to experience some kind of personal growth in her loss, it will help her to counter the idea that she has given birth to death.

Precondition Factors

Until recently, health care professionals gave little systematic attention to the bereavement needs of the mother and family of a stillborn infant. However, dramatic changes have occurred in the past 10 years. Today we know that people must actively grieve a loss in order to reach some sort of resolution. Strategies to encourage grief work have been identified and put into practice. It is recommended, for example, that parents of a stillborn child view, touch or hold the dead body of their baby. They should name the baby and make arrangements for the funeral and a marked grave site. These measures are directed at transforming the emptiness of a stillbirth into a tangible reality. Recent research findings suggest that when parents create memories of a child, the loss is acknowledged. This acknowledgment facilitates the emotional expression of their grief and, over time, leads to a better resolution of the loss.

Karen was denied this tangibly expressed grieving. At the time of her loss, management of a stillbirth was characterized by denial and secrecy. These measures were intended to spare the mother emotional pain, but they served, in effect, only to reinforce her unexpressed negative thoughts and feelings about herself. Inadvertently, these measures caused Karen's grief work to be delayed. Karen's account of her hospital stay illustrates several factors that contributed to her failure to grieve:

> When I was told my baby was dying, I told myself I would do whatever was necessary to keep my psychological distance from him. That was the only way I could bear it. I wanted general anesthesia at delivery. I didn't want to see the baby, know its sex, or know about the disposition of the body. The physician and my husband allowed me to make these decisions. Indeed, it was my right—but those decisions were neither informed nor wise.
>
> After the delivery, I was put in a private room. The nurses kept my door closed. I guess they didn't want me to be reminded of my loss by hearing other babies crying. I don't remember much of those two days. I asked for sedation, often. I cried when my husband visited: he looked so defeated. We didn't discuss the baby, we both just needed to hold each other. The next day I went home. It was hard for me to believe it had really happened.

Karen's need for psychological distance was achieved: anesthesia and sedation effectively blunted her awareness of the ordeal. Memories of her child were not created. She didn't know the child she conceived; the baby was only a dream unfulfilled. She couldn't grieve the baby she didn't know. The isolation and silence by the hospital staff supported her denial. Clinically, it is known that if we allow mothers to withdraw, we are confirming that their shame and guilt are justified. No one encouraged Karen or her husband to express their sorrow or assisted them in their mourning of the baby who didn't live. The stage was set for Karen to have unresolved grief.

Identifying the Problem

All outward appearances suggested that Karen and her family had survived the tragedy of a stillborn loss. When Karen was still in the hospital, her family removed all reminders of the expected baby. After she returned home, any reference to the baby was tactfully avoided. After a brief recuperation, Karen resumed her household duties. Family life was essentially business-as-usual.

Karen's first symptom of unresolved grief surfaced as a sexual problem. She recalls avoiding sexual relations. "I just never felt aroused. I knew my husband was disappointed, so at times we would make love. But I dreaded it. I could never predict my response; sometimes I'd start crying and spoil everything."

With time, her problem intensified. Karen began to experience pain during coitus, followed by uterine spasms the next day. She consulted her gynecologist. He assured her that nothing was physically wrong. For a time the symptoms abated, only to return about a year later. This cycle of symptoms and absence of symptoms repeated itself. Finally, five years after the stillbirth, her doctor ordered an exploratory laparoscopy. Again, no signs of pathology were detected. Karen's physician recommended psychotherapy. According to Karen, "I was really frightened. Was I going crazy?"

Remedial Grief Work

The task of Karen's therapy, as outlined by her therapist, was to grieve the loss of her baby. This is Karen's recollection of those four months:

> I cried instantly when he discussed grieving. I knew he was right but I was afraid. I didn't want to stir up all the turmoil I'd so carefully suppressed. Part of me wanted to leave well enough alone; the other part of me felt relief. I really yearned to talk about my baby. Also, I needed to find explanations for things that had been happening to me over the years. Things I didn't dare tell anyone: the uncontrollable crying spells, frequent nightmares, unprovoked rages at my husband and a sadness that was always right below the surface. I didn't know myself at times. I remember being at a shopping mall and seeing a mother soothing her crying infant. I wanted to hold that baby. I envied that

mother. Fighting back tears, I rushed to my car so that no one would see me. I sat there sobbing and telling myself how ridiculous I was. Lots of women have lost a baby. Get over it! I wanted to talk about these experiences, but didn't. A worried look from a chosen confidante was enough to silence me.

Karen's case suggests that the conspiracy of silence initiated in the hospital became an established pattern that inhibited her grief work for a long time. Only years later through therapy—in which she was encouraged to experience acute grief and to mourn her dead baby—was she able to break through that silence. In telling and retelling the event, Karen expressed many thoughts, feelings and concerns that she had never before addressed. This catharsis permitted her to acknowledge her loss and examine her feelings about it. Emotionally and intellectually, Karen began to understand and come to terms with her loss. Denial was no longer necessary. According to Karen, "Breaking my silence in therapy was a relief; I felt comforted. But my anger work was hard for me."

Karen, not accustomed to expressing anger, feared she would lose control. With her therapist, she explored this rage and the guilt and depression that invariably followed these episodes. Karen was diagnosed with a pervasive low-level depression that responded to antidepressant medication. Karen took the medication for a year after completing her therapy. Once Karen's individual work was completed, her family entered therapy to deal with the loss of the baby from their perspective. The family decided to have a memorial service for the dead baby so that they could publicly express their grief and so that they could integrate the loss into their lives. Karen and her family had finally given their grief some expression. Their grief work as a family brought them closer together, thereby giving the loss new meaning and importance.

Ongoing Resolution

Karen worked through acute grief and achieved some resolution of her loss. Does this mean Karen was done with her grief work? Some clinicians adamantly hold that grief work is never really completed. It is argued that resolution of a major loss is an ongoing process of healing and growth. Such a resolution may have to be repeated if life's circumstances change and the grief is reactivated. Karen's case lends support to this position.

I became involved in Karen's case four years later when she entered therapy for the second time. Again she manifested somatic symptoms: migraine headaches and mild hypertension. Because thorough medical examination suggested that her symptoms were not organic in origin, an underlying psychological problem was suggested.

Karen admitted to having experienced depression for some time; however, it had not motivated her to seek treatment. This fact underscores how early patterns of responding to grief may set a precedent for a patient's later responses. Karen's inclination to repress negative emotions and to deny problems eventuated in the development of her physical symptoms. Through her second course of therapy Karen was able to recognize this pattern. It was one of several discoveries.

Karen also learned that her anger could be an ally against depression. She finally understood that it was normal to experience grief responses periodically, that these did not mean she was going over to old hurts. Further, she realized that it wasn't pathological to want to talk about her baby; in fact, in the retelling of her story Karen was both honoring the importance of her baby's death and continuing to let go of her grief, which would ensure a more lasting resolution.

From Karen's initial perspective, if she talked about her baby, she was "dwelling on old stuff." Gradually she learned that the need to talk was normal and she learned to talk with someone about her feelings and to look for new meanings for herself. At this point in her life, Karen needed permission to remain open to new levels of understanding about the loss and to her responses to it. During this phase of therapy, Karen made a major decision; she wanted to adopt a baby. One school of thought suggests that a loss is not successfully resolved until it has been replaced. This may have been true for Karen: she seemed to feel a continued void in her life. However, she disagreed that her adoption of a baby was a substitute for her stillborn child. "No one could replace John, but because of him I feel differently about children. I have more to give now and want to invest in a new beginning."

Recently, Karen entered treatment again because of new and anticipated losses in her life. Her father was diagnosed with lung cancer and in the fall her oldest child was going away to college. Karen wanted assistance to work through these pending losses. This time she didn't have physical symptoms or any signs of depression. It was clear that Karen had developed new skills and insight from her earlier losses. She saw grief work as an opportunity for developing increased self-awareness.

Following Karen's latest work on her losses she decided to return to the field of nursing. As might be expected, she chose an area in which her own experience would serve her well—a hospice unit. "I think I've learned a lot about compassion, the importance of the gift of life and letting go in a healthy way."

Discussion

Examination of this case with respect to known risk factors suggests that a delayed grief response was predictable. However, as a therapist I would have expected that Karen's initial grief work would have been sufficient to allay future problems. The resurfacing of her symptoms raises the question of whether this was really a case of unresolved grief (a patient-specific phenomenon) or a normal aspect of ongoing resolution following a significant loss. This case suggests that until more is known about unresolved grief, healing may be facilitated by accepting the premise that it may never be complete and that recurrences can, in fact, trigger growth.

One hopes that Karen's protracted journey to resolution of a major loss will continue. Her case demonstrates that the work of grieving is not to "get over" something and forget. Rather the aim of grieving is to remember and to grow—in other words, to find birth in death.

Living with Dying:
A Young Man Takes Charge

Some young patients can live for many years with a terminal illness. The ways in which adolescents and young adults cope with having a terminal disease are influenced by their level of development, by their families and by the nature and course of their illnesses.

When Edward was 16, he was diagnosed with a cerebellar medulloblastoma (a tumor at the base of the brain). Edward had one sister and he lived with both of his parents. The family was of Japanese descent and their extended family lived in Japan.

Edward and his family were referred to me for counseling and support. I first met them in the neurological intensive care unit where Edward was recovering from a subtotal resection of a cerebellar medulloblastoma. His devoted parents were quietly grieving for their son who seemed to be in the terminal stage of his illness. His mother became the family's spokesperson because she spoke English very well and she was comfortable expressing her feelings. She described Edward as a bright, diligent boy who had worked hard to compensate for a mild congenital paralysis of one side of his body. Prior to his hospitalization, Edward had been achieving academically and was beginning to have some success playing tennis. The family was concerned about what they perceived to be Edward's imminent death and they worried about Edward's response to his diagnosis and treatment plan. Edward's sister, who was two years younger than he, found the situation so threatening that she withdrew from him and became totally involved in her own activities. Soon after his diagnosis, she moved out of the home.

When Edward heard the diagnosis and learned about the plan for cranial radiation treatment, he was concerned for the immediate interruptions in school, tennis and his friendships. Later, Edward became angry but directed it toward the delays and inefficiencies of the complex hospital system. For example, he readily complied with the radiotherapy treatment but railed against the delays and seeming insensitivity of the treating personnel. As he became more dependent on his parents, he became increasingly resentful of his family's attempts to protect and help him. The changes in his physical appearance, including hair and weight loss and an altered gait, were sources of great shame for Edward. Yet even in the face of these changes, Edward insisted that the disease would not return.

Edward completed his course of treatment, resumed his academic work in the fall and became more physically active. He also learned to drive. My contacts with Edward and his family became sporadic during this time. Even though he expressed interest in continuing to work with me as an outpatient, he did not call to schedule appointments. Because counseling cannot be effective without the individual's initiative, I respected Edward's decision.

Edward enrolled in college two years after I first saw him. He moved away from home and became totally involved in school. He was doing well academically and he made friends. He had a splendid semester. Then in December of that year, a massive seizure heralded the return of his tumor.

When I saw him again in the intensive care unit, Edward was sad and very angry. At times, he could not remember certain words and this frustrated him immensely. He mourned his many losses, but held on to the hope of returning to school in the spring. In the end, he was not able to do this, but his parents drove him to school to see his friends and to get an official medical leave of absence.

As a treatment plan was outlined for him, he began quite realistically to alter his plans to include courses at a nearby community college. His driving was curtailed so he began to work with his parents to develop a small business that he could manage from their home. Edward told me that he was concerned about his growing dependency on his parents, that he resented his sister's health and freedom and that he was worried about being able to continue his education, obtaining insurance coverage and establishing financial independence. These problems are very hard for a young man who has reached an age when he would ordinarily be getting ready to plan for his future and becoming financially independent.

Edward was able to resume a reasonably high level of activity in the next two years. He maintained relationships with friends from college, developed his home business and achieved a manageable balance between dependency and independence. While living with his family, Edward was able to maintain some degree of autonomy. My contact with him was sporadic during this time because I saw him only when he chose to see me.

After this two-year period Edward's tumor returned again. He was devastated and spoke sadly of his impending death. He requested regular sessions with me and utilized the time to review his experiences and how he had handled them over the past five years. He spoke of his desire to become more active in the decision-making process regarding his chemotherapy. He was determined to resolve the antagonism between himself and his sister in the time he had left. Indeed, he traveled out of state to meet his sister to begin this process.

Edward, in the face of his grim prognosis, announced that one thing he could control was how he would live during the time he had left. He was determined not to be immobilized by depression, but to live and work as fully as he could.

Edward did just that. During an admission for chemotherapy, he commented that while the side effects were awful, they were preferable to being dead. Eventually, however, he acknowledged the futility of further treatment and decided to stop the chemotherapy. He gave up driving (at the insistence of his physician and his parents) and used a wheelchair to get around outside of his home. Although he often became enormously angry and argumentative with his mother over minor issues, she was able to acknowledge his anger without retaliating or hurting him.

Edward decided that he wanted to remain in his parents' home and die there. His parents respected his wish and made plans to care for him at home. His mother made arrangements to get the equipment they needed and they received help with Edward's care from a local hospice.

Edward participated fully in the decisions about his care and his family fully supported him. He made the decision to continue his chemotherapeutic regimen, believing that the drugs contributed to some stabilization and control of tumor growth and that the treatment was preferable to death. He abhorred his debilitating symptoms and his growing dependency. At age 22 Edward died at home, supported by his mother, father and sister.

Discussion

The recurrence of Edward's tumor reminded us all of our failure to stop the disease that was robbing him of his life. His decision to continue chemotherapy following the final return of the tumor was questioned by the nursing staff. The chemotherapy given to him during a three-day hospital admission was rigorous and caused many severe side effects. The caregiving staff thought Edward should not have to go through this and displaced their anger onto the oncologist, accusing him of "forcing treatment" upon Edward. But Edward's decision to continue chemotherapy and then finally to stop represented his need to control. He took charge of the way he lived during the final months of his life.

Living Life to the End

As a clinical specialist in medical oncology, I encounter hundreds of patients who are in constant crisis, who are dealing with a devastating illness that will probably defeat them. For the majority of my patients, the period following the diagnosis of cancer is the worst and most trying time of their lives. It is a time that taxes their strength, emotions, finances and coping skills, a time of constant struggle, frustration and usually defeat. A few patients, however, possess some inner strength and courage that turns these struggles into moments of challenge and victory. Theresa was one of these patients. Today the record of her years of illness and suffering has been reduced to a few sheets of microfilm, but those of us who witnessed her ordeal remember it in vivid detail. More than that, the memory of Theresa's courage is un-diminished.

Theresa was a short, pudgy, pleasant-looking woman in her late fifties. She was widowed at the age of 27 and was left with two preschool-aged children to raise alone on her factory-work salary. Her children and grandchildren were as loving and devoted to her as she was to them. She also had a long-time boyfriend, Jim, who was her frequent companion.

When Theresa came to the medical center for treatment, she already had metastatic disease. Her primary cancer was an angiosarcoma (a tumor arising from the blood vessels) that was growing in her lungs. There was little to offer her in terms of treatment except chemotherapy which had little effect on her tumor growth and which she did not tolerate well. Each chemotherapy session was an exercise in patient pain and nurse frustration. Because Theresa had poor veins and there were no venous access devices at that time, it was difficult to insert an IV. Her nausea and vomiting were also difficult to control.

Over the two years of her illness, her lung lesions continued to enlarge and Theresa coughed up blood with increasing frequency. Eventually the tumors began erupting all over her skin. They resembled clusters of grapes and had to be surgically removed when they became too large or bled too much. Her chronic blood loss rendered her anemic and she was chronically fatigued. Almost a year prior to her death, her hemoptysis became so constant that the doctors felt obligated to advise her and her family that she might experience a sudden fatal hemorrhage. Blood was a constant reminder of Theresa's cancer.

At first, she did not seem to be an unusual person. She was friendly and cheerful. With each visit, we would discuss her symptoms, problems and possible remedies. Then she would talk of things such as her grandchildren's activities, her planned trip to California with Jim, or Friday night's bingo game. She had never been to California, so that was going to be a big event. They planned to go in the summer when Jim had vacation time, but summer was then eight months away and we all had reservations about whether she would be able to make it. Still, we certainly did not want to deny her the fun of planning.

Bingo games were Theresa's love and a constant source of entertainment for her. She went every Friday. As far as she was concerned, her nausea and vomiting were no reason to miss bingo. "You just have someone watch your game while you go to the bathroom," she told me. When she needed oxygen, she took a portable tank along to the game. When she was too weak to walk, she went in a wheelchair—but she always played bingo.

As the months turned into a year, Theresa's true strength became apparent. She was able to face her limitations and the disappointments that resulted from them without missing a step. When the time finally came for her to go to California, she was too weak. Undaunted, she and Jim went on a shorter trip to Michigan.

Despite her physical limitations, Theresa continued to live her life. She simply altered the way she did things to adjust to her new limitations and she kept her life on course. She made a strong effort to maintain her relationship with her family. In earlier days she had done things for them; as time went by they did things for her; she was always a part of the family.

Theresa died on a Friday evening. She was in the hospital for pain management and removal of more cutaneous metastatic tumors. We all remember the day because she called Jim to come and have supper with her as it had been their custom for many years. She didn't eat much and then around eight o'clock she asked to be put to bed because she was tired. One hour later her respirations became labored and she could not be aroused. Shortly afterwards, she died. There was no hemorrhage, no unusual or different pain—only tiredness and a peaceful sleep.

Discussion

In the seven years since Theresa died, I have often focused on how unusual the circumstances of her death were. We all had the impression that she knew she was going to die that night. At the time there were no symptoms to indicate an acute physical event that would precipitate her death. Though they were probably there, the symptoms were so subtle that to an observer it seemed that Theresa was merely tired and wanted to sleep.

As I review these events to write this story, it has become apparent to me that it really wasn't Theresa's death that was unusual, but the way she lived her life. Theresa's ability to maintain her mental equilibrium despite her physical difficulties was unusual. Most people who are tired and nauseated most of the time withdraw from activities, but not Theresa. She was like a soldier on the battlefield who keeps getting up each time she's wounded. Her ability to endure was exceptional.

Somehow she had learned to accept any adversity, adjust to it, integrate it into her life and continue living the best she could. Had she learned this when her husband died and she was left with two toddlers? Or was it at another point in her life that she mastered this skill?

Theresa conveyed a sense of peacefulness to others. She knew "what she was all about." She accepted the limitations of her life and made the best of whatever she had. Occasionally she would be depressed, sometimes frustrated or sad, but overall she handled most of her problems with equanimity. Theresa is remembered for her courage and endurance and for her mastery of the art of daily living.

Sudden Death in the Emergency Room: How Staff Can Help

As an emergency nurse and a parent, I know that no parent can experience a nightmare more horrible than receiving a call from the police telling her that her child has been in a fatal accident. I have experienced first-hand many of these situations and always find them incredibly heartbreaking. But over the years, I've discovered that there is something that we, as nurses, can do to assist these parents during their darkest hours of grief. That is to allow and even to encourage them to be with their dead child for as long as they need to, regardless of the circumstances of the accident.

I remember when I was a novice in the emergency department and Tom, a man in his early 20s, was brought in DOA (dead on arrival). He had had a car accident and his head had been crushed. Because he was so horribly disfigured, my first instinct was to protect his family by not allowing them to view the body. But other staff members with more experience thought otherwise. They quickly went to work preparing Tom's body for viewing by applying bandages to the gaping wound on his cheek and wrapping the top of his head in towels. Amazingly, in a few minutes he was presentable and his mother was told she could go in to see him. She sat with him for a long time, held his hand, kissed him and talked to him. She asked what was under the bandages and towels, and accepted our answers without apparent distress. When she left, I was so glad we had given her the chance to be with him to say goodbye.

Sudden death is always difficult for loved ones to comprehend. But when a child dies suddenly, it seems so impossible and so horrible that parents can't believe it is true. As parents, we expect our children to outlive us; losing a child goes against the natural order of things. Seeing their dead child is a first step for parents in the necessary process of making the death real and ultimately learning how to accept the loss.

Carol was another patient. She was 22 years old. No one knew she was depressed until the day she shot and killed herself. Because the gun she used made a huge hole in the side of her skull, we used towels to cover her injury. After spending some time with her family, we took them to her. I learned from Carol's mother that parents are somehow not offended by their child's blood. Carol's mother stood there a few minutes wringing her hands and moaning, "My poor baby, my poor baby." And then, with Carol's head cradled against her bosom, she rocked and comforted her for a very long time. It was difficult for the staff to watch. Being able to hold her child for the last time was very important for Carol's mother.

Some parents are not satisfied with only looking at their dead child and want to touch, hold and comfort as well. Parents often appear stricken and bewildered. So total is their involvement with the child that time stands still for them and they are oblivious to their surroundings. A nurse's instinct may be to protect parents from such an extremely intense encounter. Or perhaps it is our own frightening sense of identification with them that scares us. I'm convinced, however, that for the benefit of the parents, we need to overcome our own fears and do whatever we can to help them be with their dead child. Most parents seem to benefit immensely and for this reason, so will we.

Little Mike was the worst. While riding his bike on a warm summer evening, he somehow slid under a bus. His body was perfect, with not a mark on it, but the bus had crushed his head so severely that it was flattened. A horrified police officer brought the brain matter to the hospital separately. We all agreed that Mike's parents simply couldn't see him—we could hardly look at him ourselves and we were nurses. But John, an emergency department technician and the father of three boys, felt differently. He asked us if our child had died, was there any situation in which we wouldn't want to see him and we had to say no. So John did what he could for Mike. He used washcloths to fill out Mike's empty, flattened head and he reshaped his skull as best he could. With almost half of his face and the top of his head covered with gauze bandages, Mike once again looked like a nine-year-old boy. Mike's parents sat with him quietly for hours. They held each other and they touched Mike gently, tenderly. They talked about how he loved his bike and how he was riding on a forbidden street. They reminisced about his birth and his toddling antics. At times, they smiled and almost laughed. Their grief was so deep, so moving, we felt awed by it. Once again we were glad that we hadn't sent the parents home without a chance to be with their child and express their grief.

Tom, Mike, Carol and their parents taught us some powerful lessons. I have never seen parents look at their dead child in horror or disgust. Even though we always tell parents how bad the accident was, including how severely their child was injured, they never seem to be repelled or frightened. They do not focus on the trauma; instead, they see the child they knew. And they need to comfort that child: to touch and hold and be with him for a long time. Hopefully, by allowing parents a final chance to be parents, we lessen the nightmare just a little.

And Now She is Gone

Judy was 16 years old and I was eight when she became my brother Carl's high school sweetheart and a member of our family. Four years later, just three weeks after she finished nursing school, I played "Here Comes the Bride" as she walked down the aisle to become my sister-in-law. Judy recently died after a nine-month battle with leukemia. I mourn for her now, for all the things that would have been, could have been, and might have been. We had 25 years together, and now she is gone.

Judy and I shared not only our family, but also our careers in nursing. Because of our age difference, she was always a few steps up the career ladder from me. She tried to prevent me from making mistakes, but I was not always willing to listen to her. When I was a nursing student, she was a nursing instructor, so sometimes I felt like I had a teacher at home. Later, I entered a graduate program in Community Health Nursing at the same time that Judy was getting her doctorate, a goal she achieved just before her death.

Judy and I also shared the joys of motherhood. Judy's only child, Chris, was born when she was 37. Because I had my children earlier in life, our little ones were about the same age. We shared the joys and the problems of raising children. We both also suffered the loss of miscarriage.

I first knew something was wrong when I called my mother to tell her we were home from our Easter vacation. She said, "Judy has leukemia. I wrote you a letter about everything." The letter came the next day with a pamphlet on adult leukemia. Judy had provided copies for all of us.

I made a call to Judy at the hospital the next evening. She was very tired and weak, but wanted to talk. She said she had to choose a long course of chemotherapy or die within a few days. Because she wanted to see Chris grow up, she chose to have treatment.

During the days that followed she talked to me as a sister-in-law and as a nurse. She talked to me about her fears of dying and admitted she was keeping up a front for most people. She also talked about her colleagues' response to her life-threatening illness. Judy was still in the process of finishing her doctorate and she said that her professor was devastated about her illness. Her life touched many people. So did her illness.

I called Judy after a week and she told me she wanted to keep up her work. She said that when she told her colleagues at the university she wanted a desk, one had been delivered within a few hours. She laughed, "Do you know how hard it is to get something in a university? They not only got me a desk, but they got it moved across town to the hospital." At this time she seemed hopeful and determined to survive. Later, she defended her dissertation in that hospital room and was granted a Doctor of Education degree, although she never lived to use it professionally.

Judy returned home and I made a trip to see her in June. I spent a lot of time with her, and relieved my brother of some of the responsibility for her care. For me, Judy was still the teacher. She was the first patient in the rural area where she lived to have intravenous (IV) medication at home. She taught the home health care nurses how to start the IV medication, and supervised her husband and me as we discontinued it.

That summer her struggle for life went on. She had complications from infections. I saw her again briefly in September and then went for what was to be our last visit in November. By then I was deeply involved in my studies, and I took my books along so we could talk about nursing. Judy enjoyed our talks because she had been away from the university for quite some time, and, even though she had difficulty remembering because of the chemotherapy, she was always very involved in our discussions. At this time she was in remission and improving, and my hope was renewed.

In early December, a blood test indicated that Judy's disease had become exacerbated and she had to go back to the hospital. She decorated the house for Christmas and insisted she would be back in time to celebrate the holiday. I still had hope, and with my family I prepared for a short trip home for Christmas and arrived just as Mother was ready to serve Christmas dinner. Carl needed to eat fast and get to the hospital which was 50 miles away, because Judy was not doing well. He stayed very late that night because he said, "I hate to leave her."

The next day, Judy called and wanted Carl to come as soon as possible. He called the doctor and was told that there really was nothing more to be done for her. Carl and my other brother went to the hospital. Carl called about 5:20 p.m. and said, "She's gone." The next morning we all went to the little church where my family had grown up and Judy had been a Sunday school superintendent.

During this time, I could only think of all the things Judy had wanted to

do and would never get to do. She had wanted to see Chris grow up. She had
wanted to see the students she had recruited for her program learn and
graduate as nurse practitioners. She had wanted to continue in her career
and see nursing move forward. But instead she died. I wanted to share with
her all the things I was learning. I wanted to share what our children were
doing. But now she is gone.

The minister, who had been with Judy so often during her illness, was just
as devastated about her death as the rest of us. Still, his funeral sermon
conveyed a message of hope and happiness. "She is out of pain. She is with
Jesus." The funeral was large. In addition to the pastor's sermon there were
four other speakers. From her family of origin, a nephew's wife spoke. From
her family by marriage, one of my brothers spoke. From the university, the
Dean of Nursing spoke. From the nursing profession, a friend and colleague
spoke. The chapter of the honorary nursing society she helped organize put
a beautiful note and orchid in her casket. I learned a lot more about Judy
that day.

We said our final goodbye at the cemetery. Judy had asked to be buried
in the little country cemetery where most of her husband's family is buried.
The name plate on the vault read, "Dr. Judith Cattron." Most of the
newspapers had refused to use the Dr. designation for her obituary because
they said it was reserved for the medical profession. So on her vault, to be
buried forever, she received recognition for the goal she had worked so hard
to achieve.

Life goes on for Judy's family and friends, but an empty spot will always
remain. When a person dies in the prime of her life, it is hard not continuing
to see all the things she would have done. I know that at each family gathering
we will feel the emptiness without her. As her son Chris celebrates milestones
in his life, we'll think of how Judy wanted to be a part of his growing up. She
left me some of her nursing books and I feel she is with me as I continue my
education and career. Her memory lives on in the many nurses she helped
train and in the many memorials given in her honor. But I can't help feeling
sad for all the things she would have done with her family and with friends
and in nursing if she had lived.

Nan's Choice to Live and Die

Nan was my good friend and my colleague for 10 years. She was a nurse, a diabetic and an epileptic and she died at the young age of 31. She died just as she had lived—defiantly. She worked with other diabetics and taught them how to live with their disease. She also taught the people close to her about living (and dying) with a chronic illness. I was privileged to have shared her life.

The way Nan died mirrored the way she had lived. She was attending a conference in Boston when she was found unconscious at the foot of her hotel bed. She died shortly afterwards. Prior to the conference, friends, family and physicians had been divided about whether it was wise for her to go to a conference so far away from home. She had just been discharged from the hospital for the partial amputation of several necrotic fingers. Nan decided to take the risk and went to the conference, even though her illness was continuing its relentless destruction of her body. I was one of the people who encouraged her to attend. Even though she never came back to us, I was glad to have supported her decision to keep on going. She fought to live as a "normal" person; even though she lost, she died doing what she wanted.

When I saw her for the last time, we both knew that she was dying; however, I never imagined that her death would be only weeks away. Her philosophy on life had been shaped by the fact that she had been living with diabetes ever since she was nine months old. For Nan, a high quality of life meant having control and engaging in satisfying activities. Nan used to say, "A short life where I have control is better than no life at all."

In the years since Nan's death I have often wished that we had talked more about the fact that she was dying. Because we didn't, our friendship feels unfinished. There never seemed to be a good time to discuss the subject with her. Maybe I had more of a need to talk about it than she did.

I also used to want to tell her to take better care of herself. I was angry that I would be losing her; it was a helpless, vulnerable feeling, that scared me. I would have liked to have scared her into living life less recklessly, but Nan was not about to live for other people. She needed to live her life the way she wanted, and if that meant encouraging death, then that's the way it would be.

Nan's life and death affected her friends deeply. Her death made us look at how we lived and how we took care of ourselves. Her life made us examine our own behavior. Nan rarely complained about feeling bad or about her pain and that was a measure of her courage. It seemed absurd that we should complain about our minor physical ailments while she was suffering without a word.

Nan also made us look at the pros and cons of certain kinds of denial as a coping mechanism. She denied her pain and the special needs of her body in an attempt to live life to its fullest. She struggled to rule her disease, to avoid becoming a slave to it. While she had a struggle that we didn't have, like the rest of us there were times when she lived self-destructively. It has been said that people in their twenties do not possess great insight. Like so many others, Nan had not made wise choices. She drank too much—maybe to forget about her diseases, to make them go away for awhile. Actually, at that time we all drank to forget about life's disappointments. It was during those years that Nan became pregnant. Her physicians told her the pregnancy would be very hard on her body, but she chose not to terminate it. Then, two days before she was to have a scheduled cesarean section, her little boy died. We never knew why. He was a beautiful, perfectly formed baby and the autopsy found no reason for his death. His mother would die two years later.

Nan had the courage to make her choices and suffer the consequences quietly. She learned the price of self-destructive behavior and taught us this truth. I also learned that our own sense of indestructibility is a myth. All of us could easily die young. We learned that life was unfair, but one needs to do one's best. There are no acceptable excuses for giving up, or feeling sorry for oneself.

Nan's death also taught me about living with the unknown. I never knew why Nan died. I only knew that the diabetes had finally won, and that she hadn't committed suicide. I never saw her body; it was a closed-casket funeral. During Nan's funeral service, a frightening lightning storm caused the lights to flicker several times, as if God Himself was mourning her passing.

Perhaps because I never saw Nan's body, I had more trouble getting on with my grief than I would have had otherwise. It helped when a granite stone was placed on her grave; it seemed to make her death official for me.

Nan's life was a gift to me. I learned so much about myself through her. As a mental health clinical specialist, my work with chronically ill patients has benefited from the struggle I witnessed in Nan. I've come to understand the nature and freedom of personal choice.

Disney World,
Dolls and Dreams:
A Little Boy's Death at Home

Jimmy was a six-year-old boy who died as a result of acute lymphocytic leukemia. Diagnosed at the age of four, Jimmy's treatment course was difficult from the time of its initiation until his curative treatment was halted in the fall of 1987. At that time, as hospice/home care coordinator, I was asked to meet with Jimmy and his mother, Linda, to describe the supportive care services available to them. My recollection of Jimmy at that first meeting is that of a very tired, pale, bald little boy curled up on his mother's lap.

Jimmy rested with his eyes closed through most of my first meeting with his mother, but he was quite alert and responsive when my questions were directed to him. I asked Jimmy if anything worried him now that his treatment to keep his leukemia under control was no longer working. He looked at me directly and said, "No, I'm going to visit my friend, Matt. I talked to him the other day in my dream and he said he had a special place for me. I told him I would be coming to see him soon." I looked at his mother and then asked Jimmy where Matt lived. He responded quite matter-of-factly, "In heaven."

His mother explained that Matt had been Jimmy's clinic buddy who had died of leukemia just six months before. I asked Jimmy if he wanted to do anything before he went to stay with Matt in heaven. "Yes," he responded, "I want to meet Mickey Mouse." It had been arranged that Jimmy was to meet Mickey that very weekend on a "Make-a-Wish" trip to Disney World.

Jimmy's entire family was supposed to go on the trip despite the fact that Linda and her husband had separated some months earlier. Linda reported that she and her husband had been on "rocky ground" before Jimmy's illness and that the stress of his illness and care had made things between them even worse. After their separation, Linda had the primary responsibility for

Jimmy, his eight-year-old brother J.J. and his four-year-old sister Christie. Linda did not work and was dependent on state funds for financial support.

Linda had to contend with the effect Jimmy's illness had on her other children. During the past year, J.J. had been unable to concentrate or focus his energy and was performing poorly in school. His teacher reported that he "acted out" in class and that he disrupted other students. Christie had become withdrawn and less communicative as Jimmy became more and more ill. She would sob when Jimmy had to go to the hospital for treatments. She had also started to have "accidents" occasionally, even though she had been potty trained two years earlier. Linda felt that these other problems would be resolved when she had the time and energy to deal with them after the trip. In spite of these seemingly overwhelming circumstances, Linda appeared to be quite calm and controlled. Her primary goal was to help Jimmy realize his dream trip to Disney World and then to return home to prepare for his death.

During the time Jimmy and his family were in Florida, I was making arrangements with a local nursing agency for a hospice/home care plan to start after Jimmy's return. On the Saturday before the family's return, I received a frantic phone call from Linda. Jimmy had apparently suffered a significant central nervous system (CNS) bleed during the night and was semi-comatose in a Florida community hospital emergency room. After I spoke with Linda and the Florida hospital's staff, it seemed clear to me that Jimmy's death was close. Linda did not want Jimmy to die so far away from home and requested that Jimmy be given a blood transfusion and other life supports so that he could return to die in the comfort of his own bed.

Eight hours of long-distance calls, arrangements, pleading and bargaining with the hospital administrators, airline reservation agents, ambulance company owners and Jimmy's family finally resulted in his safe transport home on Sunday evening. When I arrived at their home, Linda was sitting with Jimmy in her lap. He was extremely pale and thin, conscious but irritable. Linda was totally exhausted but relieved that they were home. Neighbors had taken Jimmy's siblings so that we could get him settled comfortably in his own bed. We moved Jimmy to the couch and reviewed the previous 24-hour period. Linda repeatedly said, "I can't tell you how happy we are to be home. We'll be OK now. Everything will be OK."

Once Jimmy's waterbed was warmed, we gently placed him on it and removed his shoes. He immediately sighed and drew an enormous breath. Both Linda and I thought he had died at that moment. Instead, he fell into a totally relaxed and comfortable sleep.

Moments later, Linda's friends and key support people arrived. The community home health nurse also arrived and the five of us sat down to discuss a plan of care for Jimmy. We reviewed the possible complications Jimmy might experience—bleeding, seizures, pain—and we developed appropriate interventions for these problems, should they happen. Arrangements for routine home visits and emergency on-call services were also discussed. At the end of the hour-long discussion, Linda seemed calm and controlled again.

In the following week, Jimmy slept most of the time. Occasionally he watched the videos of the family's trip to Disney World with his brother and sister. Linda and her three close friends provided all of Jimmy's care during that week. Jimmy's father telephoned him but did not visit or participate in his care. The hour before Jimmy died, Linda and her friends held him, talked about the good times they had shared with him and watched his favorite "He-Man" video with him. At the end of the video, Linda looked at Jimmy and saw that his face was relaxed into his old familiar smile. She realized that he had died and everyone in the room understood that Jimmy had left their lives.

At the wake, the casket was open. Jimmy had "He-Man" embraced in his arms, but the old familiar smile was gone. J.J. and Christie had drawn pictures that were put inside the pocket of their brother's jacket.

While working with Linda, I became aware of the tremendous inner strength she possessed. Somehow, despite unpredictable circumstances in her life, she was able to maintain a sense of control. My interventions of teaching, counseling and lending support were useful only because I accepted Linda's priorities for Jimmy and the rest of her family.

Discussion

As a health care professional, I do not believe I would have recommended the trip to Disney World because of the risk that Jimmy might die before he returned home. However, as a hospice nurse, I knew the trip represented a sort of closure for Jimmy. If he had died away from home, his family's grief response may have been different—less healthy. By helping Jimmy achieve his wish to go to Disney World and by having him at home for one week before he died, the family had a feeling of satisfaction, accomplishment and control.

Parents who are able to give their dying child something he wants can experience a sense of fulfillment. Parents can feel that their child was able to reach some completion in his life if an effort is made to achieve a certain goal. In Jimmy's case, the Make-a-Wish Foundation enabled him to see Disney World and all the efforts to allow him to die at home enabled him to be supported and cared for in a safe, familiar environment until the very end.

Having Jimmy die at home helped Linda maintain her role as her son's caregiver. The hospice program helped her with the obstacles she faced. Her involvement with her son's care proved to be crucial in her adaptation to and eventual resolution of her loss. Everything possible was done to provide comfort, security and a sense of control for this family. The relinquishment of the parental role as caregiver and protector in an inpatient hospital setting may intensify the grief and loss associated with the death of a child. I have found that parents who have been supported and encouraged to care for their dying child at home feel they have given all that is possible for a parent to give. As one mother said to me, "I was there when she was born, and I was there to help her die. She knows that I will always be with her."

Situations such as these help me find meaning in the losses I have experienced during my life. The parents and children I work with help me appreciate the strength of the human spirit.

My Father's Death

One evening I received a telephone call from my father's second wife, Pat, who told me that my father was behaving strangely. He was having a hard time talking and seemed to be drooling. Her youngest son thought that my father should be taken to the hospital, but she refused to do anything until either my sister or I came over. I called my sister, picked her up and immediately drove to my father's house across town.

Dad was sitting in the living room with a rather unfocused look on his face. His speech was garbled and he was drooling. I suspected he had had a stroke. We called an ambulance and had him brought to the emergency room. The physician on duty in the emergency room was unable to contact my father's physician and told us to take our father back home. My sister and I insisted that he be admitted to the hospital, and we left him in the care of the hospital staff for the night.

When we went to the hospital the next morning we found our father in bed with his legs and arms tightly tied down. He seemed confused and frightened as he pulled at the restraints. We were told that he had climbed out of bed during the night and was found in the bathroom. He had been trying to urinate despite the fact that he had a urinary catheter in place. Because of this incident, the staff had decided to tie him down in bed to prevent him from injuring himself. After seeing this, Pat, her daughter-in-law (who was a nurse), my sister and I arranged our time so that Dad would have someone with him 24 hours a day. That way, the restraints could be removed. With family members beside him and his extremities free, my father became oriented and cooperative.

My father was diagnosed with a bilateral carotid occlusion and was given a poor prognosis. After his first day in the hospital, Dad had voluntary movements of both of his legs and right arm and limited voluntary move-ment of his left arm. Although there was some speech impairment (he had some difficulty getting his words out), his verbal communication was understandable, appropriate and coherent. After a week of testing and treating my father, his physician was planning to transfer him to the hospital rehabilitation unit. He told the family to begin making plans for our father's eventual discharge.

While our stress over my father's illness united my family into a caring unit, planning his discharge from the hospital tore us apart. Pat was a small woman and would not be able to manage Dad's physical care alone. Which of us would be willing and able to help her over time? My sister and her husband both worked and they had three young children. My brother and I were self-supporting adults living alone. We all lived about an hour's drive from Dad and Pat's home. Pat's three children were all married with families and working spouses, and one of them lived in a distant state. It was difficult to know what to do. Could we manage Dad's care at home?

We agonized. In previous years, we had devoted ourselves to our mother when she was ill and dying. We had also witnessed the struggles of our parents, uncles and aunts as they cared for our grandparents and other ill or elderly family members. It had always been our family's way to care for our own and in the past we had always followed that rule. In this situation, though, we could not find a way to care for our dad at home by ourselves. It was not possible for anyone to change residence or give up employment. Dad's wife was hurt and angry. She believed that we were abandoning our father and this added to our guilt. I was a nurse, and went out daily to help strangers, yet I couldn't provide care for my own father. Our only solution seemed to be to admit Dad to a nursing home, at least temporarily.

Although my father's wife insisted that his children should make the decisions about his care, she couldn't agree with them. Pat insisted that she would care for our father herself. Finally, we conferred with her children and asked them to help her see reason. They finally convinced her that the only solution was to place Dad in a nursing home for a temporary stay.

We began searching for a nursing home that provided good care and was a reasonably short distance from my stepmother so she could visit her husband daily. All the while we continued to talk about our awful dilemma. We feared that Dad would be frightened and feel abandoned in a nursing home. We were plagued by stories of poor care and neglect of nursing home residents. We were also concerned about the cost of care and thought that some of us would have to consider taking a second job to help pay for Dad's care. We still felt guilty about turning over the care of our beloved father to strangers.

We finally selected a nursing home and scheduled a visit to get further information. When Pat, my sister and I arrived at the home, we were given the message that a call had just come from the hospital for us. My father had developed renal failure. We canceled our appointment and rushed to his bedside.

My father experienced various complications during the following weeks, but through it all he remained conscious and alert. We continued our 24-hour family vigil at his bedside. My sister and I sat with him each night. While we were there, one of us always held his hand because without human touch, he would awaken to seek assurance that he was not alone.

Finally, one month after his admission, my father died in the hospital. We all grieved. When we think back to that time, however, it is not only our grief we remember but the difficulties surrounding our decision to place our father in a nursing home. At 72 years of age our father had lived a full life. And because our mother had died at an early age, we were somewhat mentally prepared for the death of our father. We were not, however, prepared for what felt like an abandonment of a basic set of family values, or the fear that our father would not receive individualized quality care in an institution.

Our father's death relieved us of that particular grief and the guilt we were feeling. It also precipitated an ongoing discussion among us as to how we would like to be cared for if and when we become ill. All of us said that we would like to die quickly and not linger, but of course we have no control over this, and there is always the chance that we will become ill and not die quickly. If or when this happens, someone will have to deal with the same problems that we were faced with during our father's illness. If we can't be cared for at home, a nursing home is the only option and that is a big concern in light of the fact that the cost of quality nursing home care is exorbitant and the care provided is in need of major improvement.

Past, Present and Future:
The Death of Rachel's Daughter

"My life is over," wept Rachel as she walked into my office. Then, through her tears, Rachel told me that she and her husband had been sailing in the Mediterranean when his brother called to tell them to come home immediately. Even though her brother did not want to tell them over the phone what was wrong, her husband insisted: their nine-year-old daughter had died in her sleep.

Both parents were in shock and despair. What had happened? Friends met them at the Rome airport so they would have support on their way home. Rachel described the following 48 hours as a living hell and admitted that she drank a lot. They would have to make arrangements for the funeral, and the shiva, but the haunting question about the cause of her daughter's death still remained; they would have to wait for the autopsy results for the answer.

As it turned out, the little girl had died of Leigh's disease, a congenital metabolic disorder resulting in poor muscle coordination, seizures and eventual deterioration of the central nervous system. No one even knew that she was sick, but she had been athletically awkward. In hindsight the doctors were able to identify this problem as a symptom of the disease from which she died. During this period shortly after her daughter's death, Rachel began to have feelings of persistent guilt and depression. When they showed no signs of stopping, her daughter's pediatrician encouraged her to seek counseling. Reluctantly, she came to see me.

Before beginning therapy with Rachel, I met with her husband, Tom, who fully supported his wife's decision to seek treatment. Tom was also terribly shaken by the whole experience. His daughter's death had impressed upon him the preciousness of life and he was determined to fill the rest of his with more pleasure and less work.

Entering treatment, Rachel could not accept what had happened and could not forgive herself for being "a lousy, social lady" mother. Her background had been difficult. Her mother had been controlling and guilt-provoking and her father had died when she was young. Her previous marriage, from which she had a son, had ended in divorce. Her husband, Tom, had also been married before and he had children from that marriage.

The daughter who had died was the only child of their present marriage and she had been a binding force in their union. A kind, sensitive child, the girl had always been interested in helping others and she hoped to become a teacher.

Rachel was skeptical about what a psychiatrist could do to help her reconcile herself to what had happened to her daughter, so she looked for a spiritualist who might be able to help her reconnect with her daughter, or at least offer the hope that she would one day meet her again. The people she consulted were members of religious sects, card readers and others committed to the notion of past and future lives. Some asked for large donations and because Rachel was so upset and anxious for help, she was very vulnerable.

At the same time, Rachel, who had been a heavy social drinker, began drinking daily, by herself, in increasing amounts. This was a separate issue. I took the position that although it might be good for her to hope, in religious terms, for an afterlife reunion with her daughter, her frantic search for a supernatural solution to her daughter's death was no substitute for a success-ful adaptation to her daughter's loss. Her increased drinking indicated to me that she had not yet dealt with the earth-shattering pain of losing her child.

Rachel mocked my stance, increased her alcohol intake and stopped treatment with me because "I did not understand." I informed her husband of her decision. Two weeks later I was asked by her husband to arrange for her hospitalization, as she was drinking constantly. Rachel entered an al-cohol and drug rehabilitation center.

After being discharged, Rachel was advised to join Alcoholics Anonymous and return to treatment with me. When she telephoned me a month after leaving the hospital, she introduced herself by saying that this "bad" patient wanted another chance. I was grateful for a second chance to help Rachel work through her problems and once again accepted her for treatment.

When Rachel came to my office for her first visit, she started by saying that she finally had come to the realization that no one could bring her daughter back to life. This realization, she said, was too horrible for her to bear. She talked about the history of her relationship with her daughter and expressed the view that she had not been as good a mother as she might have been. In fact, she said that if she had been a more diligent, sensitive parent, her daughter's illness might have been identified sooner.

I pointed out to Rachel that her regret, although understandable, was leading only to self-torture, and that it could not bring her daughter back. I also suggested that as part of the therapeutic process Rachel should revisit the director of the department of genetics at the hospital in order to develop some understanding of her daughter's illness. Usually Leigh's disease is diagnosed between one and two years of age and progresses rapidly. Death occurs several years later. Children affected by the disease usually have intractable seizures and periodic episodes of irregular breathing. Failure to thrive is also a symptom.

This cognitive therapy was very effective, for Rachel was reassured of the reality that she could not have kept her daughter alive; the child's condition had been fatal from the start.

Rachel also found it very painful to accept that in her preoccupation with herself—her overinvolvement with social life and shopping and her frequent trips and fights with her husband—she had not spent as much quality time with her daughter as she would have liked. She realized that the time her daughter ran a lemonade stand outside their house demonstrated the child's wish to be useful and to divert some of her mother's attention from herself to her family.

Rachel gradually recognized the difference between the past and the present and began to accept the pain of her child's loss. By working through her difficulties in relation to her own past she was able to develop greater intimacy with her son and her stepchildren. Her marriage also improved. As she came to terms with her own pain, Rachel also became deeply involved in working for a children's charity.

Discussion

In addition to facing the death of her child, Rachel faced the pain from her past and present life that she had not worked through and integrated. The therapeutic task was to not deviate from the fact that Rachel needed to face the reality that she would not see her child again in this world.

Rachel's search for supernatural solutions only increased her anxiety and she attempted to escape from this feeling through the use of alcohol. Hospitalization and the return to treatment brought a meaningful result. She was able to work through the issues of separating from her own controlling mother and mourning the loss of her father.

As Rachel proceeded to repair her life and develop a sense of self, meaningful improvements occurred in her relationship with her son, her stepchildren and her husband. Her commitment to charity work continues to give pleasure. As her therapist, the most difficult task for me was to avoid collusion with Rachel's need for "magical solutions" and to deal with the character problems that had not been previously resolved.

Cancer of the Soul

Flipping through my old high school yearbooks a few weeks back, I discovered her hilarious little messages scrawled in the margins. It had been years since I'd seen her neat handwriting: the "t's" always crossed, the "i's" always dotted. I'd forgotten how much she loved perfection.

These messages, written to me by my sister Nancy, startled me at first and sent a cold shiver down my spine. In all these years I'd never seen them. I couldn't imagine when she would have written them. But they were hers, all right—the biting humor, the snide remarks that always made me howl with laughter. Nancy always knew how to make me laugh.

Seeing those messages made me think of a summer night many years ago when Nancy and I sat on our front porch for hours squealing with laughter as we made up songs about the neighbors. Nancy was 19 then; I was four years younger. We were in our pajamas.

They were silly songs, actually kind of cruel. But the crueler the lyrics, the funnier we thought they were. That night it was late and after a while our father yelled at us from upstairs to quiet down. This only made us laugh louder. Then it occurred to us that if he could hear us, certainly the neighbors could too. Well, that was more than either of us could bear. We laughed until our stomachs ached and tears streamed down our cheeks.

I hadn't thought of that night in years. Suddenly, I missed her so much. Staring at the messages she wrote in the yearbook made me feel so lonely. I wanted Nancy to see me laugh at them. More than anything, I wanted to see her laugh again. She had such a beautiful smile.

I don't know why she killed herself. But I do know that toward the end of her young life my sister wanted nothing more than to die.

She was 16 the first time she tried to commit suicide. Late one night, without warning, she swallowed a bunch of pills she had found in the medicine cabinet. The dose was enough to kill her but she panicked and told my parents, who rushed her to the hospital.

At first the doctors said she was just having a tough adolescence. Nancy was the second in a family of eight children. There was a lot of pressure on her to set a good example, the doctors said. And there was a lot of competition from the rest of us. Pay more attention to her, they told my mother and father.

And so we blamed ourselves. My parents were convinced that they had neglected Nancy and each of us thought that, in our own way, we had driven her to despair. I used to think that it was my fault, that if only I hadn't worn her clothes all the time without asking she wouldn't have gotten so upset and swallowed those pills.

But as the years wore on, it became increasingly clear that her erratic behavior and violent mood swings were caused by something more severe than typical teenage anger. Nancy was a very sick young woman.

One sunny June afternoon, a few days after our front porch sing-along, Nancy's quest for death began in earnest. A few months earlier, midway into the second semester of her sophomore year at the University of Colorado, Nancy packed her bags and came home. She said she couldn't stand the pressure at school anymore. Once she was back home, she moped around the house most of the time in her pajamas. She also cried a lot.

Caught up in my own teenage world, I couldn't understand any of it. I thought she was being a spoiled brat. Then one Thursday, my mother promised she would take me out in the station wagon to practice for my driver's test. I was waiting impatiently behind the wheel for my mother when the commotion began. Nancy, I later learned, had locked herself in the bathroom, swallowed a bottle of sleeping pills and was lying in the bathtub as it filled with water. When I ran yelling in the house to find out what was taking my mother so damn long, I found her on the phone with the fire department. My sister, Mary Kay, was pounding on the bathroom door, shouting at Nancy to open it up. Sometimes, I swear I can still hear that pounding. But Nancy wasn't answering. All we could hear was the sound of rushing water.

While Nancy lay in the bathtub drowning, I stood crying in the next room, hating her. I was 15 and incapable of understanding. Why was she putting us through all this? How could anyone be so mean and selfish?

She didn't die that day. The firemen arrived just in time. They had to break down the door with an ax. We all watched as they loaded Nancy onto the stretcher. She was naked, her face bloated and white. The humiliation of it all! I buried my face in my hands.

When she came out of the coma two days later, Nancy cried, not because she nearly died, but because she had lived.

The next five years were pure hell for her. She spent her life in and out of mental hospitals, while the rest of us wondered if we were crazy too. We were trying so hard to help her, but nothing worked. Just when it seemed that she was getting back to normal, something would trigger her again. And again, she would swallow a bottle of pills. Each time she did, someone would be there to call the ambulance and rush her to the emergency room. It became a tiresome routine. Apparently, Nancy thought so, too.

One sunny June afternoon, now nearly nine years ago, Nancy swallowed another bottle of pills. Only this time, when the paramedics came to cart her away, she convinced them that she was all right. Because she was over 21 and in no apparent danger of dying, they said they could not take her to the hospital against her will. My mother got her things together to make the familiar trip to the hospital. But when she went upstairs to get Nancy, she was no where to be found.

While my mother was on the phone with someone from the hospital, Nancy had skipped out the back door and headed for the nearby railroad tracks just as the rush-hour commuter trains were coming into the station. She was 24 years old.

The newspaper article said she had just stood there with her back to the engine, ignoring the train's many whistles. The engineer tried to stop, the article said, but it was too late.

They played Beethoven's "Ode to Joy" at Nancy's funeral, which was oddly appropriate, I thought. We had gathered to mourn our loss, our helplessness at saving her from a life of pain. But, at the same time, there was great joy. At last, I thought, Nancy got what she'd wanted for so many years. Finally, she was free from the turmoil that had consumed her life.

Our pain over losing her had just begun, but the sorrow we felt for her had come to a welcome end. In the back of my mind, I guess I always knew she would succeed in killing herself someday. At least after she died we didn't have to dread it any longer. There would be no more worrying about who would find her dead.

A few weeks before she killed herself, I asked Nancy why she wanted so desperately to die. "Because I'm nuts," she said with a smile. The brutality of her honesty caught me off guard. We both laughed. I told her that I loved her. She said she loved me, too. We hugged and then we cried. I thank God we had that conversation and I cringe for all those people who lose loved ones without having the chance to tell them how they feel.

Exactly what was wrong with her, we never knew. I used to say that my sister had cancer of the soul; various doctors called it acute depression mixed with paranoid schizophrenia.

Time is kind. It dulls the memories of all those nights I lay in bed and listened to Nancy crying in a low whimper like a wounded animal. It eases the pain of remembering her crazy talk of voices, nonsense she would utter through a mouth made dry by medication. It fades the feeling of my father's arms around me as we stood in the emergency room, his voice choked with tears as he told me, "She's gone now."

But time is also cruel. I have trouble remembering how her laugh sounded. I strain to recall the jokes we shared.

I don't know why she had to suffer as she did. Why her? Why not me? Why, for that matter, does anyone have to live like that?

But as troubled and brief as her life was, it was not without meaning. I like to think I live my life with more zest because of Nancy, that I have more compassion. In a strange way, I consider myself lucky to have had a sister like her. I saw what it was like for her to suffer so much and my problems seem insignificant in comparison.

It hurts to remember Nancy. But it's worse to forget her. My memories of her and the lessons she taught me stay alive as long as I can see her in my mind. Maybe that's why I keep her beat-up red ski jacket in my closet and her picture by my bed.

I miss her a lot. Sometimes I go to the cemetery to visit. It's only a few miles from my house. I plant flowers in the spring and put a wreath there at Christmas. I even took my baby son there to "meet" her. But the gray headstone seems so formal, so unlike her. I usually leave feeling empty.

As time passes, I worry that she will fade from my memory. I would hate that. I guess that's why I was so glad to discover those notes in the yearbook. It was as though Nancy had come back from the dead for just a few minutes to share a laugh with me. For just a moment, I felt as if we were back on that front porch, howling and cackling. And I remembered her more vividly than I had in years.

God, she had a great laugh.

9231 Days: A Father Grieves

Seared into my mind and every fiber of my being is 6:30 a.m., November 4, 1983—a Friday. That cataclysmic day would forever change the course of my life as I knew it.

I was at home in Hollywood Hills in Los Angeles. A phone call came from my stepfather who was at Roosevelt Hospital in New York City. His shaking voice said to me that I should immediately come to New York because my daughter Robyn, who at the time was visiting him from California, was "critical."

Critical. The word raced home over the long-distance phone lines. Logic made me reply, "How in the world could she be critical?" Hadn't it been only yesterday I spoke to her, heard her, consoled her? I had tried to understand her pleading words to me, "Daddy, I hurt so much and…no one…believes me. No one." With fatherly words I had tried to soothe her, "Everything will be OK…your doctors will help you, sweetheart. I'll call you again later."

After the call from my stepfather my mind started to race and I began to plan the things that I had to do. I had to go to New York on the next flight. Then, a little after 10 a.m., I got the second call. The phone rang and my heart stopped. I knew it would be from New York and I hoped it would be good news: that everything was going well, no need to rush, she's doing better.

But my stepfather's voice was broken: the devastating words that I could not really comprehend started with, "Son, I don't know how to tell you…."

At that moment the dreadful truth smashed into my head like a bludgeon, swift, punishingly painful. The unbelievable…the unthinkable had happened. Robyn was gone; a victim, at 25, of pancreatitis.

Then I was in a plane heading for New York. Neither the never-ending roar of the engines nor the numbing alcohol I kept drinking would dim my pain. My dear son Ron, 18, one of the prides and dreams of my life, was with me. My younger daughter Elianna, my other blessing, stayed home. My children were my life, my reason to live and to go on.

As the miles droned by, I was dazed and in full denial that this had really happened. I felt betrayed by God that he had taken my vibrant, extremely beautiful, bright and caring daughter in the prime of her life. Why should a just and caring God do this?

Only 9231 days before had she taken her first breath. I remember her joyous cry saying, World, I am here. Only 9231 days before—9231 days filled with our dreams of her living a long and happy life in a beautiful world. As loving parents we had all the dreams, all the thoughts, all the plans for our daughter. Now they were gone, tossed in an instant into nothingness. Why? Why? I could take losing everything—possessions, money, limbs—but not my child, my precious daughter. Questioning God, I wondered why it hadn't been me that died, if it could only have been me. Tearing off my limbs couldn't have been more devastating than losing Robyn, more painful, or more final.

We flew for miles and time elapsed, but I had no awareness of this; I was oblivious to everything except the pain. Then, strangely, God came to me in a very unexpected way. Sitting next to my son Ron was a man named Robin, and sitting next to me was an understanding, deeply concerned young lady also named Robin. Could this have been mere coincidence?

Trying to pass time and ease the pain I was reading the *Town and Country* horoscopes for November 1983. I looked up Leo since Robyn's birth date was July 27. The horoscope read, "Once you have coped with the winds of change, which will reach gale force around the time of the new moon, November 4, the most traumatic and emotionally draining period of the year for you finally will have come to an end." How prophetic, how painfully true it was.

The section for my sign Capricorn stated, "November 4, an emotionally disturbing phase...November 6 and 7...a major upheaval in the working pattern of your life." How true these words were, for when I arrived in New York only my most basic instincts were operable. I was in pain, hurting very deeply for myself and my son who was undergoing shock that would only manifest itself years later. After the last shovelful of dirt hit the casket, the pain of reality set in. Robyn was gone. My dreams for her were gone. My hopes for her were gone. The desire to be joyous in her joy was also gone. Buried with the last shovelful on a cold and rainy day in November 1983. It was as if the heavens, too, cried at this earthly loss.

The unbearable, unfamiliar healing process started with mourning, grieving, yelling, drinking, depression and self-recrimination. I asked myself what I could have done. Was life worth living? The pain was unbearable. I questioned my beliefs. Everything I had suffered for, worked for, fought for, was now in question.

Lightning hit again, months later, when I thought I was through the long grieving process. As I drove to meet my wife for dinner, a radio talk show host began speaking about a chalice. Everything suddenly collapsed upon me as I recalled an engraved silver wine chalice that we had used to make our wedding vows. We had planned to give this chalice to Robyn because to us she was heaven's blessing from that marriage.

At that moment I remembered that this wedding memento had been tenderly wrapped in Robyn's first bootie and placed safely in a vault to wait for her. I was tearful as the hurt stabbed at me again and again. Now who would have this cup, this chalice of love, this heirloom? Robyn was gone and it was meant for her only.

I raged, screamed and cried in my lonely tomb of a car. But the world remained unaffected by my grief. It moved steadily and efficiently by. It was untouched by my pain and loss. The whirlpool of despair sucked me down to the bowels of a worldly hell. I questioned life, God, the universe.

Then, at a meeting of The Compassionate Friends (a group for parents whose children have died), I continued to discover indications that I was perfectly placed to receive still more pain. I felt as if I had been hit by a ton of bricks when the speaker noted that "some 95 percent of all marriages break up after the loss of a child." Was I not on target in this arena, too?

Robyn had been the child from my first marriage. Because of her death my long second marriage ended with bitter and deep resentments. During this time of crisis, I resented that my second wife was not supportive, not to mention other problems we were having. For example, she did not help to heal the trauma, the emotional and spiritual disaster that followed Robyn's death. Her comment to me was, "When are you going to stop this grieving?" I wondered how anyone could give a time frame or a condition to another's hurt, confusion and helplessness. How could anyone else know the pain of losing my child, my Robyn, my flesh and blood and dreams?

Some people tried to console me with the words "I understand." How could they understand the pain of losing my child? Sure, they might understand the loss somewhat, because they once lost a mother, father, relative or friend. But how could they ever understand the horrendous feeling of losing a child, especially my child? I acknowledged others' losses, but I felt no one could grasp mine.

Friends may leave you at times like this, perhaps because of their fears about their own mortality. Or perhaps they fear that this tragedy might be contagious. Who knows? The truth is that in a situation like this, you are alone. Very alone. Swiftly and deeply, you are sucked into the caverns of despair. You must endure this trial alone. I not only grieved the loss of my child, but also the loss of a once-understanding wife. I grieved the loss of many "what could have beens." Everything collapsed. Everything was lost. I found no answers—only more and more questions.

How much pain can a loving God give one man? Looking back I would say that God does not dole out more than a person is able to handle. God then introduced me to a new life force, a woman who appeared at a time when I needed love, understanding, compassion and a hope for tomorrow.

Now there is a tomorrow. I was forced by this woman to take new paths and return to being a living part of the world's fabric. Now I have a new purpose in my life, a new center. The dreams of what could have been are now replaced by what will be. I am also trying to build new bridges to my children.

I have decided to give my experiences with loss to others as support to those who are trying to recover from grief. I am also using my skills as an executive. I am creative and blessed with God-given talents in marketing and communications. I have a new reason to live—an important, dynamic reason to be alive.

My new life is the finest "living monument" I could give to Robyn. I now understand and am grateful that her life force will always brighten my days and those of her brothers, her sister and all who knew her. We are happy to have had her in our lives, short as that time was. In my mind she will always be with me.

Stillbirth:
Attachment and Loss

The spring of 1982 arrived full of promise. The chinook winds blew across our southern Alberta home. The air was fresh with the aroma of damp soil and new grass as the last traces of snow disappeared. My husband and I were excited about my pregnancy. Our second child was due to arrive on June 1.

My pregnancy was so normal and we had no idea that there were going to be problems. In fact, aside from the usual first few weeks of nausea and other minor discomforts, I had an easy pregnancy. My last appointment with my doctor was May 5, and he told me all was well. But on the evening of May 6, I realized that I had not felt the child move for almost 24 hours. I rushed to the hospital and when the doctor examined me, he heard my baby's strong heartbeat. Relieved, I went home. The next day, I felt the child move slightly in the afternoon, but after that it was still. Early on Sunday morning, May 9 (Mother's Day), I discovered a reddish discharge and realized I was in labor. We left for the hospital. I remember driving through town; we were so excited about the moment we would see our second little one.

It's hard to describe the shock and horror we felt when they examined me and couldn't hear a fetal heartbeat. My labor lasted the rest of the morning and Mitchell was born dead at 12:45 p.m. From that moment on our lives were completely turned upside down. My husband and I were faced with the most difficult and painful situation of our lives.

The death of someone close to you is such a difficult thing to deal with. I think most of us prefer to deny that a crisis is real because it is just too painful. When you are in denial, it often seems that everything others say and do is wrong, at least that's how we felt. Everything that was said and done for my husband and me during this time made an already horrible situation worse. At the stage of my labor when the nurses were sure that Mitchell was dead, things got worse. They left me and my husband alone, except for an occasional brief visit by a nurse who asked if my contractions were increasing and who made comments like: "By the way, the lady beside you just had a baby girl! Just thought you'd want to know" and "We've had one patient who lost three babies before she had a live one, so don't feel so bad. You can always try again." I was numb with shock and fear and I didn't want to be ignored. Neither did I want to be bombarded with flippant remarks that implied that my child's death was an insignificant event. I mean, I hadn't even delivered him yet and already he was being referred to as some experiment that had failed and we should just ignore this effort.

I remember having feelings of great terror during my labor. How was I going to face the pain of labor with no baby to make up for it? I was also worried about what they were going to do with my baby's body. For all I knew, they might just throw him out.

At one point earlier, I had noticed several nurses standing in a group talking about something. As we walked by, they stopped talking and stood and watched us. When we had gone a little way down the hall, I glanced back and noticed they had started to talk among themselves again. I had the feeling that they were discussing our situation and what to do with us. It made me feel like I had some terrible disease, that everyone was afraid to come close to me in case it was catching.

When I finally had delivered my baby, I was taken to the recovery room where two other new mothers were enjoying their babies. I couldn't believe that the hospital couldn't find another room where I would at least have been spared the pain of listening to these other parents with their babies. I felt helpless and at the mercy of the hospital staff. After all, it was kind of hard to get out of bed and run to someplace where I wouldn't have to face what was happening.

For the rest of my hospital stay, I felt the nurses looked at me with real disgust. They couldn't seem to understand why I was crying so much and making such a fuss. I was treated with very little dignity and respect. Against my wishes, the staff called one of my friends and invited her to come and try to "snap me out of this depressed state of mind." After all, they told my friend, they couldn't send me home like that. The staff did little things that were very inconsiderate of my pain, like throwing open the curtains to "let the sunshine in," after I specifically requested that they leave them closed. These things left me feeling furious and humiliated. I walked out of that hospital not only without my child, but with a lot less dignity as well.

The months that followed were depressing and, most of all, lonely. My husband and I often felt like we were separated from the rest of the world by a glass wall. We could see our friends and family carrying on with their lives as if nothing had happened, while our lives had come to a sudden stop.

We wanted so desperately to feel normal again, but it was extremely hard to accept the fact that things would never be the same for us. I developed a severe sleeping problem and many nights went by when I didn't sleep at all. It was only through the patience and support of a few close friends and family members that either of us managed to cope at all.

Approximately two months after Mitchell's death a concerned friend brought us a tape to listen to, featuring Joyce Landorf, the author of *Mourning Song* (a book about grieving). This was the first time we had ever understood the stages of the grieving process. It was a great comfort and relief to hear that what we were experiencing was a normal reaction to the death of a loved one. Several family members listened to the tape as well, and as a result knew a little better how they could be of the greatest support to us. I will always be grateful to them for allowing us to repeat over and over the details of Mitchell's death and the pain we were feeling.

Our daughter Carleen, then just five years old, was due to enter a preschool program that September. By chance, her teacher had also just lost an infant son. It was nice to have at least one other mother who knew exactly how I was feeling. We took great solace in sharing our losses with each other. Also, her husband was the only other male besides one brother-in-law to provide a sounding board for my husband, Vern, to share his grief on a man-to-man level. Within days after Mitchell's death, I began to keep a diary. Many times I took out my frustrations by writing down the feelings and thoughts I was having on that particular day. I also began to search for books written by parents who had lost a child, as well as articles in newspapers or magazines that dealt with grief. We needed so desperately to find all the encouragement we could get that someday the pain would pass and things would be joyful again.

One of the greatest steps in our healing was finding out 15 months later that I was pregnant once again. That pregnancy was one of the longest and most tension-filled times we've ever lived through! When Brennan arrived healthy two years and one month after Mitchell's death, we were on top of the world. That little boy has filled our "empty arms" and given us much joy!

Still, Mitchell will always be our second child. When asked how many children we have, we always answer three. We talk about Mitchell openly and freely and acknowledge the role he has played in making us the kind of people we are today. We also enjoy doing things in his memory. This past Christmas we purchased a gift for a little underprivileged boy who is the same age as Mitchell would have been. In addition, we take comfort in planning a special way to remember him on his birthday.

My husband and I feel privileged that we were one of the couples instrumental in forming a support group for other grieving parents. We strongly believe that no one should have to go through a loss such as ours without having someone to lean on. Those suffering such a loss need others to encourage them to hang on. At the time of Mitchell's death, when friends would say, "You'll be better people because of this," I couldn't believe that that would ever be true. The pain was just too great! Now I like to believe that they were right, that we have learned to be more compassionate, patient and tolerant of those around us. I know we have learned to keep our priorities straight. It's very easy now to say no to outside commitments in order to spend time with each other and our remaining children. We are stronger in many ways, and yet much more vulnerable because we know what it means to love someone, no matter how short the time, and then lose them.

One of the things that hurt the most was when people would say things to us like, "He was only a baby," or "He wasn't even part of your family yet," or "You didn't even know him." To them his life may seem insignificant, with no reason or meaning, but we know differently. Because of that little boy we are different, and hopefully can make the world a better place for someone else. Though short, his life did matter. Every time we talk with parents who have just lost a child and realize that we were able to give some support to them and ease their hurt just a little, we know that it's so!

The Loss of Our
Unborn Child

As soon as my husband and I found out that we were expecting our first child, we told everyone we knew. Besides our friends, relatives and co-workers, we told people standing in check-out lines, the people who fixed our cars and anyone else who would listen. We were thrilled. My nursing colleagues were very happy for me. Our child was going to be my parents' first grandchild.

Fifteen weeks into my pregnancy, I began to have cramps. I was only slightly concerned because I thought that the cramps were caused by something I had eaten. My husband and I were going to a party that evening and I was busy getting our covered dish ready. When I noticed that I had had some spotting, I called my physician. He was not available, but his associate told me that it was probably nothing to worry about and that I should just take it easy. He told me to call back if I had any more concerns.

Gradually the cramps started to get worse and I started passing small clots of blood. I tried not to worry my husband, but he noticed each time I went to the bathroom to check. We decided to call our friends to let them know we wouldn't be coming to the party. Though I had tried to deny it, the act of calling our friends made the chance that something might be wrong seem more of a reality. Nevertheless, I hoped that the cramps would just go away and everything would be fine again.

But the cramps continued to get stronger and I started passing larger clots. I called the physician again. He said that I didn't have to come to the hospital unless I started passing "large" clots. I was somewhat relieved, but really didn't know what he meant by "large" clots. In my opinion, the clots I was passing were large, but I just didn't know if they were large enough to be concerned about. As we waited, my husband was very helpful and supportive. He fixed me a big plate of scrambled eggs. I could tell that he was getting scared. I kept telling him that everything was going to be OK, but deep down I think we both knew better.

Neither one of us slept that night. Finally, at about six in the morning I admitted that things were not going to get better and that we had to go to the hospital. It was so early in the pregnancy and we were so ill-prepared that we didn't even know how to get to the hospital. We had to call a friend to get the directions. She tried to reassure me that I was going to be fine, but I could tell that she was worried.

On the way to the hospital, my husband had to pull over to the side of the road several times because I had to vomit. I felt bad each time we stopped because I knew that he hated to see anyone get sick. Besides, they were his scrambled eggs that I was throwing up. He was so patient. He would stop the car, get out, turn his head and wait until I said I was finished. The ride to the hospital seemed to take forever. I kept thinking, "Medical science has really come far. They will be able to save our baby." But in my heart I knew it was not to be. I guess I was hoping for a miracle.

At the hospital they told us that it was too late to save our baby. When they told us that I would have to have a D&C because the miscarriage was incomplete, we both started to cry. There was no longer any question about it; I had lost the baby that had become so special to us. The child that had been growing inside of me was no longer alive. My husband was taken into the waiting room so that they could get me ready for surgery. Because it was Sunday morning, they had to make a special call to the surgical team.

Although it was a matter of an hour or two, it seemed like I had to wait forever to go to surgery. My cramps continued to get worse and I started passing really sizable clots. After I had filled five or six bedpans, I knew what the physician had meant by "large" clots.

Everyone was very aware of how upset I was. My tears just would not stop. It seemed like every time I looked up, more people were coming in to tell me how many miscarriages they or their spouses had had and how many children they now had. After about the fifth person, I began to wonder if the staff had hunted for everyone in the hospital who knew someone who had experienced a miscarriage and sent them in to see me. I found myself wondering if some of them were making it up to make me feel better. Nothing seemed to help. The more they talked, the more I cried.

A miscarriage wasn't supposed to happen. I had taken good care of myself and the baby. During the pregnancy, I didn't drink or smoke. I took my vitamins every day, even though previously I had been very forgetful when it came to taking medications.

I was very worried about my husband. I had never seen him cry before. I called a friend of ours and asked her to come over to be with him when I went to surgery. I didn't want him to be alone. She came right over and it made me feel a little better.

By the time I was wheeled down to surgery I felt absolutely miserable. I remember asking the anesthesiologist if the cramps would be gone when I woke up after the operation. I was very relieved when he said yes and put me to sleep. But when I woke up, my husband was there and so were the cramps. I wanted to scream, "He lied, he promised the cramps would be gone!" But my husband looked so sad and tired, I didn't want to worry him anymore. I told him that I felt fine.

I found it somewhat amusing that the nurses and physicians were no longer coming in and out of my room at rapid intervals. For long periods of time I was all alone in my room. After I sent my husband and my friend home to get some sleep, I was only checked on periodically by the nurses. No one talked to me about my miscarriage. Maybe the staff thought that I would start to cry if someone talked to me about it. I actually would have liked someone to come in and sit with me. Maybe not to talk, but just to be there. I felt very scared and very alone.

The "what if" questions kept coming to mind. What if I am never able to carry a child to term? What if the miscarriage had been caused by something I had done? I worried about how I was going to tell everyone. Would I be able to talk without crying? How would people respond when I told them? Would people avoid talking to me because they knew I was hurting?

We called only our immediate family and a few friends that first day. Some of my co-workers came to see me while I was still in the hospital. We cried, but we also laughed. We talked about my miscarriage, but we also talked about the party that I had missed and what had been happening at work. Their visits didn't take away the pain or the empty feeling inside of me, but it was nice to be able to talk to someone.

My sister and her husband came to see us the day I came home (I was only in the hospital for a little over one day). We went out for pizza and spent most of the time talking and crying. It was great to be with them. We discovered later that they had just found out that they were expecting their first child. My miscarriage had been very hard on them. My sister kept a diary during her pregnancy, and many of the comments in it are her thoughts about me and how I was doing following my miscarriage.

When I went back to work, most people avoided talking about my miscarriage. It was almost as if my pregnancy had never been real. Then after about seven weeks, I began to think that I was pregnant again. I told a few of my close friends. They were supportive, but encouraged me to wait to see what the tests showed. My first pregnancy test came back negative and so did my second one. After the third pregnancy test, the nurse came out to the waiting room with a small calendar in her hand. She said, "Let's look at the calendar and try to figure this out. When did you miss your period?" I told her that I had not had a period since my miscarriage and her whole facial expression changed. She tried to convince me that based on the test results, I was probably not pregnant. Maybe I just thought that I was pregnant because of my strong desire to become pregnant again. The more I cried, the more determined she became. I told her many times that I was sure I was pregnant. I had the same symptoms before. I was very tired, my breasts were sore and I had morning sickness. She seemed sure that these symptoms were related to my miscarriage, not a second pregnancy. Finally she said, "OK, Mrs. Smith, let's pretend that you are pregnant and schedule you for a prenatal visit in one month." I was somewhat relieved, but sure that she thought I was crazy. I had read about pseudo-pregnancy in my maternity textbook and so had she. I was sure that she told her co-workers that I had a classic case of pseudo-pregnancy.

I didn't tell many people about my "imaginary pregnancy." Nonetheless, friends and co-workers began to ask if I was pregnant again because I had gone back to my morning sickness routine. I frequently had to leave the change of shift report meeting to vomit. I told some of them about the nurse who thought that I was "nuts." They laughed and encouraged me to take it in stride. My husband strongly believed that I was pregnant again, but he seemed somewhat afraid to mention it, just in case something went wrong again.

When I finally went in for my check-up, my obstetrician told me my delivery date and asked me if I had any special concerns about the pregnancy. I told him that I wasn't worried as much about the pregnancy itself as about the fact that his nurses thought it was "all in my head." He laughed and said, "This pregnancy is in your uterus, not your head." He was extremely supportive during the pregnancy. He seemed to be able to anticipate my concerns. He would talk about them and reassure me, even before I was able to put them into words. I will always remember how sensitive and caring he was.

This time we didn't tell as many people that I was pregnant. I think that we were both a little concerned that this pregnancy might also result in a miscarriage, but I was able to carry our baby to term. I went into normal labor. It was hard, but I told myself that it would all be worth it. I told myself that, unlike the pain I had gone through with the miscarriage, this pain was going to lead to the birth of a baby. Soon, I thought, we were going to be able to experience the thrill of holding our own child.

Then, when I reached the transition phase of my labor, I suddenly started to vomit. My husband rushed out of the room to get a nurse. Later, when we talked about it, he told me that he had feared that I was going to miscarry again. He told me that he knew I was too far along in my pregnancy to miscarry, but all those feelings from before had come rushing back.

We now have two very healthy children. When I think back to the miscarriage, I realize that if I had not gone through it, we wouldn't have the son we love so much. We still wonder a little about what the child we lost would have been like.

Time Had Run Out

When I first saw Mary she was lying in a hospital bed, a wan young woman of 23 who was shrouded in a fog of the deepest sorrow. Why? I wondered. Under the sheets her abdomen looked the size of a six-month pregnancy, and indeed, she was 26 weeks pregnant. As I pulled back the sheet to feel and listen to the child, the cause of her sorrow became apparent. She had no right leg. Instead, there was a massive incision just above where her leg had been.

A nurse brought me Mary's chart. Two weeks before I saw her, Mary had had a hemipelvicectomy (removal of a leg and half the pelvis) for an extremely malignant type of osteosarcoma. She was aware that the x-rays of her chest, which had been normal before surgery, now showed she had early metastases. She knew that she was going to die. She only wanted to live long enough—six to eight weeks—so that she could provide her baby with a reasonable chance of survival. Her husband felt the same way but both of them were worried that her cancer might spread to the baby. She was admitted to a private room on the delivery floor to provide her immediate access to emergency services for a cesarean section. Supplies for an emergency c-section were at her bedside in case Mary stopped breathing and the baby had to be delivered immediately.

After about three days in the hospital, Mary started to become very optimistic. She would say, "We're one day closer." She began to smile and loved it when people would sit and talk with her. The nurses grew very close to her and often stayed after their shift was over to do little extras for her and just to be with her. The doctors visited her often. She was permitted visitors at any time. There were frequent visits by the hospital chaplain who provided Mary with a religious presence and also gave psychological counseling to both her and David, her husband.

Things went well for three weeks. Mary gained three pounds during that time. The fetal heartbeat was heard. The baby kicked. But on the twenty-second day after admission, Mary had a massive pulmonary hemorrhage that could not be controlled. An immediate cesarean was performed. Sadly, a 980-gram girl who never took a breath was born.

David had been prepared for Mary's death, but was devastated by the death of the baby. He had been thinking that the baby would be a living reminder of Mary, but instead he lost both. For about six months he continued to visit the hospital. About a year later, he remarried a woman who resembled Mary and had three children with her. David saw Mary in all of them.

Discussion

It was important that Mary continue to maintain the pregnancy long enough so that the baby could live. At 26 weeks the baby had little chance of surviving; at 32 weeks the baby's chances were significantly improved. Depending on the time of delivery the greatest risk to the baby was the prematurity. The spread of cancer from a mother to an unborn baby is extremely rare.

When Mary entered the hospital, both she and David knew that her death was inevitable. David was fearful that his wife would suffer pain, and he was more concerned about a premortem c-section as a last-ditch attempt to save the baby than about a postmortem c-section. If the baby had to be delivered by cesarean it would be very small, compromising its chances for survival. The c-section could also tax Mary's strength and probably hasten her death. In addition to his physical and emotional exhaustion, David was overwhelmed by his unpaid bills and the need to borrow money from his parents. He worried about how he would care for the child without his wife's help.

At that time, he received immeasurable support from both his parents and Mary's; they said they would bring up the baby and even adopt it. His parents said that he could move back home with them if he needed it to.

The goal agreed upon by both sets of parents and physicians was to strive for the maturity of the baby prior to the mother's death. An agreement to this effect was signed by both parents. An operative permit signed by Mary for cesarean section was the top sheet in the chart. Frequent monitoring of the patient and the fetal heart tones was performed. If Mary's condition worsened or the baby became distressed, it would be necessary to take the baby by cesarean section. Because it was impossible for the attending physician to be immediately available at all times, the parents agreed that the resident physician could begin the operation while waiting for the attending physician. A perinatologist, pediatric resident and premature nursery were steps away.

Despite the extensive surgery, Mary's cancer had spread beyond control. She could not live long enough to give birth to a baby with enough pulmonary maturity to be benefited by the technological resources of the modern premature nursery. Time had run out.

The Case of Nakita:
A Nurse Watches a Child Die

Nakita was a two-year-old toddler hospitalized with neuroblastoma, an embryonic tumor arising from the adrenal and sympathetic nerve cells. Nakita was diagnosed at 18 months and at that time had widespread metastases to skeletal muscles and abdominal organs. Nakita was treated with extensive chemotherapy and survived both the treatment and its complications, which included a platelet count so low that her body was completely covered with bruises. Nakita's mother was a 16-year-old adolescent who could not begin to cope with her daughter's illness and never visited the hospital. The grandmother visited Nakita, but the visits were infrequent.

I was assigned to Nakita during my pediatric nursing rotation. I, too, had a two-year-old toddler, but my child was healthy and enjoying life; Nakita was sick and dying. Because of the late diagnosis of Nakita's disease, her prognosis was poor. It was up to the staff to become Nakita's family and support system. She had formed a special attachment with a day-shift nurse named Joy. Nakita was fearful of strangers and would cower in the corner of her crib and whine when approached by unfamiliar staff members. My heart went out to this little girl who knew so little about life. She had suffered so much in the time she had lived. I wanted to bring some happiness into the last days of her life, but I was a stranger and Nakita was afraid of me. She thought I would bring more pain into her already painful existence.

I did not touch or impose myself on Nakita, but I would talk to her during the times Joy worked with her. As long as Joy was nearby, she was not afraid of me. When Joy would leave the room, I would sit quietly next to Nakita's crib and talk to her as she watched the soap operas on television. Her eyes were big, wide and brown. She kept her index finger on her lower lip and because of her low platelet count, this made a bruise in the center of her lip. She had lost her hair from the chemotherapy, but it was starting to grow back, short, brown and curly. I thought she was one of the most beautiful children I'd ever known. I was angry that she was suffering.

Eventually Nakita began talking to me. She would point to the television as if to tell me what was happening in the soap operas. She would indicate to me whether she wanted the television on or off. She permitted me to bathe her, to hold her and to give her affection. When I went home and saw my own child, I would feel angry at Nakita's mother for not being there for Nakita.

I spent 10 weeks with Nakita during my pediatric rotation. The first few weeks were spent establishing a relationship with her. I formed a special bond with this child, and she with me. I loved and cared for her "unconditionally," and when she was in pain I saw that she was medicated. I loved this child as if she was my own and cried inside every time I thought about the life she would miss. Eventually, Nakita was assigned to another student. I worked with my classmate as Joy had with me, helping Nakita adjust to a new person. During that next 10-week period, Nakita died.

Nakita's grandmother invited all the caregivers to the funeral and memorial services. No matter how hard I tried, I couldn't go. I couldn't bear to say goodbye to this little girl that I had grown to love as my own child. Students who did attend told me that her mother was there. They said that the mother's grief had been so intense that she had thrown herself across her child's casket and fainted. For the first time, I realized what her mother had gone through during Nakita's hospitalization; she hadn't been able to stand by day after day and watch her child slowly die. And I, in a similar way, wasn't able to actually go to the funeral and see her dead. I no longer resented Nakita's mother; I now understood her feelings.

Discussion

When Nakita became my patient, I felt like her surrogate mother. This was very hard for me. Perhaps I felt guilty for having a happy, healthy baby while Nakita suffered. My anger at her mother for not being there was directly related to my own values and beliefs about how a mother should react to a dying child. As a result of my feelings, Nakita became my child and I her mother. I gave her the love and care that a young child needs who is going through a crisis that she can't possibly understand. Ironically, in the end, I could no longer condemn her mother for coping with Nakita's illness by staying away. She had the courage to go and say her final goodbye to Nakita. I never could.

When Death Strikes a School

Case One

Thomas Thatcher was the popular principal of a small-town elementary school. He knew every child's name and all the children smiled when they saw him coming. His school was like a family. One night after evening prayers with his wife he said that he did not feel well, clutched his chest and fell dead from a massive heart attack. The next day a school full of children had to be told what had happened to a man they all loved.

The next day the schoolchildren were brought together in the auditorium and told what had happened. They sat in small groups with their teachers and shared their emotions. Together they decided that they wanted to do something so that everyone would know what Principal Thatcher had meant to them. With board approval, the school was renamed Thomas Thatcher Memorial School and bears that name today. In regular classes during the next month, the themes of loss and grief were dealt with by discussing current events and children's literature. Names and addresses of local support groups were made available to families and staff, but these appear not to have been utilized. The students in this school displayed no unusual behavior problems as a result of the principal's death.

Contrast this scenario with another school in a nearby district whose officials refused to name an athletic field after an athletic director who was retiring. Even though this man had not died, like the principal at the other school, his departure was a form of loss to the students. This man had guided a generation of students. The officials justified their refusal by saying, "If we start doing this, we may end up making a habit of honoring everyone who has been a part of this district."

Staff members, students and alumni expressed anger at the board's decision and asked what was wrong with showing teachers and students that their presence in the school system mattered—that their contributions might indeed make a difference. There was an increase in fighting and vandalism and a lot of absenteeism in the two-month period following the board's decision.

Case Two

Sally was a highly motivated student about to begin her senior year at a local parochial high school. She was described as a bright young woman, a devoted daughter and a good student. Although she did not have many friends at school, she did have a few friends at home. She felt pressure to succeed in high school and was anxious about the approaching year of college applications. During the summer vacation following her junior year, she killed herself by taking an overdose of drugs.

Sally's principal, who held an advanced degree in psychology, ordered the teachers in Sally's school *not* to discuss her death with their students. A school funeral mass, standard procedure for most parochial schools when a student dies, was not said. By foregoing the mass and requesting that teachers keep quiet, the principal desired to avoid the possibility of copy-cat suicides. She also wanted to avoid the "scandal" of suicide. However, every student in the school knew what had happened. Faced with silence by their teachers, they could only conclude one of two things: that their teachers knew how to answer their questions and help them deal with their feelings, but chose not to, or their teachers were helpless to do anything for them and so they dared not try. The first reaction produced anger on the part of many students and the second fostered feelings of helplessness. The students were left to deal with these feelings on their own.

Almost one year later, a staff development day was devoted to teacher concerns. It was not announced in advance that these meetings would have any connection with suicide, but that was their subject. There was a lecture and discussion, after which most teachers remained silent. But after the conference several teachers contacted the lecturer to discuss their concerns about how Sally's death had been dealt with. Because the school had offered nothing and probably even made matters worse by being silent, many teachers and students had attended community support groups for help. They stated that they no longer saw the school as a place where they might receive support in dealing with personal problems. Students at this school were unable to explain their loss of interest in classes or their falling grades. Students did not speak in school about the mounting anxiety they felt as senior year approached and they feared that they might crumble under the pressures they felt had killed Sally.

Case Three

Mr. Joseph, a school principal, had a problem dealing with the topic of death. At the time, two of his former students were hospitalized with life-threatening illnesses. Because both of these students admired him, he asked other faculty members to tell them that he would come to visit them. Though he established several specific times when he said he would go to the hospital, he never went and never called. He simply could not deal with the situation. Then one of the students died. Though Mr. Joseph might have been expected to help the school mourn its loss, he informed faculty members that no teacher could be given "official" time to attend the funeral. He said that allowing them the time would be a bad precedent, and because the student had graduated two years earlier and was no longer officially enrolled in the school, it didn't make sense.

Students and teachers had difficulty accepting this position and expressed anger, resentment and confusion. Vandalism (which had been decreasing over the previous year) increased and communication between Mr. Joseph and his staff members suffered. Some teachers reported that they were unable to speak with him. Mr. Joseph offered support to staff members who sought to establish a suicide prevention program in the school (there is often a higher risk of student suicide after the death of a classmate), but did not become personally involved. One year later he sought a position in a different school system.

Mr. Joseph coped with situations he found troubling through denial. He was unwilling to seek counseling, stating that he did not have a problem that needed to be resolved. In his new position he has continued to use denial as his chief means of coping with death-related events. His successor at his former school supported the suicide prevention program that had started during Mr. Joseph's administrative tenure and he expressed a willingness to discuss issues of loss and grief with staff members and students. He also helped staff members initiate peer support groups and took an active role in training student counselors. He worked with one teacher to develop, implement and publish a protocol for schools to assist students in dealing with a loss.

Use of a Protocol for Schools

It was raining hard when Jim and his friend left the movie theater. Jim's mother was waiting for the boys in her car across the street. Before they crossed the street, Jim looked both ways but did not see the oncoming car.

His friend called to him to stop, but it was too late. The car struck and killed him. Jim's mother ran to him and within minutes the town's paramedics arrived. But there was nothing that could be done. Jim's mother, seeing that her son was beyond help, walked over to the teenage driver who had been behind the wheel of the car that had hit her son. She put her arm around the shaking youth and told him that there was nothing he could have done and that it was not his fault.

Later, at the funeral home, a number of parents who decided not to attend, dropped their children off, then returned to pick them up an hour later. Many of these children were facing their first encounter with death and Jim's mother was the only adult who was present to attend to their needs. Although the parents of Jim's friends were expecting their children to go on "as usual," sudden loss is not overcome so easily in children. Successful grief resolution does not happen without some intervention.

A number of resources and programs were available at Jim's school to help students deal with their grief and loss following his death. Along with the boy who had been with Jim when he died, the principal of the middle school visited each classroom on the Monday after the accident to tell the students in person what had happened. He also asked Jim's friend to talk to each class. The principal told the students that it was normal and understandable to be sad about Jim's death, but added that Jim would not want them to stay sad, but to go on with their lives.

The parents' organization had a book passed to each class. Each student was encouraged to write something about Jim, or to put a message in the book for Jim's parents or older sister who was a student in the same school system. One boy wrote that he and Jim had been trading baseball cards and attached the card that he knew Jim needed to complete his set. Others wrote poems or told of times they had shared with Jim. The school board allowed this project, although one board member did say this seemed "very morbid" and that he saw no reason to have the students "dwell" on what had happened.

An outside consultant was brought in to speak to parents of the students at an evening assembly and to address any problems they might have encountered with the responses of their children to Jim's death. During a camping trip that had been planned previously, students were reminded that they could continue to think about Jim if they wished, and that there were people who would be glad to listen to them if they wanted to talk about Jim or about any other issues that Jim's death might have brought up for them. Lists of support groups were supplied to all interested parents and several families attended group sessions or sought individual counseling.

A faculty development conference dealing with student grief reactions in the classroom was planned for late winter for administrators and staff members of all of the schools in the system. The Stevenson-Powers protocol for dealing with a student death was distributed to staff members, and methods of implementing it were discussed. Resource lists of audiovisual materials on the subject were also made available to classroom teachers.

Two weeks after the faculty conference, two more students from the same school system died in unrelated events on the same day. One freshman student died of leukemia (which had been diagnosed only two weeks earlier) and a second student, a high school senior, was killed in a skiing accident. The protocol that had been distributed to staff members was implemented and the school, rather than canceling classes, mobilized staff members to act as a support system for students. The students assumed an active role in planning a memorial service at the high school and the contact people who had already been introduced to the community were again made available to students, families and staff members.

A Nurse's Response to the Death of a
Newborn Child

The following story illustrates the range of responses experienced by both the parents and the nursing staff when a child is born with a severe anomaly.

Childbirth is generally a time of happiness for parents and those close to them. The staff on obstetrical (OB) units derive satisfaction from caring for families during this special time. But when a baby is born with major problems and is not expected to live, all persons involved feel a great loss. At the time the following case occurred, I was working part-time as a staff nurse on an obstetrical unit that specialized in providing alternative family-centered care in a birthing room setting. This case study focuses on the 16 hours that I worked with the parents of the child.

Sue and Jim were in their late twenties. Although Sue had a school-age daughter from a previous marriage, this baby would be their first child together. Sue's due date fell shortly after the new year. Perhaps, she told herself, they would have a Christmas baby!

Two weeks before Christmas Sue had an ultrasound because she seemed to be carrying too much amniotic fluid. After the test, Sue and Jim were told by their doctor that their unborn baby was anencephalic—meaning that it essentially had no brain and that this condition was "incompatible with life." In other words, their child was going to die shortly after it was born.

Sue came to the hospital to have labor induced on the weekend before Christmas because they did not want the labor to start on Christmas Day. The anniversary of this baby's birth was going to be hard enough to deal with; they didn't want Christmas celebrations to be clouded with painful memories.

On Saturday I listened to the report with the other OB nurses. Nobody really wanted the assignment of working with Sue and Jim because it was so sad, but eventually I volunteered because I believed that I could offer them support during this difficult time. I didn't want them to feel like the staff was avoiding them. And even though I wanted to help, I wasn't sure how I was going to get through the birth and death of this child. I knew it would be hard for me to put my own feelings on hold in order to be able to help this couple.

A woman in labor must trust her own body and she must be able to trust the people who are caring for her if she is to labor effectively. The labor process causes a loss of control over certain body functions, and the woman must feel that she can allow that to happen. Emotional conflict and the tension it produces prolongs labor and makes it more difficult.

Spontaneous labor presents a unique challenge to a mother's ability to cope; induced labor can be even more challenging. A drug called prostaglandin was used for Sue's induction. This drug can be, in a word, wicked. It causes intense labor contractions, nausea and vomiting, elevated temperatures, diarrhea and more. In addition, the knowledge that the baby was deformed and would not live long produced an extremely draining situation for all of us.

Sue's labor was long and hard. It was no wonder that she asked for painkillers to help her deal with the pain. I spent most of my time meeting Sue's physical needs, though I knew my being there helped her emotionally as well.

Jim seemed unsure of his role. He stayed in Sue's room but had to be encouraged to help her. He looked lost. We talked some and he told me that he had gone to the library to read about anencephaly. He said he knew their baby would not live. He had seen pictures: the baby would probably have a "froglike" head. Some medical books still used the word "monster" to describe a fetus of this kind. Jim seemed bewildered, wondering whether his genetic background could have somehow caused this problem.

We all seemed to be engaging in self-protection. In many ways my behavior paralleled theirs. I had many concerns and in some ways I hoped that Sue would end up delivering on another shift. That way I wouldn't have to be there for the child's death. But what if she did deliver when I was there? Would the baby live? What would I do if it did? I was very anxious.

At the time, the Baby Doe legislation controversy was at its peak. I tried to find out if we had to provide "hydration, nutrition and medication" to the baby if it lived, but I found out that infants with conditions "incompatible with life" did not have to be treated.

Jim told me that they did not want to see the baby or to know its sex. I explained that often one's fantasies about the baby were more frightening than reality, and that they were free to change their minds at any time.

Pictures and mementos, I told them, would also be kept on file at the hospital and could be claimed at a later date.

When I reported for work on Sunday morning, I was distressed to see that Sue had been in labor for nearly 24 hours and that her progress had been very slow. This was normal. It was also normal for the delivery to happen all of a sudden. Perhaps Sue sensed that she could trust me to be with her during the birth. I had just reintroduced myself to Sue and Jim when Sue felt the urge to push. Soon she gave birth to a living boy.

Another nurse stayed with Sue while I took the baby to a secluded nursery area. For the rest of the day, I had little contact with the other nurses. I sensed that they were staying away from me deliberately. They really didn't want to know anything about this couple and their baby that was going to die shortly after birth. They didn't even want to be near me because of my involvement! None of them volunteered to help me with either caring for the baby or any of the paperwork associated with the case.

After the baby was born, Jim decided he wanted to see him. When he saw his son struggling to breathe, he started sobbing. I stayed with Jim and allowed him to express his grief. The baby lived for about two hours. When Jim saw his son again after his death, he seemed relieved that he was no longer struggling.

While I was cleaning the baby's body and preparing it for tests, the secretary went into Sue and Jim's room to get birth and death certificate information. She came out angry because the couple had become upset when she asked for the information. I felt a variety of emotions: anger because the secretary had gone in without consulting me, frustration because I could not be in two places at the same time and guilt because I had assumed that the parents would understand that their baby might live for a time after the birth and that we would be required to report the birth and death. This made me realize that the thoughts and feelings of patients should be evaluated on an ongoing basis.

Toward the end of my shift I had completed the required volumes of paperwork about Sue and Jim's case. Sue finally decided to look at the baby. Before she saw him, I put a hat on him to hide the majority of his deformity. Then we looked at and touched the baby together. In the process we discovered his many normal baby features, and both of us got teary. I realized that Sue did not know that they could name their baby. I encouraged her to discuss names with Jim so their son would have an identity. She also accepted the hospital's mementos of the baby's birth. Sue's daughter had been staying with grandparents during Sue's labor. Sue and Jim were not sure how they would discuss the baby with her.

My shift was over. The nursery coordinator would later call Sue and Jim to assess their adjustment. After the holidays I would return to the night shift.

I had contained my emotions for two days. It was my way of getting through the crisis. However, on Sunday night I went home and sobbed.

Discussion

During pregnancy a couple fantasizes about their child's features and be-havior. They expect that their baby will be born perfect and healthy. The death of an anencephalic baby represents the loss of that wished-for child. This loss can be more profound for parents than the loss of a normal baby because it brings into question their ability to produce a "perfect" child.

The birth and death of a deformed child is heartbreaking not only for the child's parents but for their caregivers as well. Caring for these families takes a tremendous amount of energy, both physical and emotional. In these kinds of circumstances, the parents rely on the caregiver to provide supportive and somehow healing care.

My role as caregiver was difficult in this case. During the short time that I was with Sue and Jim, I believe I offered them as much support as I could. During Sue's labor, I stayed with them as much as I could. My main focus was Sue because she was showing the most noticeable and medically critical symptoms. However, I now see that Jim should have been offered more support. There were times during the labor when he left the room and had no one to talk to. I couldn't talk to him because I was always busy with Sue. There should have been another caregiver available to meet his needs.

The nursing tasks involved in dealing with a neonatal death are time-con-suming. Providing emotional support for the baby's family, completing case paperwork, caring for the baby's body and dealing with my own confusion and grief required my full attention and the entire eight hours of my shift. I now give myself permission to ask for help from other staff members when I need it. Perhaps I did not do this before because I wanted to show the other nurses that I was able to handle everything by myself. Clearly I could have offered much more to this couple if I had had help.

On a unit that is so geared to life, provisions must be made for the times when there is loss of life. Ongoing sensitization programs for OB/GYN staff are needed. In the case discussed here, having a clinical nurse specialist (CNS) on the unit would have been an asset. Unfortunately, many hospitals do not have a CNS for obstetrics. A CNS might have been able to coordinate aspects of care, supported the father while the nurse was caring for the mother and counseled the parents and nursing staff during and after the crisis. Also, care for a couple like Sue and Jim should not be limited to the time they spent in the hospital. While much can be done for a couple in two eight-hour shifts, mechanisms for continued support must be available to the parents who have to deal with the loss for a lifetime.

In a case that involves the death of a newborn, the behavior and reactions of the attending staff are often similar to those of the parents. Helplessness, grief and self-protection are common. Throughout an experience such as the loss of a wished-for child, all participants must try to make sense out of the situation and must find some meaning from the experience, even if it seems at first to make no sense at all.

Shelley's Death:
Five Sisters Remember

Twenty-eight years ago our sister Michelle, or Shelley as we called her, was killed in a car accident when she was 18 months old. We (her five sisters) ranged in age from 5 to 11 years. Four of us were at school when the accident happened. Dad, Mom, Pam and Shelley were in the car when it was hit by a dump truck. Shelley was killed instantly. Dad and Mom were seriously injured, and for a time we worried that they would die too. Pam only had a broken nose and a broken ankle.

While we have shared some of our memories of the accident with people outside of our immediate family, we have never really talked about the accident among ourselves. Maybe we hurt too much to talk about it. Maybe we didn't want to make each other cry. Maybe the feelings were just too raw. Maybe the thought of re-experiencing the tears and overwhelming sense of loss was just too frightening. Whatever the reason, rather than share our thoughts, feelings and memories, we kept them inside. Now we are making an effort to share them, not only with each other, but with you. Writing this has been a long and painful process, but it has given us a sense of relief and a sense of hope.

Pam: When I came to, it was snowing. There was lots of blood. Someone was helping Dad. I rode to the hospital in an ambulance and Dad was on another stretcher in the same ambulance, but all I could see of him were his cowboy boots.

Roxanne: Our Aunt Eleanor came to school to tell us about the accident and take us back to our grandparents' house. She said my parents had been in an accident, but that they were alright. As she talked, all kinds of thoughts rushed through my mind. Terrible thoughts that they might be dead and then relief that they were OK. Then she said that my sisters, Pam and Shelley, had also been in the car and that Shelley was dead. My first reaction was to ask myself why I hadn't remembered that they were also in the car. I felt guilty for not remembering.

Vickie: This is terrible. It just can't be. They were in a car accident. Mom, Dad and Pam are in the hospital. Shelley is dead? She's just a little kid. I just saw her this morning. She was laughing in her high chair. She's always laughing. Shelley has curly hair like me. Marcia and Pam have blonde hair and Rocki and Cheri have brunette hair, but no one else has curly hair. Each big sister has a little sister like them—and now I've lost mine.

Marcia: She said that they were in an accident, but that they were going to be OK. Now she says that Shelley is dead. That can't be. She said that they were going to be OK. Shelley was sitting in the high chair just a few hours ago. She had cereal all over her face and she was laughing. She is my favorite; she's everyone's favorite. She can't be dead.

Cherie: When Aunt Eleanor told us that she was going to take us with her, I thought it was great that we got to get out of school. I thought we were going to go do something fun. When she said there had been an accident, it just didn't sink in what kind of accident it was. I didn't realize that she was talking about a car accident. To me an accident is when someone falls, or drops something, or spills something. Everyone kept asking how everybody was. She told us that Mom, Dad and Pam were alright. My older sisters kept asking how Shelley was. When Eleanor told us that Shelley was dead, I didn't think she really meant it. I didn't cry right away. It bothered me that everyone else was crying. I don't think I really understood how serious it was.

Vickie: Grab some clothes, try not to cry. Oh, why didn't I clean my room. When will we come back here? Who will be coming back? Will things ever be the same? Finally we are at Grandma's, but no one is here. They must be at the hospital.

Marcia: Everything will be OK once we get to Grandma's. She isn't here, no one is here. Now what do we do? They say we can go to the hospital. I'm so scared.

Cherie: Marcia and I kept praying that Shelley would come back to us alive. I thought that since she was so little and had never done anything wrong, God would let her live again. It wasn't until the funeral that I figured out there was no chance of her coming back.

Roxanne: I remember arriving at the hospital. When we walked in the door, it was dim, cool and shadowy. Then we walked up a small flight of stairs. We waited while they decided if we could go in because we were under age. They decided it was OK and we went down a corridor to a room on the right. A nurse pointed to a person in bed with bandages and said that he was our dad. He was unconscious or asleep, so we couldn't go in. Then we went down the hall to a room at the end. Mom was awake and asked if we were OK. She was very sleepy; we didn't talk much. Then I remember being in Pam's hospital room. She was standing up in a child's bed with bars. She asked if Shelley was coming back. I quietly answered "No." Then she asked if Shelley was in heaven and I answered "Yes." She seemed very perceptive for her age.

Vickie: We waited on the steps of the hospital while our uncle talked with the nurse. Finally he said something about how much we had gone through and how it might be the last time we would see our parents. Then they let us in to see Mom. Mom looked so beat up. I don't remember seeing Dad.

Marcia: Mom's eyes were black and blue. She looked tired and sad. Dad's room was dark. I couldn't see very much of him. All the bandages blended with the sheets. I really didn't see his face. He didn't talk or move. Pam was in a crib, high off the ground. She was too old for a crib. Why did they put her in a crib? She looked scared.

Cherie: They said we could only see Dad for a couple of minutes. He had stitches in his eyelids. They said the car key had been pushed into his knee. I kept imagining a big key sticking out of his knee. Dad seemed weak and tired. Mom talked to us, but her eyes were all black and blue. She also had something around her head. Pam was in a room with a crib, a rocking chair and two books (Huckleberry Hound and something about a tree house). I kept thinking Michelle was somewhere in the hospital.

Pam: I kept getting out of the crib because I was too big for it. It was cold in the room. There was a big white toy chest there. I kept asking about Mom, Dad and Shelley. When they brought me back to Grandma's, they forgot to bring my clothes, so I left the hospital wrapped in a big blanket.

Roxanne: I was the oldest, so when my parents were in the hospital, I felt responsible for the family. I felt that it was my duty to be strong and to get us through this. It was my duty to help everyone else deal with the situation—I could deal with my feelings later. Instead of being together during this time, we were split up. Marcia and I at one aunt and uncle's, Cherie and Vickie at a different aunt and uncle's. It was hard to be apart, even though we were staying with our cousins, which normally would have been a treat. We were worried that if something happened to our parents we would be parceled out to relatives. I was not going to let that happen.

Vickie: Cherie and I stayed at our aunt and uncle's. They were very nice to us, but it wasn't home. If I had known it was only for a couple of days, it would have been OK, but I was afraid it might be permanent. Many people stopped in to bring food and say how sorry they were. When the adults talked, they often forgot that we could hear them. The "what ifs" were frightening. What if Mom and Dad didn't come home? What if we were separated? What if things were never the same again? Trying not to cry or panic was so hard. It blocked out everything else.

Marcia: Rocki and I stayed with our aunt and uncle and their two children. Usually I loved to go visit my cousins, but this time was different. I wanted to be with my sisters. I didn't want to be separated. My aunt tried to be so nice to us. She didn't make us go to school and we didn't have to do barn chores. But I wanted things back to the way they were before the accident. I didn't want people to treat me extra nice. I wanted my family back, my whole family.

Roxanne: My sisters went back to school. Being the oldest, I went to the hospital every day. I lost my voice for the week.

Vickie: We went back to school the next day. Everyone was so polite to us, even kids who normally weren't. As long as I didn't think about it, I was alright. We were playing and a boy slugged me in the stomach. Normally this was not a big deal, but I started crying and couldn't stop. Our teacher hugged me and kissed me on the top of my head—and she didn't even like me. My aunt came and took me back to her house. I knew it wasn't the boy's fault, but I needed an excuse to cry.

Marcia: I was glad to be going to school, because I would get to see Vickie and Cherie. Everyone was too nice. My teacher told me that Shelley was God's special angel, that he had let her come down to us for awhile, but now he needed her. It didn't make sense to me. God just didn't take people back, especially little children. Besides, I didn't want to give her back; we needed her too. She had been our little sister. I cried whenever anyone mentioned Shelley and the accident, so the other children stopped talking about it around me.

Cherie: Riding the bus to school was fun (we usually walked to school), but when we got there it seemed strange not to see Marcia and Rocki. I missed being all together. I wanted our whole family to be together again.

Roxanne: Mom asked me to take care of my sisters. She asked me to pick out a pretty dress for Shelley and dark dresses for the rest of us to wear for the wake and the funeral. She had tears in her eyes. I bit my lip so that I wouldn't cry. I had to be strong. Vickie and I got matching dresses. Marcia's was navy plaid with red trim. Cherie and Pam's were alike. I don't remember Shelley's dress at all.

Vickie: We went to an expensive shop to buy dresses for the funeral. As we were leaving, a lady asked my aunt, "How many girls do Jack and Virginia have?" My aunt said "Six." I was so glad that she included Shelley.

Marcia: The store we went to was expensive. I didn't remember shopping there before. I didn't want to get a new dress, especially if it was for Shelley's funeral. I didn't want to ever wear that dress again.

Roxanne: The wake was the worst. Five sisters sitting in the front row of the funeral home, with their youngest sister in the casket in front of them. Our parents couldn't be released from the hospital for three weeks, so our relatives were with us. It seemed like hundreds of people walked by, patted us on the head and said, "She looks just like she is sleeping." I heard that phrase over and over. She didn't look like she was sleeping; she looked like she was dead. Pam walked up and touched Shelley. When she came back she said, "Shelley is all powdery and cold." I hugged Pam and tried to ease her pain. Women walked by saying, "You poor things." Then they would walk to the other side of the room, put a smile on their face and start talking about things like pumpkin pie recipes. At times it seemed like they really weren't concerned about us, like they just came to gawk. The words they said didn't help, because they didn't sound sincere. I wanted to stand up in the middle of the room and shout, "Leave us alone! We don't need you." I wanted to gather all my sisters in a big hug and close everyone else out, but we had been taught to have good manners and to be polite. I decided that I would never have a funeral or a wake. I never want to put my family through that kind of pain.

Vickie: We all sat on a little couch in the front of the funeral home. There was a continuous line of people. Many of them, especially old ladies with powdered cheeks and blue hair, seemed to feel the need to pat our heads and kiss us. They made comments such as: "Oh, the poor little orphans," and "Do you think that Jack and Virginia will make it?" and "Poor kids." The only thing worse than these women was when there was a break in the line and we stared at Shelley's body. I just wanted to wake her up and take her home. Then everything would be OK again. One of our uncles picked Pam up at the hospital and brought her to the funeral home. She went right up to the casket and touched Shelley. "She's cold," she said loudly. Then she started crying.

Marcia: Only four of us would fit on the couch, so I sat next to my aunt. People just kept walking by, shaking our hands, patting our heads and kissing us. I tried hard not to cry. I thought, Please don't talk about Shelley or Dad and Mom. If you don't mention them, I won't cry. Once I start to cry, I might not stop. I was doing OK until Pam started crying very hard after she touched Shelley. Then I started to cry. I don't know if I've ever cried so hard.

Cherie: At the wake, we were all lined up in the front row. Many people came by shaking our hands, patting our heads and pinching our cheeks. When I touched Shelley and felt how cold she was, I knew that God wasn't going to bring her back to us.

Vickie: The church was full of people for the funeral. Just before the service started, they wheeled Mom and Dad down to the front part of the church. They both looked so sad. Mom was wearing a black hat and veil. The veil had little black dots on it. I think it was supposed to cover up her black eyes. I really didn't hear what the minister said. I was trying so hard not to cry. I was sniffling constantly until they shut the casket lid, then I burst out sobbing. It was so final. After the funeral we all went to our grandparents' house. It was like Thanksgiving or Christmas, with all our aunts, uncles and cousins, but there was a major difference; this was my little sister's funeral. I just wanted to cry and run in my mother's arms, but I couldn't because she had to go back to the hospital. Roxanne reassured me that no matter what happened, we would all be together. She told me that Uncle Gerald would take care of us. I didn't have to worry, she said, Gerald would know what Mom and Dad would want.

Marcia: People were packed into the church. There wasn't enough room for everyone to sit. We sat with our aunts. Mom and Dad were wheeled in right before the service started. I was so glad to see them, but they looked so sad, like they hurt all over. I cried a lot, but I cried the hardest when the minister spoke Shelley's name. I really tried not to cry, but I couldn't help it. My heart sank when they closed the casket. God wasn't going to give her back. He was going to keep her. I knew that he would love her, but I wanted to have her back. I wanted to see her smile and I wanted to hear her laugh. She didn't belong in a casket. She loved to run and play.

Cherie: The funeral was big, I think everyone came. The church was full. At the cemetery it was snowing. It was cold and very final. The reality of everything really set in.

Pam: I remember all the people at the funeral. One big lady in black, that I didn't know, came up to us and put a big wet kiss on my cheek. She kept saying that she knew what we were going through. She kept trying to hug me. I disliked her a lot. I remember kissing Shelley. I still find it difficult to attend funerals.

Roxanne: I have good memories of the day Dad came home from the hospital. I think that Mom got out of the hospital earlier, but stayed at our grandmother's to be near Dad. A friend of our family had been staying with us. It was much better to be all together in our own home than to be separated. Dad was pale and walked with a cane. Mom's eyes were back to normal, but she looked tired. I was so glad to have them home. Men from the church had chopped a load of wood for our furnace. Women from the church had cooked casseroles, pies and other food. They didn't stand around, patting our heads, saying meaningless words. It was much better than the wake.

Vickie: Once we were home, everything was sunshine. Our babysitter was still there to help out. Dad walked with crutches initially and Mom's face turned 10 shades of black and green. Pam limped around the house, not always on the same leg. Our house had been cleaned from the furnace to the attic before we came home. It was a little tough finding things, but it was sure nice of our relatives and friends to do it. My shoes were in my closet, arranged in a circle. We had a new car. The biggest black station wagon I had ever seen. It had seatbelts in every seat, even in the far back.

Marcia: Things were much better once the five of us were back together. Uncle Gerald and our grandparents knew that we needed to be together. Grandma had taken care of all of us before, and she saw no problem doing it again. Once Mom and Dad were better and we went home, things improved even more. Things weren't back to the way they had been, but they were better. The Christmas holidays came around six weeks after the accident and they were difficult for all of us. People were super nice to us and we got more presents than usual. I knew that it was because of Shelley's death. But I wanted Shelley back much more than I wanted the extra gifts.

Roxanne: If I had to choose one event that had the biggest impact on my life, this would be it. I experienced a depth of emotions never before felt by a happy 11-year-old. I experienced real anger for the first time. Most of all, anger at God for allowing this to happen, for causing unnecessary pain, for taking the life of a wonderful, innocent little girl who hadn't yet had a chance to live, and for allowing the driver of the dump truck to continue to drink and drive. I felt so helpless and confused. Everything was out of control. It wasn't supposed to happen like this. If you were good, and my family was, then bad things weren't supposed to happen. It wasn't fair. I wanted God to realize that he made a mistake and correct it. I wanted it to be a dream that I would wake up from and everything would be OK. I prayed that God would make it right. My belief in God had been badly shaken. But there was nowhere else to turn.

I couldn't fix it myself. I remember kneeling on the back stairs at my grandmother's and praying. I told God I would do anything if he would let my parents live and keep our family together. Over the years my feelings have mellowed: I no longer blame God for what happened. I now accept the fact that bad things can happen to good people. I still don't understand why it has to be that way; I don't like it, but I have learned to live with it. I've learned from this experience that it is never too soon to tell your family that you love them. I still think about Shelley and what she would have been like. It is difficult to write down the memories and feelings that I have kept inside so long. The tears still get in the way.

Vickie: All of us kids prayed to God like we had been taught. I started out asking that it just be alright again. I think I then realized that God couldn't do that, so I asked God to help Mom and Dad get better. I just didn't know what to ask about Shelley. When they shut the lid of the casket, I decided that Shelley hadn't died. I constructed a fantasy: the funeral home director kept all the little kids in the back of his funeral home. They had something like a nursery school there. They were happy and healthy and they could stay there as long as the funeral director didn't tell anyone about them. I'm sure that I knew this wasn't really true, but it made losing my sister easier to accept.

The car accident has affected my life in many ways. The thought of losing Mom and Dad made me appreciate them more. Uncle Gerald will always be number one with me. As I got older I realized how young my aunt Eleanor was when she had to tell us the news. I really felt sorry for her. As a mother, having my children pass the age of 18 months became very important. I have thought a lot about what it would be like to lose one of my children. Seatbelts are required in our family. My husband and I made out a will soon after our children were born. Choosing a guardian was very important to me. I wanted someone who had similar priorities. Thanksgiving always reminds me of sadness and death.

Marcia: Shelley's death made me very aware of how vulnerable we all are. Even if we live a "good life," we can't be sure that we will live a long and happy life. I still have no good answer to the often-asked question, "Why does God let children die?" Although I have been working as a nurse in maternity and pediatrics for the last 15 years, I still find it hard to accept the death of a child. I find it especially hard to accept a child's death if I can't make sense of it. Some children die for a scientific reason. In the case of others, I just can't make any sense of their deaths. Although it still hurts me to see children die, I feel somewhat drawn to critically ill children and their families. Maybe it is because I want to help make this experience a little less difficult for them. There is no way to make it easy for them, but maybe I can help them to identify and mobilize their individual and family strengths.

My family has always been very important to me, but Shelley's death made me realize how much I really love them and how lucky we are to have each other. Shelley's death has also had an impact on the type of mother I am. I hope my children always know that I love them very much and that nothing could ever take their place in my heart. After I became a mother, I gained a new understanding of how hard Shelley's death must have been on my parents. I hope and pray that I never have to go through an experience like they did.

Cherie: After Shelley died, I felt as though there was something missing. I missed having a younger sister. Because Pam and I were very close in age, she seemed more like an equal. I wished for a new baby, not to replace Shelley, but to fill in some of what was missing. When our brother John was born, it was perfect. He added what was missing, but he didn't replace her. I know that because of the accident, I have always been strict about the use of seatbelts. I wonder, if car seats had been available, would Shelley have been killed? Shelley's death has made me realize how important it is to tell my children, everyday, how much I love them. You never know what might happen.

Pam: After Shelley's death, I spent a lot of time with my grandparents. Grandma talked a lot to me about death. We talked about why I didn't want to play with dolls, babies or other children. I loved Shelley a lot: she had been my baby. Mom and I made pinch pots together after the accident. I guess it was a form of therapy. I am not sure if Shelley's death is the reason why I have never wanted children of my own. I love my nieces and nephews, but I have never had the desire to become a mother. I still think about Shelley now and then, and I wonder what it would have been like to grow up with a younger sister. When I go back home, I never go to the cemetery. I don't like to look at that cold slab. I don't like funerals and I don't want them to have one for me when I die. I still have a fear of dump trucks and can picture the dump truck coming toward us.

We hope that reading this has helped you as much as we were helped by writing it. As we mentioned earlier, it was a long, painful process, but we think that we have grown because of this experience. We think that by sharing our thoughts, feelings and memories, we have gained a much deeper understanding of ourselves and of each other.

Viewing Death in the Emergency Room

Sandy

One summer evening, the emergency department in which I worked was notified that a 21-year-old DOA (dead on arrival) was en route. We were told that the police would be notifying the man's wife, Sandy, and we thought that she was probably on her way to the hospital. We were told that Sandy was pregnant and due within the week.

When Sandy arrived at the emergency department, her movements were slow. She didn't say a word except in response to our questions. In the next few days we realized that her family was more upset about their only son-in-law's death and worried about the future of their unborn grandchild than they were concerned about Sandy and her loss of her husband one week before she was going to have a baby. During the next three days Sandy's family and friends expressed overwhelming concern for the unborn baby and they kept telling Sandy that she needed to be strong for the baby.

In the emergency room, Sandy was offered the opportunity to view her husband's body. She was told that because of his massive head injuries, her husband's head would be covered. Sandy viewed the body with her parents and then spent some time in the room alone. She touched her husband's body all over and lingered over his abdomen, raising his shirt so that she could stroke his lower chest with her palm. I made sure she had privacy, but made a point to check on her regularly. I encouraged her to talk to her husband, but she didn't.

Sandy's husband was buried three days later. At the cemetery, Sandy went into labor and delivered a healthy son six hours later. After the birth, Sandy did not speak of her husband.

Bonding between Sandy and her baby has been minimal. Sandy's mother takes care of the baby and she reports that Sandy often displays indifference or resentment toward her child. Sandy has also developed numerous physical complaints including stomach pains and severe headaches.

The Andrews Family

Mrs. Andrews was in the kitchen preparing dinner when her 19-year-old son, Jim, hung up the hall telephone, went into his bedroom, closed the door and ended his life. She heard the "pop" and found Jim lying on the floor. The rescue squad and emergency department staff failed to resuscitate him.

At the time of the suicide, Mrs. Andrews was alone because Mr. Andrews was traveling home from northern Wisconsin. When her son's death was confirmed, Mrs. Andrews wept. She expressed shock, surprise, guilt and some anger. She also expressed concern for her husband and how he would deal with his only son's death. Mrs. Andrews was joined by her pastor and by friends when they heard about Jim's suicide.

Two hours later, Mr. Andrews arrived at the hospital understanding only that there had been some type of accident. When told of Jim's death, Mr. Andrews' shock was profound. His face registered total bewilderment. He had very little to say. His only tears came at the funeral three days later.

The family viewed Jim's body together and then individually. Because all external damage was to the back of Jim's head, a full viewing was possible. Family members and friends hugged and touched Jim's body. Mrs. Andrews talked to her dead son when she was alone with him.

The Andrews family chose to be honest with the community about how Jim had died. Luckily, this well-liked family found that their friends and neighbors were very supportive of their circumstances; many families find that this is not the case when a family member commits suicide.

On the staff's subsequent contacts with this family, we realized that Mr. Andrews was having a very hard time coping with the suicide of his son, while the rest of the immediate family was grieving openly (which can be very healthy and healing). After the funeral, Mr. Andrews never referred to his son or spoke his name and he would leave the room if anyone discussed or even mentioned Jim. It was agreed that support services would have been beneficial, but no one in the family, including Mr. Andrews, chose to attend a grief support group. Mr. Andrews was adamantly opposed to seeing a therapist. Mrs. Andrews and her mother helped each other deal with their grief; they both read extensively about suicide and grief during the first year after the suicide and both talked openly about Jim and reminisced about his life. This kind of behavior indicated that they were adjusting well. In the second year following his son's death, Mr. Andrews developed several health problems. His initial complaint was a "closing up of his throat." Six months later, he was diagnosed with chronic obstructive lung disease.

Pat

Pat and his fiancee, Linda, were walking along a road at dusk one summer evening three months before their wedding date. Suddenly a car struck Linda and threw her 20 feet into the air. By the time Pat reached her side, Linda was unconscious and dying. Despite his desperate attempt to stop the flow of blood from her head, she died.

Now Pat relives Linda's death through flashbacks of the accident and asks himself why she was hit and not him. He reviews their two years together and feels remorse about many things that he wishes he had done differently. He also mourns the loss of the life that he and Linda would have shared (marriage, children and a home).

Early on, Pat sought help by contacting and meeting with me and then moving into bi-weekly therapy sessions with a psychologist. Because he had experienced a significant depression following the breakup of an engagement five years ago, and knew how horrible it felt, he was determined to avoid a repeat of that depression.

Pat feels that he has just recently moved out of the profound shock and is now beginning to feel the extreme sadness and loneliness caused by Linda's death. Sleep continues to be a problem for him and weekends represent lonely, sad blocks of time that he is learning to endure.

Discussion

In one of our sessions, I asked Sandy to evaluate her experience in the emergency room on the day her husband died. Sandy said that the help she received was beneficial and that the hospital staff was very supportive. However, she expressed sadness and anger that she had not been allowed to see her dead husband's head. She asked me to describe how her husband looked. My discussions with Sandy have caused me to re-evaluate my decision not to allow a family to see their dead loved one when there is significant body damage.

On reflection, I believe that Sandy's stroking of her husband's body was more important than I had realized at the time. I had a vague, intuitive feeling that she wished to touch or examine her husband's body in more detail. In retrospect, I wish that I had verbally given Sandy permission to further explore his body. I also would have provided totally private time so that the exploration could have included his genitals if that had been her desire. This could have provided a final closeness as well as a distinctive identification that may have been valuable for her.

Mr. Andrews' refusal to acknowledge his son's suicide may have been a form of denial of the death. If it was denial, there was some hope through the Andrews' only grandchild, a boy born four months before Jim's death. This grandson, now two years old, has resembled Jim from infancy and is commonly believed to have many of the personality and behavior traits of his dead uncle. Both grandparents spend as much time as possible with this child.

In Pat's case, because of the intervention of the medical examiner's office, minimal emergency department time was available for us to work with him (Linda's body was taken away very quickly for autopsy). Pat resisted viewing her body initially and there was no time for him to work through his early feelings and fears. Given time, survivors will often reconsider and view the body. In my five years of experience, I have never known family members to be sorry that they viewed the body, but have known many to express remorse that they had not. Viewing the body helps the bereaved accept the reality of the loved one's death. It also helps them to release emotions that might otherwise be denied until the funeral.

Summary

As different as each of the people in the three cases appears, all of them faced the sudden death of a loved one and all had similar needs. Most survivors are thrown into an instant state of shock when they hear about the sudden death of a loved one. People in shock are often so stunned that they must be helped to make the most basic decisions such as who to call and what to say to them. Because I work in an emergency room, I am often right in the middle of this painful situation. Often I must tell survivors that their loved one is gone and how they died. It is hard to see their pain and I want to do whatever I can to make things less horrible.

Survivors need accurate information, not only about the cause of death, but about what is expected of them (i.e., contacting a funeral home, considering an autopsy or organ donations). Survivors need adequate time to begin functioning. In many ways, viewing the dead body is a very important first step in acknowledging a death. Rushing families through this phase may increase anxiety or generate anger that isn't easily resolved.

Once the survivors leave the emergency department, they need resource information such as the name and telephone number of a person at the institution who will be available to answer questions or assist with other issues related to the death (i.e., how to reach the medical examiner, how to get a copy of the medical records and how to apply for social services). Survivors also need information about grief support groups.

My co-workers and I check on all the families within a week, and then monthly on the anniversary of the death. Some survivors need or request more frequent telephone or personal contacts. The contacts serve to support and reassure, and act as a liaison with appropriate community resources. Recovery from a sudden death takes a lot of time. Those who work in the emergency room are able to provide very critical early support to survivors—that is, if they take the time and care enough to make the extra effort. To me, doing this is well worth it.

OVERWHELMED BY LOSS

Rehearsals for Death:
When a Troubled Son
Has Vanished

Pat and her husband, Don, do not know if their schizophrenic son is dead or alive. Greg disappeared three years ago and his parents do not know where he is. Greg's last contact with his parents was from a pay telephone outside of Richmond, Virginia. During that call he asked them for money and gave them an address in Washington, D.C. where he expected to be the following day. His parents sent him a check for 300 dollars and a plea to come home. Strangely, the check was never cashed and they have not heard from Greg since then. They live with fear that Greg is hurt, sick or dead. One thing they know, however, is that Greg's future, if he has one, will not be the one they had in mind for the handsome, sensitive son who grew up in their home. The parents grieve not only for the loss of their son, but for the loss of their son's future.

I learned about Greg's disappearance from Don and Pat in a support group for families with mentally ill family members that we both attended. As a graduate student in psychiatric/mental health nursing, I joined the group to learn more about the experience of mental illness from the family perspective. Don was very quiet and did not have much to say to me or anyone else. On the other hand, Pat and I became friendly during the weekly meetings and eventually volunteered together for a subcommittee assignment. Our task was to visit the state mental hospital and report back on discharge planning for patients leaving the institution.

We made an appointment with the state mental hospital discharge planner who later met and talked with us and offered us a tour of the hospital and grounds. The hospital was like most other state mental hospitals: a solid, yellow-gray brick building with long halls, high ceilings and corridors with tiled walls. In spite of the hospital's attempts to humanize its care facilities, it had too many patients, too few staff and too much time was wasted by both on meaningless activities. Although we saw no evidence of what we read in the papers (charges of violent patients terrorizing other patients and over-medicated patients living in stupors), it was clear that mental health was as absent as sunshine behind these thick, brick walls and covered windows.

It was with some surprise, then, that I listened to Pat say "God! I wish Greg were here." When I asked her to explain what she meant, she said, "As bad as this place is, at least I would know where he was and that he was alive." That day she began to tell me about her son. We agreed to meet weekly over the next few months because she needed someone to talk to about her grief.

Greg, she explained, had been diagnosed with schizophrenia. The diagnosis came after two years of erratic behavior (paranoid thinking and emotional eruptions followed by withdrawal and isolation) and auditory hallucinations. Although he was in treatment with a psychiatrist during those two years, Greg would frequently stop taking his medication. When he stopped, voices and psychotic thoughts would overwhelm him. When this happened, he would withdraw further from treatment and everyone else. Pat would tell the doctor about her son's behavior, but Greg was an adult, and therefore legally responsible for voluntarily seeking treatment. The doctor could not force Greg to take his medication unless he was a danger to himself or others. This pattern of treatment, refusal of treatment, psychotic thinking and withdrawal is all too familiar for families of the mentally ill.

Finally, after a suicide attempt, Greg was admitted to the state hospital. He stayed for seven months, stabilized, and was discharged with a treatment plan that he was responsible for following. But instead of maintaining his treatment, Greg would leave the city and travel by bus to other parts of the state, sometimes staying with people he met en route and sometimes staying at shelters for the homeless. Pat and Don heard from him every few months or so when he called home asking for money. Not only did they send money, but they often tried to find him at the addresses he gave. They found him once or twice, but were unsuccessful in convincing him to come home, to get help or even to contact them regularly. Greg's trajectory was clearly downward and they felt helpless to stop it.

As I got to know Pat better, she told me about her visits to the morgue. These visits started during a period of time when they had not heard from Greg for over two months. They knew he was in the vicinity of the city in which they lived because friends had reported seeing him. A small column appeared in the newspaper one day describing the body of a young man that had been pulled from the river by police. He had no identification and police were asking citizens to come forward if they had any clues about his identity. The description of the body matched Greg. Mustering all their emotional strength, Pat and Don went to the police station and asked to see the unidentified young man. As they walked to the morgue, Pat silently berated herself for ever thinking death would be easier to accept than chronic illness. The thought that this could be the body of her son was more horrifying than anything she could imagine. The guilt she would feel over his dying alone, his suicide or homicide and her failure to be able to help her child flooded her consciousness.

Pat explained to me that in the morgue, she and Don were ushered into a side room. The cart carrying the body was rolled in and the sheet over it was pulled back. She saw that the body was not Greg. They cried and they thanked God for the reprieve. They have since repeated this nightmare four times. The only difference is that now the police call them whenever an unidentified body that resembles Greg is brought in. The police have a file photograph of the smiling, handsome high school graduate and a few family snapshots that Don and Pat have supplied. To Pat, the morgue visits seem like rehearsals for what may one day be the real thing. She cannot imagine that Greg is ever going to return to them or that he will ever have a college education or a job or a family or a future—things that had seemed so certain when he was a child.

Knowing that one-third of schizophrenics will improve and one-third will stabilize is of little solace to families of the one-third who will deteriorate. Pat knows there is a slight chance that Greg is all right and living safely somewhere. However, Pat's fear is often stronger than her hope, and she is weighed down by the tremendous sense of loss that takes over. Pat grieves for the loss of her son and simultaneously hopes for his return. Neither Pat's grief nor her hope disappear. They just go on.

Discussion

As I listened to Pat talk about her son, I marveled at how strong she was to be able to function at such a high level while carrying such a tremendous emotional burden. She said that the support group she attended was very helpful and that she would continue to go. It meant a lot to her that the other members had similar problems and that they understand her fears. They also understood that the disappearance of her son was similar to having lost him to death, and this was especially important to her. She was considering working as an advocate for services for the mentally ill because she thought it would help her. I agreed. Such work would allow her to feel like she was doing something for Greg, even if only in a general way.

I suggested that she keep a journal in which she could write down some of her happy memories about Greg. I knew that most of her good memories had been overshadowed by the sadness of the last seven years and it was important for her to remember them.

Although my meetings with Pat spanned only a few months' time, my learning from this experience goes on and on. I had professional experience with schizophrenic young adults before, but had no clear idea of what their parents were experiencing. No amount of reading about the grief and loss associated with serious mental illness could provide me with as much insight as did Pat's story.

"777 Maternity Stat!"

Disbelief and shock momentarily immobilized me as I heard "777 stat maternity ward" come over the hospital's intercom. The announcement meant that somebody's heart had stopped, somebody coded postpartum. Could this be true? I listened for another announcement. Again I heard the dreaded "777 stat maternity ward." Was this about the new mother, Sara, who had been transferred out of the recovery room only 30 minutes earlier? Was this the same patient whose difficult delivery my colleagues had just been discussing? This was horrifying; maternity patients are not supposed to be that vulnerable. They certainly don't die! But this patient did die. The expert resuscitation efforts of our specialized high-risk birthing center were not able to help her.

As we were cleaning up after the code, I found it disturbing that we were required to charge to the patient's account items that had been used in the resuscitation attempt. It was unnerving because all of the items had been used unsuccessfully. It seemed senseless to charge for life-saving equipment when all our attempts had failed. Making up the bill only served to intensify my feeling of failure.

The maternity ward is usually a happy place to work. Most of us expect that a pregnancy will result in a healthy baby and mother. When we think about the birth of a child we generally don't even consider the possibility of death. If someone does die it is usually the child, not the mother. To a medical professional a maternal death after childbirth is equated with failure.

I identified with this young mother who was about my own age. I, too, had recently had a child. But my child had a mother; Sara's child did not. I was left searching for answers—and meaning. I looked for someone to blame or a way to prove that this death had somehow been an accident. I wanted to reassure myself that such a tragedy couldn't happen again.

I was not alone in my search for meaning after Sara's death. Jack, Sara's primary physician, described his relationship with her as close, and he said that she wasn't just an ordinary patient. "I lived through her miscarriages, her abortions, her Title XIX [public assistance], her private insurance problems and her divorces. Periodically, she would call me up and say, 'Hi, honey, this is your pest.'" Jack said that he had begun caring for Sara when she was 16, when she had developed a pelvic mass. He had also cared for her sister and mother. Sara's death was his first and only experience losing a maternity patient.

Because Jack considered himself an exceptionally well-trained physician, a perfectionist and the possessor of a God-given talent for recognizing a sick patient by just looking at her, he kept questioning how he could have failed Sara. He reviewed obsessively the sequence of events that led up to her death. He has never been able to discover why Sara died and to this day he agonizes over losing her.

Upon hearing of Sara's death, Jack broke down and cried. He was devastated. He badly wanted to attend her funeral, to say goodbye. But suddenly he was faced with a dilemma. The insurance company advised him it would not be in his best interest to attend the funeral because of the possibility of a malpractice suit. Therefore, Jack did not go to the funeral and he still feels pain about that decision. "I wanted to go—because she was more than a patient—she was a friend."

Missing Childhood

During our interview, Edith told me about a television program she had just seen that gave her a little bit of hope—hope that she thought she would never feel. She said that the moment she saw the show, she found herself holding her breath. If she breathed, she said, she feared that what she was seeing and hearing might disappear. The program was about adults who had suffered severe abuse as children. I could feel both her hope and her pain in her velvety soft yet sorrowful voice. She told me that all of the special care and attention that she had given to her troubled husband Carl for so long had not helped him deal with his pain.

She talked about Carl's gentleness and kindness and how he had been loved by all the people who knew him. She said he was very kind to her and "painfully" grateful, but that he could not make clear to her—at least in any way that she could understand—why he would go just so far toward emotional intimacy and then stop. He simply could not take that final step that would allow him to feel, or even to touch, or to be close to others. He just could not accept the love and caring even though he needed and wanted it.

Edith knew that there was something very wrong about her husband's life. There was something missing and she had no control over it and no way to understand it either. I could feel the immense amount of frustration she felt. She couldn't quite grasp what it was about Carl and his childhood that caused so much trouble. She told me how she longed to understand what prevented Carl from living without misery. It was obvious she loved Carl more than anyone else in the world and that the shadowy angst in their lives caused her great pain.

Carl, Edith said, was a laborer who could neither read nor write. They had been husband and wife for over 20 years. She begged me for information about where she might find help so that she could understand her husband's problem. She wanted to be rid of her feelings of restlessness and anxiety. If nothing else, she wanted to find something to help her accept Carl as he was and let go of what could never be.

I spoke with Carl the next day. His voice was much lower than Edith's, but it had a similar, melodious resonance. There was a note of pain and hopelessness in his voice, too. I couldn't help thinking that Carl must possess a beautiful singing voice. But at the same time I was saddened by the suspicion that he never sang because he wouldn't know how and perhaps he was never happy enough to want to sing.

With difficult pauses, Carl began to talk about his childhood. It was clear to me that Carl didn't realize that his life was any different than anyone else's. At times, he said, he tried to make some sense of it. He did recognize that his parents treated his siblings differently than they treated him, but he wasn't sure why. Beyond that, he didn't remember thinking much about his feelings—the constant confusion, the consistent sameness—until he was older. He did, however, remember very well that each and every day his parents told him that he was a very bad and very evil child, and that they treated him the way they did so that he would be "saved." Carl said he heard this, but didn't understand it. He didn't know what "saved" meant, but he wasn't allowed to ask questions.

Carl never went to school and did most of the housework for as long as he can remember. His parents drank heavily in the evening and they often woke him up in the middle of the night to clean up after them when they became sick. He was frequently forced to kneel with his head down for hours in front of his family. He was not allowed to speak without permission. He could not flush the toilet unless he asked. He was not allowed to walk on the rugs in the house; instead he had to walk around them with socks on so that the rugs could be spared his "filth." Carl had no shoes and he never left the house. He was fed infrequently and when he did eat, it was what was left over from the others' dinner. His brothers were taught to fasten a chain around Carl's neck and attach it to a doorknob, leaving him just enough length to reach the feeding dish on the floor from which he ate on his hands and knees. He ate in this manner without knowing why and he didn't think about it. He was forced to keep his eyes lowered at all times so that he couldn't look into his family members' eyes. He was often left alone; it was always either very hot or very cold and it was always dark. Carl couldn't remember how long these solitary periods lasted, but he did remember being in a small, closet-like room and that he was given some sort of food and liquid. At times, he said, he felt better knowing that the others were gone.

Carl's beautiful voice carried a sense of hopelessness that was both glaring and subtle. He told me that he felt no purpose in living and that he would kill himself were it not for his wife and children. He was careful to tell me that he had never hurt his children, but that he could not be emotionally or physically close to them in the way he wanted to be.

Carl never reflected on his childhood until after he became an adult. He said the first 20 years of his life contained nothing that he wanted to remember, but nothing he could ever possibly forget.

Carl remembered times when he was older that he had tried to find help for himself, but he was never able to follow through because the memories were too painful. He told me of his need to "accommodate" the early years of his life by placing the memories in "boxes," putting them in "another room" and locking them up. He said he was glad that he could not get into this "room" and that was his security, his source of sanity. He added, "When I do think about it, as I am right now, I find myself wanting to cry forever, but also wanting to hope…to try to find something, but then there's always that other part of it. I'm so tired of living. I'm tired of depression and wish I had never been born."

A few people have tried to help Carl by helping him grieve for the loss of his childhood, but he maintains that he doesn't know how, or even where, to do this. He once asked me, "How can you lose something you never had?" He then expanded on this: "I never owned my feelings. I never owned a place or even a tiny space of my own. I never owned anything. There is another person inside of me, and after some 40 years I don't own or understand that person. I don't know how to want or to hope for something better or for something different because I don't know what something better or something different is. I just know that I can never, ever forget this, and that just brings more sadness. I think it's better that I keep it in the other room. I went into the other room only once and it was too painful and too frightening and I had to put it back and I can't unlock it again.

"Lately I think about how it is when I wake up in the morning. The one thing that is always the same in my life and the one thing I can trust will never change is the dawn. The dawn is always the same. It is grayish and dull, just like it has always been. I know that some dawns have a yellow sun, but I can't look at that sun. I think that what I hope for most is that someday one of my dawns might not be the same grayish, dull color, but that someday one might be a very dark black and that will mean that one dawn I will not wake up."

Discussion

My purpose in relating this story is not to stun or to upset, but to inspire. I believe that people need to know that countless numbers of children in the world experience the horrors of child abuse and neglect. Worse still, this horror continues and most of it is kept behind locked doors as a vicious secret from everyone, most especially from those who could help put an end to it.

Because of Carl's abusive childhood, he is now a man full of severe hopelessness and unyielding pain. Carl's story, which is also the story of many others, changed me. It took a long time to get past my own anger over how some people treat their children. I have been able to let go of that anger, but my sadness continues.

I can only hope that Carl will find something that will help him. Some people don't recover, but I would like to think that for Carl, a brighter future is possible. I find comfort in hoping for him and also in believing that my hope might reach him. I have no doubt that some of you who have read this story are survivors of child abuse. Please share your experiences and your understanding of them with those who were fortunate enough to have the free, innocent and wonderful times of childhood that should be every child's right.

Every Child: A Cry for Help

Sure I look a lot like other people but that depends on where I am and what I'm thinking at the moment and yes I can smile and maybe you've seen my smile but I don't think so because it is still such an effort and it took such a long time to practice because I spent most of my life crying or sitting and staring or staying in bed or drinking too much or eating too much or just hiding and sometimes it was spent hurting myself because the pain was so familiar and the smile was not and if you have seen my smile you will easily forget it because most of my life was hiding inside of myself.

I was too tired to do anything and I was too frightened to try anything because I was terrified of making a wrong move or a mistake because I knew I could only do things badly and even *that* at times was not bad enough for them and if it was good then I had to say it was bad even though I knew it was good and then I got so mixed up that I wasn't sure if I did it or didn't do it because they were always so angry and it was always my fault and I was always doing everything wrong and because I wasn't sure of what they wanted me to do in the first place.

You're going to have a lot of trouble understanding this because I don't understand it myself and it was a long time ago and it went on for such a long time and I was trained by those who are supposed to love me to assume a major role in the destruction of my own life and to know that I was their target practice and it wasn't that I wanted to be bad because I tried to be good but I got it all mixed up and that was the beginning of all of the dreadful monuments.

I built my life to support the abject poverty of any feelings that reinforced the constant mixing up of the good and the bad. Please listen to me when I tell you that I tried to be good and I tried very hard to wash the plate just right just one time and I know that I did that and I washed that plate in that way 10 times and you could take that plate and place it under a microscope and find nothing that didn't sparkle clean but they would tell me that it was dirty and that I better not come away from the sink until the plate was clean and I knew the plate was clean but they kept it up and kept it up until I saw dirt on the plate that wasn't there and I pointed it out to them and I said I was sorry for the dirt that wasn't there and that was their signal or their reason to begin beating me and the beatings went on and on.

What I saw in their eyes was worse than the beatings because the changes in their eyes frightened me and it was only when I could pass out that I would wake to receive the plate smashing over my head that I didn't feel but felt the stinging of alcohol being poured over my head to cleanse the cuts and where were you then and why did you never say a word or notice that I was bleeding and hurting and please remember I haven't forgotten any of this because I have the nightmares with me and I have the will not to forget any of it but then I do forget a lot of it because sometimes I can't stand to remember it and I know I am mixing you up and I see that you are trying to be nice to me but please remember I don't trust you and you'll just think I am crazy like they do and I am you know.

There's a fine line between craziness and saneness and sometimes I choose to be crazy because it's easier and I'm going to mix you up like they mixed me up and because I am mixed up how could I not mix you up and this is the way I talk to myself a lot of the time and please listen to me because you see it is like a reflex to me and I automatically say yes, no, no, yes, and I still am not sure of the right order whether it should be yes, yes, or no, no, because they never would explain the order to me or the reason they made me like this.

I am angry and are you wondering why I spend most of my life inside of myself and do you wonder why my husband beat me just as they did and that I had a child that died and no one cared and the child I left behind that no one knew about I have just started to think about and that I had another child I almost lost because I nearly killed that child and are you now just beginning to notice that this is not sounding like a story with a power that transcends misery.

Please wait a minute because it gets better but I get worse and you may stop reading if you want to because it doesn't matter and I don't know if I should be trying to say this in this way or if you will understand why I am so angry and do you think you could understand if I would tell you that sometimes I think even grownups do things that they don't understand.

I will get back on track and will start over again to tell you that now I think I may be getting better and that I want to believe this but if I say this I am not sure because it is so hard to say it in the first place because I am not used to it so let me mix you up some more and maybe then you will wonder if you heard me right and if that doesn't work for you then maybe you will have to listen to me very carefully because you would have to have lived this way for a long time to understand me and to know that I ran away many times and that some of the other homes were not as bad as I made them out to be and that some people may have tried or cared but if they so much as raised their voices or said something that reminded me of them I ran my race as fast as I could but then I always had to come back to them and for a time it didn't matter any more because I had my other friends that I made up for myself that I kept in the hiding place of my life where I thought a lot and wondered a lot and wrote about all of this and then I realized that writing all of this down was not the best thing for me to be doing and that maybe I needed to be erasing the bad things.

I couldn't understand why I was always trying to forget and why I couldn't until I thought about erasing what I had written down and I think that for about 10 years I didn't remember many things at all.

I do remember climbing out of my bedroom window or hiding under my bed or going to bed with all of my clothes on and that nothing worked because he would always be there and she never took care of me and why was I taking care of everyone because she had to work because he was sick and that he would get better some day and I kept telling her that he was not sick and couldn't work but that he was horrible and that he hurts me and please let this stop please help please if you didn't see the smile that was never there you must have seen my eyes and you must have noticed me even if you were always working so hard and why were you always in your room and why was he always in mine and you and he became they who always hurt me and sometimes I think that even grownups do things that they don't understand.

When I was cleaning the plates so hard again you and he came in and smacked me in the face for something I did three hours ago that I couldn't remember and where were you and why did you not notice me and do you understand why I can't do anything and why I am so crazy and so bad and why I can't do anything right and why don't you understand this and why did I have to sit in a closet and watch you beat each other up and now do you understand some of this and please tell me why I should have to get it when my sister is bad and my sister is only two years old and I am 13 and I am not bad either but I just think I am.

I don't pay attention in school and do you know why your eyes are glazed over when you beat me and that I'm not going to run anymore and that none of this makes any sense and that I can't stand it any more and I remember how you smiled at me when they brought me home from the hospital after

I tried to kill myself as if you were glad that I couldn't do that either and the doctors said I am sick for thinking that way and that mixes me up more because I saw your smile and I can't smile and do you think that is why you did not see my smile that was never there and that is why he has to hurt me when my sister is bad and he says it is because he loves me.

I keep telling my sister to please be good and I'm tired and afraid and keep thinking please don't let her be bad today because I am afraid of him and I am afraid of his heaviness on my small self and I hate him and the way he smells and you don't listen to me and I am mixed up and please listen to me because I am trying to tell you something and I didn't smile in the hospitals or with the helpers either and I was with them forever and it seems as though it will take forever to begin to unmix the mixup and then I will be dead.

If someone took 37 years of your life and made each day a devastation of years and created a crazy mixed-up puzzle for you to put together and then stripped you of any and all of your dignity and made you so afraid and made you spend all of those years in the misery of your own company and then another eternity of hours scratching in the concrete-like dirt of your life's puzzle to find an answer or a reason.

No one helped you because remember they did that once and you didn't get better fast enough so we know you weren't trying and we know you need to do this all on your own and now please look at me and ask me why did you do poorly in school and why did you marry the man who half killed you and why did you hurt your child and why did you never do anything right and now please tell me who would hire me when I do everything wrong and with all the cuts on my wrists and the marks on my body and the scars that don't show and will never go away and then ask me where I have been for 37 years?

I am tired of running the race and I can't run anymore because it made me even crazier trying to outrun the hurricane of fright and confusion and now to continue to duck and avoid the afterwinds of sadness and the funnel of shame that constantly scoops me up and makes me dizzy in my attempts of recovery and please remember that recovery means rewriting all that I have so carefully erased that it seems ludicrous to me to relive all of the races and frantic pace to survive the sickening whirlwind of memories I don't want to recall.

I told you that I wrote all of this down and then I erased it and then I took all of it and tightly squeezed the pieces of paper of my life into tiny little wadded-up balls of nothingness and threw them away and now please don't ask me to pry them open again only to relive those torn written erased mixed-up feelings from the attic of my mind.

I think even grownups don't understand some of the things they do but they will never remember them and they will never concede that this happened and maybe that is why I think that my suffering may differ profoundly from my feelings and that I am slowly taking only a squinted look at that because it hurts me so to open my eyes and look at it starkly and clearly.

You didn't have to finish reading this and I am not sure you will understand what I have said or what I have told you and why I am so mixed up and I'm not sure how to say all of this in a better way and I'm not sure I care if you understand or not but please remember that I am angry and I hurt and that I was hurt by them and by him and by you. I still wonder where you were and that I don't trust you and that I never will and that maybe I am getting better but I am not sure and maybe I will never be sure.

I really did try to smile but you chose not to see my smile that wasn't there because you chose not to look at me and you chose not to notice me and I don't trust you and I wanted to trust someone and I needed to trust someone and I wanted to pay attention in school so please don't send another letter to them saying I am not doing well in school and please understand that I am trying and please ask me why I am not doing well in school and I do try because every day on the way to school I tell myself that I have to pay attention in school in order to get away from this and please remember when you send a letter to them that they are not who you think they are and you don't know what sending those letters to them does to me.

Please believe how hard I try to pay attention and that if I could survive just two hours in school I might make it but then I lose all of my promises to myself and I lose my dreams because I can't seem to make it for two hours because all I can do is to wonder what will happen when I come home today and then I get sick to my stomach and all I can think about in school is please don't let my sister be bad today because if my sister is bad I have to be with him and I don't understand this because my sister is only two years old and I am only 13 and every hour I keep trying and hoping to let me get through today because I have to do well in school to get out of this so please don't let my sister be bad today.

Now listen to me please! Because now...just now...I am beginning to wonder if I have been too mixed up to understand that I've been asking all the wrong questions and what I had a right to ask everyone was, Please tell me what I did to deserve this?

Imprisonment

I wake up in the morning, get out of bed and step forward to the cold steel bars at the front of my cell. I cannot move past the confines of my five- by ten-foot cell until the guards open my door for breakfast. The guards also dictate when I go to work, when I return to the cell, when I go to recreation or the library and when I take a shower. All of the time that is not consumed by these activities, I am locked in my cell (14 hours a day on weekdays, 20 hours on weekends). I have been in prison for the past eight years.

I am deprived of all freedom, as we generally understand that concept. However, I retain one very important freedom, as do all prisoners. I have the freedom to decide how to spend my time while I'm locked in this cell.

There is a wide variety of options available. I could spend all my time watching television, which is probably the most popular activity among prisoners (thousands of hardened criminals, believe it or not, become completely engrossed in the day-to-day developments of soap operas). Or I could spend as much time as is physically possible sleeping. When awake I could lie in bed daydreaming. I could also choose to become lost in the cloud of drug abuse, spending all my time whacked out on marijuana and pills. I could spend hours on end conversing with the other prisoners in the cell block, yelling up and down the tier, giving amazing accounts, most of them lies, of my romantic-dashing-outlaw-type adventures before I was imprisoned. I could even spend all day playing chess, yelling out the moves cell to cell with other chess players. Or like many others, I could become deeply involved in the intrigue of rivalry between the various inmate cliques and gangs, spending my time creating and carrying out intricate plots to undermine rival groups.

All of these are common activities among prison inmates. I choose, however, to spend my time reading, writing and studying. That may sound like a disciplined regimen, but it's a highly effective form of escape. When I'm in the midst of a captivating novel, I break free from prison. I could just

110

as easily be sitting in a public library or in my own apartment; the experience of reading a novel "on the outside" would be no more rewarding or enjoyable than it is in my humble prison cell. When I'm deep in the turbulent throes of the creative process, working on my own novel, following my muse and reveling in its gifts, the fact that I'm in prison never occurs to me. When I'm studying philosophy, wrestling with the concepts of logical positivism and dialectical materialism, the concrete walls fade away and the steel bars cease to exist for me.

In terms of my ability to learn, to grow and to create, I have defeated my imprisonment. In the world of ideas, I roam as freely as any person who is not in prison.

In this manner I manage to satisfy my intellectual needs in spite of the physical constraints on my liberty. There is another aspect of my loss of freedom, however, that has proven far more difficult to satisfy: my emotional needs.

Every person has a need for friendship, for companionship, for other people with whom to share the myriad burdens of human existence. Because of the weight of their woes, there is possibly no group more in need of companionship than those condemned to prison, yet no group in society is more completely denied such relief.

I find that it is virtually impossible to find friends in prison. The social environment is so harsh that prisoners tend to build up a tempered shield between themselves and others in order to avoid being emotionally injured. From behind this shield of emotional invulnerability, most prisoners project the tough, uncaring, antisocial attitude they are so renowned for. This steadfast denial of their feelings has become a necessary element of survival for inmates in American prisons, but it also creates a social atmosphere in which meaningful interaction cannot take place. Prisoners end up being as isolated from each other as they are from the outside world.

Because of the almost total absence of interaction between inmates, they rely on their relationships with people on the outside for their personal and emotional needs. While some inmates manage to maintain closer relationships with people on the outside than others there is one trend that almost invariably holds true for everyone. The bonds that an inmate has with friends and loved ones grow progressively weaker the longer he remains in prison.

My own experience is typical of this trend. During the first few months of my imprisonment I was given a lot of support from my friends and family. I received a steady stream of letters and visitors. But the visits soon became less and less frequent and eventually they stopped completely. The flow of letters also dwindled. Nowadays, some friends send me no more than a Christmas card and I haven't heard anything in years from most of them.

The result of all of this is that I'm a very lonely person. Desperately lonely. The emptiness in my life rips at my psyche, so much that I relentlessly search and strive and grasp at straws in an attempt to achieve even the most limited degree of fulfillment of my emotional needs.

Just the other day I happened to receive a letter from a woman I had dated before being incarcerated. I hadn't heard from her in several years. This woman kept in touch with me for the first year or so of my imprisonment, then dropped out of sight. I later learned that she'd gotten married. In her recent letter she writes that things have changed in her life. I believe this means that she and her husband have split up, especially because she also says that she's now living with her sister. She says that she would like to come and see me.

I wrote back to her and told her I'd be happy to see her. Then I submitted the forms necessary to have her name added to my list of approved visitors. I know precisely what will happen. She will visit me a few times and keep in touch for a few weeks, maybe months. As soon as she develops a new relationship with a man on the outside or reunites with her husband, she will discard me like a worn-out shoe. I know this because I've experienced the same pattern with several other women over the years.

The only use this woman has for me is as a purely temporary means of filling the emptiness in her own life, in the absence of a "real" relationship. She is actually insulting me, but I will welcome the insult and be happy for it. I will be thankful for whatever miserable crumbs of affection she throws my way. Or maybe I should shift to another metaphor. Whatever affection she gives me will be like cool, clear water to a man dying of thirst. I will rejoice in her insult and pray for more.

I am a person existing in grace and harmony on one level, and at the brink of disaster on another. Intellectually I am healthy and strong, ever striving for greater understanding and continually expanding my horizons. Emotionally I am a patient in critical condition, weak and faltering, dying of starvation. Prison is tearing me apart.

A Policeman's Loss

During my career, I've been involved in many cases—well over 100 homicides and attempted homicides, suicides and numerous assaults. The first couple of death cases I worked on (whether homicide, suicide or accidental) took some adjusting to. But then something happened inside me; now the sight of a dead body doesn't get to me like it did before.

In 1980, a number of women in the inner city area were murdered. All of them had either been beaten or stabbed to death. The killer's MO was to leave his victims covered with clothing or a piece of furniture.

While we were on this particular case, my partners and I got a call about an incident concerning a woman being beaten. We were the first squad on the scene and when we got there, the front door was open. Inside we found that the living room was a mess and the furniture was tipped over. When we uprighted a couch and looked underneath a sheet that was covering the couch, we found a black woman who had been severely beaten about the face.

I checked for the woman's pulse and listened for breathing. I found none. She had been beaten so severely that her eyes were nearly gone. Paramedics responding to the call soon arrived and confirmed her death. We then began to protect the crime scene. The victim's 10-year-old son had found his mother this way when he came home from school. He had then run to his aunt's house. She had also seen the victim before we got there. It was part of our job to help the family, all of whom were in a highly emotional state, with their grief.

One part of protecting a crime scene is to make everyone who is not investigating leave the area. But as was the case with this situation, we had to deal with family members who were screaming and trying to get to the victim. They want to know what's going on and what is being done for their loved one. It is an extremely tense position for a police officer. You're unable to devote much time to the family because your duty is to the investigation.

You'd like to take the family to a quiet area, sit with them and talk. You'd like to give them time to ask questions and not have to rush your answers. Unfortunately, that kind of time is hardly ever available.

People expect the police to show stability in the face of trauma. At homicide scenes, the family and witnesses need someone to control the situation, someone who will not break down, someone who is level-headed. I try to be that for them.

I guess the way I've been able to get through murder cases is by playing mind games. Sometime during my early years as a police officer, I stopped seeing the bodies for what they really were and began seeing them as mannequins. This was not a conscious decision—it just happened. Maybe one body had taken on a waxy look, or its position in death did not look natural. I'd take it one step further and imagine that it wasn't real at all. I'd try not to think of this body as a person who has a family or emotions. Later, however, I could not help but think about things like life after death and heaven and hell. I wonder why a victim's last moment on earth had to be violent and what they might have done differently if they had only known what was going to happen.

After being at the scene of a murder, I found that it was helpful to talk things over with my wife. I would leave out the gruesome details and explain my feelings to her. We've since been divorced, so that outlet is not available anymore.

I've had several deaths in my own family. My 15-year-old sister-in-law Beth choked to death one Christmas Day. I had to identify her body at the county morgue. Nine years later, my 18-year-old son Tom committed suicide in our house. I found his body and administered CPR until the paramedics arrived, but he was already dead. I wasn't able to use mind games to separate myself from the reality and pain of those two deaths. Those bodies weren't manne-quins, they were family. I have never really had anyone to talk to about these two deaths, so I've never really adjusted to them. Along the way I have experienced nightmares, bouts of sadness, loss of concentration and loss of energy. It's been difficult.

My 17-year-old son Mike lives with me. He is my main source of stability, so I'm not looking forward to when he enters the military after he graduates from high school. When Mike leaves, I know I'll be facing the loneliness of loss again. Because my son and I have grown very close in the last three years, it will take a lot of adjustments when he leaves. I'll be coming home to a quiet, empty house instead of one filled with loud music and car magazines. There will no longer be an auto repair shop in our garage. But what I'll miss the most is the sense of family. When my son leaves, I will lose my family.

Alcohol has become part of my way of coping, but I don't feel I use it as a crutch. Yet, looking back, I realize that I escaped a lot of my pain after the divorce and the deaths in my own family by drinking, even though I did it moderately and always off-duty.

Being a police officer is not hard. Having a personal life as a police officer is. The job has made me suspicious of everyone and everything. It is extremely difficult for me to trust anyone.

I'm not proud of the way I look at things and wish I could change my attitude, but the deaths I've dealt with on the job, my own personal tragedies, and the way I've been programmed to think have all taken their toll.

A Daughter's Duty

Clyde was a 77-year-old man who had suffered from emphysema for over 10 years. Even though he had physically deteriorated quite a bit in the past year, he continued his efforts to be active: he rode an exercise bicycle at home and although it was difficult, he did some gardening. He lived with his 72-year-old wife of over 40 years and their 33-year-old single son. They had another son and daughter who lived in another state, and also an older daughter who lived 30 minutes away.

Shortly before Clyde's last hospitalization, his daughter Sara, a resident physician, came to see him. Clyde had been seeing a local physician, Dr. Norris, whom no one else in the family liked. Sara shared the rest of her family's negative opinion about the doctor, but she did not want to interfere with her father's right to choose the doctor he wanted. However, when Clyde himself began to express doubt about Dr. Norris ("I don't think he cares much about me anymore"), Sara helped by obtaining her father's medical records so that they could be forwarded to a new doctor, someone Clyde had seen before. At this time Sara noticed how apprehensive and depressed her father was.

Four weeks later, before he had changed doctors, Clyde went on a long walk that left him with unremitting abdominal pain. Twelve hours later, his son-in-law decided to take him to the hospital. By the time Clyde was admitted, he had become slightly confused. The admitting diagnosis was an allergic reaction to medication. When Clyde's wife and son-in-law left him, he was feeling somewhat better, but by the next day he was in restraints, bruised and talking incoherently. Clyde was confused and unable to recognize his wife or son-in-law. Clyde's wife became alarmed and the son-in-law called Sara.

Sara thought her father's behavior sounded like he was having an acute drug reaction and instructed her husband to find the resident in charge and ask him or her to review her father's chart. (Her own attempts to telephone the hospital and reach a resident or the attending physician were met with endless holds and disconnects.) A resident physician told the son-in-law that Clyde had suffered a toxic reaction to lidocaine, which he had been given for a ventricular arrhythmia, a condition he had had for some time. This information was not given to Clyde's wife or any of the other family members.

Haldol was given to counteract the drug's effects and Clyde was put in restraints. Toward the end of his first week in the hospital, Clyde began producing green sputum and experiencing shortness of breath. Although Clyde's wife thought he seemed worse than when he was admitted, Dr. Norris told her that Clyde probably would be able to go home in a couple of days. He then told her that Clyde's behavior was due to Alzheimer's disease. He did not mention the admitting diagnosis, the possibility of a drug reaction, or the results of any of the diagnostic tests that had been conducted.

After being told that her husband had Alzheimer's disease, Clyde's wife became hysterical. When she got home she called her daughter Sara, who then called Dr. Norris. When Sara reached him, he made no mention of the Alzheimer's diagnosis and stated that her father would more than likely be discharged in two or three days. He also told her that he did not think it was necessary for Sara to fly out to be with her father. Sara, however, didn't agree. She was concerned about the attending doctor's contradicting stories and worried because her father was being cared for by a doctor he had wanted to discharge. She decided to fly home.

On the day Clyde was supposed to be discharged, he had to be intubated for deteriorating blood gases and was admitted to the ICU. He was given large doses of prednisone because he was now diagnosed with aspiration and intercurrent asthma. When Sara arrived, her father was lying comfortably in the ICU and her brother and sister were with him. The intern on duty said he could not give Sara much information about her father because he had just arrived on the case. When Sara told her father that they were all working to bring him home, he grabbed both of her hands and brought them to his face as if to kiss them.

At this point, Clyde was not thinking clearly and he pulled out his breathing tube 36 hours after it had been put in. After doing so he appeared dazed. He was still receiving Haldol and prednisone. The x-rays and physical findings showed a persistent pneumonia. By the time he was in his second week at the hospital, there had been no meeting between Clyde's family members and his physicians about his diagnosis and prognosis. Sara noticed discrepancies between the attending physician's reports and what her mother assumed was going on, and discrepancies between the attending physician's diagnoses and those of the resident. When he became increasingly short of breath, her father appealed to all those around him for help, even though he himself had taken out the breathing tube. He was quite confused.

At Clyde's bedside, Dr. Norris said that Clyde should go to a nursing home instead of to his own home, and suggested that Sara and her mother see about placement. Out in the hall, away from Clyde's wife, Dr. Norris asked Sara for permission to make him a DNR (Do Not Resuscitate). When Sara asked his reason for doing this, a decision she thought was rather premature, Dr. Norris said that her father was "senile and would be hard to handle." At this point Sara realized Dr. Norris had made up his mind that Clyde was terminally ill. Sara had seen physicians fail to treat elderly patients as aggressively as they might younger ones, and knew that they sometimes lost interest in patients they thought would never recover. Dr. Norris, it seemed, was one of these doctors. Nevertheless, she gave him the benefit of the doubt, thinking that perhaps he had suggested a nursing home in an attempt to spare the family the financial hardship of 24-hour home care.

Sara felt her father deserved another opinion. She called her training hospital and spoke to several neurologists and cardiologists, and to the pulmonologist who had seen Clyde two years before. After relating Clyde's history as completely as possible, she asked them to advise her as honestly as they could. Was Dr. Norris correct in the prognosis he had made? To her surprise, not one doctor agreed with making Clyde a DNR or with barring further ventilator use.

Sara tried to broach the issue of a second opinion with her mother. Frightened and exhausted, her mother told her that Clyde had suffered long enough and that he should be allowed to die. After having met with the social worker to discuss nursing home placement, she feared she might be left totally without money.

Her mother now began asking Sara when she was going to return to her own home. Sara and her husband had been sleeping in her mother's bed and were unwittingly contributing to the mother's exhaustion. Sara felt increasingly isolated and helpless in her attempts to do the right thing for her father, and yet she did not want to alienate her mother and the rest of the family. Therefore, she attempted to enlist her sister in persuading her mother to secure another opinion on their father's condition, but her sister's response surprised her. She told Sara that she was being selfish and not thinking enough about their mother. She also said that Clyde had never told her he loved her! It was obvious that her father's illness had also taken its toll on her sister.

Because Clyde's physical condition appeared somewhat more stable, Sara decided to return home in hopes that family emotions would cool. Neither she nor her husband had been contacted by Dr. Norris since he had spoken with her about making her father a DNR.

Several days later, Sara's mother called her to say that Clyde had appealed to her in such an anguished way for help with breathing that she had decided to allow another doctor to see him. The consulting cardiologist had told her that Clyde would have to be intubated for the evaluation. Sara's mother had decided to consent and Clyde was evaluated. The results of the evaluation pointed to his lungs, not his heart, as his main problem. Because this diagnosis seemed to reveal little that was not known about Clyde's condition before, her mother decided Clyde should be extubated. Sara was devastated at her mother's reasoning; she felt the doctor's assessment clearly indicated that Clyde needed a ventilator to breathe comfortably. Sara was aware that her father's emphysema would ultimately kill him, but she still felt he deserved the chance for a little comfort that was being denied him. In addition, she knew that because he was denied the ventilator, he would be in terrible distress for some time to come.

During one of her many calls to the hospital to find out about her father's condition, Sara was informed that her father had been officially classified DNR and DNV (Do Not Ventilate). She expressed her disagreement but heard nothing more from the hospital for several days. Then the hospital's social worker called to tell her that her disagreement with the rest of the family was causing them distress and that Sara should "stop acting like a doctor and start acting like a daughter." Sara called her sister and attempted to convey her dismay over her father's suffering, which could go on for some time. She told her she felt he needed the ventilator because he had acute pneumonia. Her sister told her that he would not get the ventilator and that their brother and mother were going to meet with Dr. Norris to determine how his death could be hastened. Sara's sister declared that their father was not going to be like Clare Conroy, a family friend who was in a persistent vegetative state, and that Sara was just playing God and couldn't accept death.

Sara called Dr. Norris and was told that her mother had authorized the ending of NG (nasogastric) feedings. (They had just recently been initiated, at Sara's suggestion to the resident.) When Sara told Dr. Norris that she did not agree, she was told that she was not next of kin and had to talk with her mother. Sara was in despair over her father's condition and her mother's apparent decision to hasten his death. She finally got up enough courage to call her mother. When they talked, Sara discovered that her mother had never meant to authorize the end of her husband's NG feedings. She had been confused and thought what she was authorizing was the removal of the ventilator tube. This apparent confusion on her mother's part only saddened Sara more. During the conversation, her brother broke in on the phone and accused Sara of wanting their father to live on the ventilator in a nursing home forever.

It became obvious that everyone except Sara and her husband hoped her father would die. Over the next week, Clyde continued to live in an agonizing condition, slowly deteriorating. Sara knew that the longer he continued without proper nutrition and respiratory care, the less likely it would be that he could survive. He was somnolent or delirious most of the time, and she was told at one point that he had even asked if he were dead yet. This news, which she assumed was meant to show Clyde's concurrence with the hospital's course of action, only served to crush her. She knew how her father had wanted to live. His wanting to die showed only how great his suffering was.

On Father's Day she was told that Clyde had a mucus plug obstructing his right mainstem bronchus, and that his blood gases were deteriorating quickly. In the hospital's view, only intubation and suctioning could save him and that was being done.

Dr. Norris asked the family to have Sara call him. Sara obliged and told Dr. Norris how displeased she was with his treatment of her father and lack of complete disclosure to her family. Dr. Norris countered with, "If you were so concerned, why did you leave? Do you want me to withdraw from the case now?" Sara was aghast at his comments and their timing.

Two hours later, her father died. Shortly thereafter Sara was informed she was not welcome at her father's funeral. Her sister felt that she would probably make a scene if she came. Sara was devastated. Her husband sought the name of a therapist and offered to set up counseling for the whole family. But when he tried to get the family together, Sara and her husband were told no one except Sara had a problem. Sara's sister told him that she was writing a living will to protect herself from her doctor-sibling.

Sara sought advice and comfort from her friends. They all advised her not to complain about the medical or psychological care rendered to her father. Since he was dead now, they reasoned, such a claim could only serve to hurt her mother. Sara took their advice. She and her husband have remained in contact with her mother, but family relationships are no longer what they had been. Eight months after her father's death, Sara is still depressed and confused.

The Purgatory of
Being "Barren"

I was a ripe old 21 when I first became aware of the difficulty I was having becoming pregnant. My husband and I had been married for two years and both of us felt that it was time to start a family. I had never been regular with my periods, even when I had weighed more and did not exercise regularly, but I never imagined that fertility would ever be a problem for me.

I had been off the pill for approximately one year when I decided to seek medical advice about my "supposed" inability to conceive. Almost immediately the physician placed me on fertility pills. I was also told to check my temperature every morning before getting up to go to the bathroom. It became a morning ritual for four years. It also became a barometer for my moods; if my temperature dipped after being elevated for over two weeks, I knew that my period was coming and, of course, that meant no baby was coming.

After more than nine months of taking a fertility drug called Clomid, I began to experience intense breast tenderness and abdominal bloating. I felt pregnant, but it had only been one week since I had my period. At that time the home pregnancy test was not available, so I waited. After a week of this, I suddenly began to have intense lower abdominal pain that radiated to my shoulders. I also began to bleed moderately. I thought it was a miscarriage, even though there had been no confirmation of the pregnancy. It was a hot September evening, a Sunday, as I recall, and I had just finished cleaning up after dinner with my in-laws. Finally, after several more hours of this intense pain, I decided to call my gynecologist. When I could not reach him, I spoke with the chief of the department and persuaded him to let me come to the hospital for an examination. He was very reluctant to do so.

The emergency room staff were kind to me and I was admitted for observation. I spent the next 48 hours in the hospital with nothing to drink or eat. I also had numerous tests to check to see how much blood I had lost, the results of which indicated that my blood levels were below normal. The pregnancy test was negative. Nothing else was done. I was told that I probably had an ovarian cyst. I went home and went back to work as a registered nurse on a pediatric unit.

Two weeks later, as I moved some cribs down the hallway at the hospital, I suddenly felt a gush of fluid from my vagina. I ran into the bathroom and was shocked to see blood. I felt light-headed, bloated and uncomfortable so I left work and went home. It was a Saturday afternoon and a University of Wisconsin football game day—a big event in Madison. I convinced myself that I was completely neurotic, so I ignored the symptoms and ate my favorite meal of beans and fish. I ignored the increasing pain and continuing flow of blood.

Finally, at six p.m. I realized that the bleeding wasn't going to stop. Desperately, I tried to track down my husband at a post-football practice session. When I finally managed to reach him, he came home and took me to the emergency room. I hardly remember the ride to the hospital. I was weak and in excruciating pain.

This time, diagnostic tests were done. A colposcopy confirmed uterine bleeding. Sick and frightened, I was rushed to the operating room. I felt like I was dying. I asked my husband to call my mother. She rushed down to see me and I just kept holding her hand. It was over before I knew it. I awoke to the feeling of knives in my abdomen; the pain was unbelievable. I threw up; the nausea was overwhelming.

The next morning, my gynecologist visited me and said, "Well, at least you got pregnant." I could not believe it; I had just been given the news that I had suffered an ectopic tubal pregnancy and was now minus a fallopian tube, but "at least I got pregnant!"

Blame it on my youth and naiveté but after I recovered from surgery I continued to take the same fertility pill. I began to have ovarian cysts on an almost monthly basis. My husband had declared that he would only have children naturally and wouldn't consider adoption. It seemed that the gods were against me.

My husband's sperm count was OK; I was the "guilty party." I honestly began to feel this way. Month after month, doctor visit after doctor visit, I suffered. Nothing worked. I took hormone pills, injections, fertility pills, went through a laparoscopy, endometrial biopsy and other procedures. And I always made sure that sex was on the "appointed" days—the best days for conceiving. During the three and a half years when I would sit in the gynecologist's waiting room, I watched mothers throughout their developing pregnancies and always, always, I left feeling as though I had done something wrong in my life to warrant my "barren" state.

The final blow to the idea of becoming pregnant coincided with the birth of my husband's child; he had his baby with a co-worker with whom he had a longstanding relationship. That was the end of our marriage. I decided that never again would I allow anyone to make me feel inadequate because of my inability to conceive a baby. It wasn't my fault, yet still I had been made to feel terrible about it. With that decision, I entered a whole new stage of life. I became an education-bound person who was going to make something of herself!

When I reached the age of 33, something happened. Suddenly, it seemed like everyone was pregnant. After achieving two educational goals and meeting a stable, wonderful man, I suddenly began to experience that old familiar feeling of loss—a profound sense of emptiness. I realize that I will most likely never experience having a child. At times I've allowed myself some hope at the thought of conceiving in vitro or by some other means, but as my current gynecologist recently pointed out, my chances of ever becoming pregnant are slim—no matter what.

My boyfriend isn't sure he can accept that he might not have his "own" natural children. Can I blame him? I can understand how he feels, but it is still extremely upsetting. It infuriates me that I am in this position and cannot do anything about it. Just because I cannot have a child, he makes me feel like an oddity to be discarded for a fertile woman.

Even though I feel such a terrible sense of loss, I am trying to concentrate on the other things in my life. I do have an interesting career, good friends and a nice family. Eventually, I want to adopt a child who needs someone to provide nurturance, care, discipline and above all, love. I know I can be that mother.

Genital Herpes:
A Life Sentence

Jim is a 27-year-old man who came to our sexually transmitted disease clinic for educational counseling on genital herpes. He had been diagnosed with this disease by his private physician about four months earlier.

Jim had been in a monogamous relationship for two years. When his relationship became as he put it "a little rocky," he would go out and try to drink away his sorrows. One night he met a woman in the bar and later that evening they had a casual sexual encounter. Seven days later Jim developed sores on his penis and his physician diagnosed him as having genital herpes. Jim already felt guilty about cheating on his girlfriend, but contracting herpes in addition was devastating. He decided to be honest with his girlfriend about what had happened, but it ended their relationship. He felt he had received just what he deserved. In other words, genital herpes was punishment for the "sin" he committed.

While Jim told the nurse at our clinic his story, he would hardly look her in the eye. He explained that even though the relationship with his girlfriend had ended four months earlier, he was still having "lots of problems." Not only did he fear that he would never have another sexual relationship, but he was also mortified because his girlfriend had told a neighbor about his disease. He just couldn't bear to face anyone so he would sneak in and out of his apartment. He was so embarrassed that he chose to isolate himself.

He said he felt "dirty" and worried that people could tell he had herpes. "I feel like there is a big red 'H' on my forehead." He no longer went to work because he thought all the women there could tell he had herpes. "When I walk into that office, I can just feel my face getting red and my whole body getting hot. I feel like a big walking herpes germ, as if I'm spreading herpes wherever I go. I don't know how much more of this I can take." By this time, Jim was sobbing. "I can forget about another relationship. No one will want me."

Another client named Kathy was sure that she had contracted genital herpes from a new sexual partner, but he denied having any symptoms related to that infection. Kathy was frustrated and angry. "I'm not that kind of person [to get herpes] and I'm not deserving of this life sentence. How could he do this to me?" she asked with tearful eyes. "Who will ever want me? I'll never have sex again."

The following month Kathy returned for counseling with a new partner, Tom. She was surprised that Tom remained interested in her after she told him that she had herpes. Kathy was very worried about the contagious period of her recurrent outbreaks and actually wanted to end the relationship with Tom so that she wouldn't have to worry about infecting him. This insecurity continued as Kathy repeatedly returned to the clinic for reassuring exams. She just felt unable to judge when sexual conduct was safe and therefore avoided sex with Tom as often as possible.

Eighteen months after her first clinic visit, Kathy attended the HELP support group for individuals with genital herpes and their partners. She said it helped her to be able to share common feelings with the other members and that it was reassuring to know she was not the only person with genital herpes. However, she also felt sad because of all the lives she felt were "ruined" by this disease. By this time, Kathy had transmitted herpes to Tom and was verbalizing guilt. Again she said she wished he had never been interested in her so that this would not have happened.

Discussion

Unfortunately, the media has sensationalized genital herpes so much that both public and personal hysteria has resulted. Herpes has been portrayed as a horrible and incurable venereal disease and because of this, those infected with the herpes virus can suffer varying degrees of psychological consequences. The infected client's preconceived image of genital herpes can prove to be the greatest hurdle in the healing process. Accurate information about the disease is crucial to psychological as well as physical recovery.

Jim chose isolation as an escape but could not recognize that this choice was the cause of his unhappiness. Several years after diagnosis, Jim occasionally attends the HELP support group and admits that he has turned to alcohol to relieve his sorrow. He does not want to seek counseling for his depression and isolation and hopes a cure will be coming soon.

Kathy chose the legal route to deal with her anger, seeking monetary rewards for past and ongoing physical and emotional trauma. The verdict was one of comparable liability, meaning that both parties had some responsibility for the consequences of their behavior, he with 51 percent and she with 49 percent. In spite of or perhaps because of this judgment, Kathy is still dwelling on her "terrible" life. In disbelief she comments, "Do you know that even after all of this, the guy is still telling everyone that he doesn't have herpes? I can't believe it!"

My work with clients who have genital herpes has been a real learning experience. Frequently I have been frustrated by my own inability to help clients resolve their feelings of self-recrimination. I finally came to the realization that I cannot be responsible for their thoughts and actions. I can be supportive and provide them with the information they need to cope, but I cannot change the world to make it easier for them. For some individuals, a single, tiny lesion can cause an enormous amount of pain—physically, emotionally and socially.

A Lawyer's Loss: The Verdict
Doesn't Mean the End

It's been over two years since it happened and to think about it still gives me a dreadful feeling in the pit of my stomach. True, I was only the lawyer in the case, but I still feel remorse over the lawsuit I lost on behalf of my client. I can only imagine the magnitude of the pain that the mother, my former client, must feel when she thinks about the loss of her only daughter, Cindy—a loss made worse by the failure of the lawsuit against the driver of the car that struck down and killed Cindy.

I extract small comfort from the fact that the jury did find the 76-year-old driver to be negligent. Unfortunately, they found the daughter, Cindy, to be more negligent and thus, under Wisconsin law, her mother was not entitled to recover damages from the driver who killed her daughter. Cindy's mother spent an excruciating week reliving the experience of losing her daughter. She had to recall watching Cindy slip from a coma to death. She had to hear testimony about how the wheels of the car ran over Cindy, leaving tire marks across her back, and see photos of a small stain of Cindy's blood on the bumper of the car. She also had to hear the treating doctor testify that although Cindy was comatose during the week after the accident, she was still capable of suffering and felt great pain up until her death. Cindy's mother went through all this pain for nothing.

Monetary damages would not have brought her daughter back or compensated her for her daughter's loss, but at least if we had won at trial, Cindy's mother would have had the satisfaction of knowing that the jury determined that Cindy was not at fault in the accident. More importantly, it would have shown that the jurors had understood my client's profound loss and had awarded the only thing the system could offer her—compensatory damages.

I had worked tirelessly preparing for the trial. I spent hours meeting with witnesses, studying the expert reports, preparing legal briefs and meeting with Cindy's doctors and nurses at the hospital. One night a few days before the trial, I went to my client's home to prepare her to be a witness since her testimony would be crucial and very demanding. She was going to have to testify about the kind of girl Cindy was, about the things she and Cindy used to do together, about her hopes and dreams for her only daughter. We needed to show very concretely what a mother loses when she loses her only daughter. I knew it would be difficult for her.

When I arrived at her home, she showed me Cindy's room. Although it had been over a year since her daughter's death, Cindy's stuffed animals were still on the bed, her magazine pictures still taped to the wall. It looked like a room to which a 14-year-old girl would return any minute. I expected her to appear, flop down on the bed, turn on the radio and pick up the phone.

I asked my client to tell me about Cindy. We were both in tears as she talked about what a loving, sweet girl Cindy was. We went through a photo album of their last family trip, and my client showed me a huge Mother's Day card Cindy had made for her the year before. She said that they were truly good friends to one another; they had never had the sort of angry, bickering relationship that many mothers and daughters have.

We talked about how she learned of the accident, the hellish experience of driving the long distance to the hospital and the shock of seeing her daughter in a coma, with tubes running out of her and equipment all around her.

Although Cindy never regained consciousness, her mom insisted that she knew Cindy had been able to sense when she was there. She thought maybe Cindy could even hear her. For a few days the doctors had thought that the coma might be lightening, that Cindy might come out of it. Cindy's mom had been thrilled. She started to plan how she could care for Cindy at home; it would be difficult, but they could manage it. And it would be so nice to have her in the house again!

But this hope was cruelly dashed. Cindy slipped deeper into the coma, and started to become decerebrate. Finally, a week after the accident, her brain stopped functioning. Then she was gone.

To this day I still ask myself, What could I have done differently? Maybe if I had asked one of the witnesses just a few more questions, if I had highlighted certain evidence more in my closing argument, if I had done something differently, would we have won?

I reacted to the verdict in much the same way that some people react to the news of a death. I was stunned and incredulous at first. I was sure there must have been a mistake. I wanted to get as far away from everyone in the world as I could. I was physically, emotionally and mentally drained by the loss. How could this have happened? What did I do wrong? What in the world will I do now?

Gradually, I became angry. Somehow I felt that I had been victimized by the opposing attorney, by the witnesses, by the judge, by the jury. Why did they do this to me? I had worked so hard and cared so deeply. I had given it everything I had and it hadn't been enough. Maybe I just wasn't good enough to be a trial lawyer. Maybe I just didn't have what it takes. I was disappointed in myself.

My anger and disappointment eventually faded, but they have never really gone away. I finally had to put the trial behind me and move on. But even now, as I write, all of the anxiety, fear, disappointment and pain from that loss come back to me. I don't know if any number of "wins" will ever erase that experience completely. I have a permanent scar.

I Don't Know:
The Confusion of Incest

I don't know what it's like for other people who grew up as incest victims. It's easier for me to imagine what it's like for children who grow up in normal homes where there is no incest. Normal families, that's what I read about. That's what I thought I visited when I went to play at my neighbors next door or went to a friend's house for a slumber party. I saw normal families on TV. But I don't personally know about normal. So when I think about incest and what kind of loss it caused for me, I think, loss of what? Innocence? Childhood? Reality? I don't know. It seems like I lost the world. In my world, there were no boundaries. That might sound trite or existential, depending on your frame of mind. But for a child, having no boundaries means it's entirely possible that someone will throw you out of a moving car if you tell. You could die and be buried in a field and no one would know. You think anyone you ever stay with, anyone who ever looks at you, may ask you to give up your body and your breath and your space. When you have no boundaries you have to give up being conscious, otherwise you cannot "be" at all. But that's just how I look at it. I don't know if it is true. Maybe no one else feels this way.

I don't trust myself. I am smart, but I say, "I don't know" a lot. People ask my opinion about the things I went through and I qualify it. My excuse is that I don't know how else to live. I don't know. I don't know. I've practiced those words forever. What happened when I was four? I don't know. How did I break my leg? I don't know. When did the abuse start? I don't know.

But I do know details. I could pick from a pile of them. There was the lace tablecloth I looked through while hiding from my cousin. And the dizzying smell of whiskey and Lysol. I know the colors of the rooms where it happened, the texture of the blankets, the breakfast I ate and the Christmas present I got just before the last time with my uncle. I know those things. And I know the cost of knowing them.

These details are not like pictures in an old album. Each one created a little bit of the lie I've been living till now. It's been like living on a miniature island of sand; there seems to be nothing solid to stand on. Each detail of what happened to me accumulated and together they eventually cost me my sense of self. And each detail reminds me of the terror of having no boundaries, living in a child's world in which there was no way to predict what would happen.

I try to think. Am I explaining this right? I went to a support group for a while. Everyone had well-developed goals: they wanted to integrate the different parts of themselves; accept what had happened and move on; or grow comfortable with their sexuality. We went around in a circle sharing goals. I was last. I said I wanted to be able to come to a meeting without throwing up first.

Maybe I'm not the right person to write this.

My Daughter Died;
My World Collapsed

I never would have believed that my whole world could change so drastically in one split second. Sometimes I feel as if someone else has entered my body, taken over my mind, my home, my whole life. Yet when I look in the mirror I still see the same face. It is not cheerful and happy as it was four years ago, but the same features are still there. I'm learning to live without my daughter, but it has been a long, hard four years. I know I will never *accept* my loss, but time has taught me how to at least *cope* with it.

Nikki was 14 years old when she died. She was excited about starting her freshman year in high school. That year would have meant parties, football games, dances and the prom—the things all young girls dream of throughout junior high school. But Nikki never got to live those dreams. After her death, I watched her friends enjoying the things she had talked about so often and my heart would break. Why was someone so young cheated out of a wonderful life?

Seven years ago my husband and I sold our house in the city and bought a small mini-farm in the country. Nikki was our only child. She made friends easily and loved animals, so the farm was never a lonely place for her. Those years on the farm were wonderful. They taught us hard work and a strong closeness developed between us as we worked together.

Then one day tragedy struck and our lives were changed forever. Nikki got off the school bus and was assaulted by a man who had been hiding behind a tree. Our little cocoon that had seemed so safe and protected was violated by terror. My husband and I promised ourselves that we would never allow harm to come to Nikki again. This promise is what made what happened next so much worse.

After the assault, Nikki was scared to be alone; she wanted someone with her every minute of the day. At night she would sneak into our bedroom and lie on the floor beside our bed because she was afraid to sleep by herself. We were frightened too and finally got a gun to protect ourselves. In the end, it was this "protection" that caused Nikki's death.

Two weeks after Nikki was assaulted, I was putting the gun away. I must have fumbled, because it fell from its holster and discharged. The sound of the shot shocked me and when I saw the look on Nikki's face, I realized that something terrible had happened. She had been struck in the chest by the bullet.

The drive to the hospital seemed to take an eternity. I remember that I prayed and bargained with God. This was my only child. Surely God couldn't be so cruel that he would take her from us. "If you just let her live, I'll take her in any condition. Just let her live."

The next thing I remember is seeing the tears in my father's eyes as he stood outside the hospital doors shaking his head. At that moment my whole life crumbled; I knew then my prayers had not been answered and that all of our dreams and hopes were now gone.

I'm not sure what happened during the next couple of days. We went to the funeral parlor to make arrangements. When my husband asked if Nikki was in the building, the funeral director told us she was downstairs. I had worried the previous night about her being by herself in that funeral home. For weeks we had done everything possible to make sure that she was never alone. And here she was having to endure the one thing she had been most afraid of.

On the day of the funeral, I saw Nikki lying in the casket and all I could register was shock. I went into a state of denial—this couldn't be my daughter. This child didn't laugh or smile and she didn't even look like Nikki. I couldn't touch her or kiss her. I couldn't even say goodbye. Instead I just kept waiting for her to walk around the corner and tell me that the horror of the past few days had been a dream.

The following year was a living hell. Just crawling out of bed in the morning was a real challenge because I knew that I had to face another day of a life I didn't want to live. I got a job to keep myself busy and worked as many hours as I could. I built a wall between myself and my thoughts, trying never to think of the past. The ride to and from work was the hardest as it allowed me too much time to think about Nikki. Some days I had to pull off to the side of the road because my tears were blinding me. At night I would be exhausted, more from trying to battle with my memories than anything else. Going to family affairs was painful because part of my family was missing. Still worse, most of our friends made a point of not mentioning Nikki or what had happened. That hurt even more. It seemed like they had forgotten her.

I turned to my family and a wonderful support group called The Compassionate Friends for comfort. In the presence of the support group, I once remarked that I wished I could wipe out the past 14 years of my life so that I wouldn't have to face the pain of my memories. But someone told me that someday I would cherish those memories. I can say that this day has not yet come.

Sometimes I still feel bitter at the thought of continuing my life without Nikki. I will never have grandchildren to spend my retirement years with. And it scares me to think that someday I might lose my husband and be completely alone.

Thinking back still hurts terribly, but now I know that I would never have given up those 14 wonderful years. Nikki was a special gift, and for that I am grateful.

Moments of Transformation:
Overcoming the Suicidal Urge

George told me that unless his life somehow changed miraculously by the time he reached 30 (in two years) he was going to kill himself. As his therapist, I knew that this was not just an idle threat; George was a high-risk candidate as the following list of factors makes clear:

- He was isolated. Although he had a number of acquaintances, most of them contacted him only to borrow money and they also made him the butt of their jokes. This made George feel deceived and exploited, and invariably he would withdraw into his own solitary world. Instead of focusing his anger at the people who bothered him, he chose to direct it at the larger world that he thought was corrupt, immoral, unfair and heartless. George did not feel safe in any of the relationships he had with other people, except perhaps for the one he had with me.
- He was unemployed. The only work George did was the sporadic renovation of a small house that his father left him. He lived off a small amount of money from his father's estate which was doled out by his lawyer. Because there had been no actual will, George was always worried about the estate being torn apart and he worried that his father's partners, lawyers and the IRS would steal from him.
- He drank very heavily. He would consume 5 to 10 shots at a sitting several times a week at lonely, local bars.
- He was impulsive and often violent. He would often slap or otherwise humiliate girlfriends.
- He was a hunter, a marksman by his own description, and had an arsenal of weapons ranging from handguns to high-powered rifles.

As a child and adolescent, George was severely abused both physically and emotionally by his alcoholic father. Unlike many parents who physically abuse young children by exploding into random fits of violence, George's father's abuse was systematic and calculated. He was also apparently motivated to abuse by feelings of envy for his son. For these reasons, the emotional aspect of the physical abuse was especially painful for George. A charismatic and prominent surgeon, George's father never endangered the life of his son, but rather filled it with helplessness, agony and inexpressible rage. He did this by insulting George, both at home and in front of friends. These incidents would end in skin-tearing wrestling matches between father and son. This abuse continued through George's late adolescence and only stopped when his parents got divorced. His father died suddenly of a heart attack shortly thereafter. George told me that at the time I was seeing him, he still hadn't mourned his father's death.

Treatment

Space permits me to give only a schematic account of George's treatment (and what seem to me to be the moments of his transformation). During two years of treatment with me, George would complain either about the "heartlessness of the world" or about how "fat, ugly and stupid" he was. About both, but particularly the latter, he was actively resistant to any argument to the contrary, regardless of how heartfelt and honest I was. George was handsome and well-built. He also had a native intelligence which, though not scholarly, was unusual with an off-beat perceptiveness and creative spark that was far richer and more interesting than the more stereotypical well-spoken intellectual that he reproached himself for not being. He rejected all of what I thought in this regard, showcasing instead his weaknesses, insecurities and inadequacies and his rage at the world. Even though this pattern would continue for a year and a half, our rapport, nevertheless, grew steadily.

Treatment began to accelerate when George became involved with a young woman who, to a striking and uncanny degree, was similar to the image he conveyed to me of his father: attractive, charismatic, aggressive, alcoholic, rejecting and abusive. After a couple of months of intense pleasure with her, George began to describe her betrayals and his self-attacks. He would describe vividly how drunk she would become, her flirtation with other men, her cocaine abuse, her impulsive spending (and asking George for loans), her verbal abuse of him and the violent incidents between them.

George would admit to me that he plagued her with his insecurities, and would continually ask her for reassurance that he wasn't "fat, ugly or stupid," even though, as with me, he would not let himself be reassured. At one point he said he repeatedly questioned her about whether his penis was long enough for her, an issue which, in light of his inconsolability and her condition at the time, would be sure to slash away at his self-esteem. He seemed determined to show his girlfriend and me what a failure he was, how impossible it was to help him and what a worthless undertaking it was even to try.

I found myself in an increasingly disturbing and bewildering bind, and, I suspect, he knew it. It was early in my career; I was supposed to be helping but he was receiving no help. Certain fleeting, satisfied gleams in his eyes and smiles in response to my efforts to reach him showed me that he was hoping for my frustration, counting on it, designing it somehow. I felt that he was directing enormously powerful and uncontrolled anger at me. He was introducing dangerous elements into our relationship.

Outside of treatment George's life was unraveling. He continued to drink, his girlfriend was sleeping with other men, furniture was broken and bruises were caused in the fights they were having. I had begun to receive calls from his sister and mother alerting me to his suicidal innuendoes. I recommended a psychiatric evaluation to determine if medication should be prescribed, but George told the psychiatrist and me that he absolutely would not take any medication. It was becoming very clear that I was being put to some sort of test (which I had never taken before), and that if I could not pass it, he would kill himself.

I sought help from colleagues and from books, but I didn't feel helped by anything. I felt that something deeper in me needed to change—something dramatic—in order for anything to change in George. I felt an enormous desire to help him, and this was only made worse by the mounting helplessness caused by his resistance to accept anything from me. The strain was becoming uncontainable; either I had to give up (and that was a horrible prospect) or I had to start seeing things in a different way.

It finally hit me that I had to do both: in a way it was necessary to give up on George and I also had to view things differently. I began to see my feelings of helplessness as no different from other feelings that I have about a patient—a communication of sorts. It occurred to me that inducing these powerful feelings within me was the only way that George was able to speak to me and what he was saying was: "Here, here are my feelings of utter, unspeakable helplessness—you feel them—see what you can do with them. Neither I nor anyone I thought I loved could do anything with them other than punish me for them. Let me see what you can do with them. I'll give it one more chance." George would be 30 in two months.

For certain moments during the sessions, the intense pressure I felt gave way to an equally intense curiosity about what I could actually do for George. I would ask him this question directly. At first he said, "I don't know" and quickly shifted back to complaining about how abusive his girlfriend was and how he couldn't live without her and whether the size of his penis was responsible for the whole mess. I asked him again, earnestly, "How can I help you, George? I want to help. What can I do for you?"

"I don't know," he would keep saying, very quickly shifting to another subject. Sometimes, before he got too far away, I would interrupt him with the question, "How come even my desire to help you isn't of any help to you?" He would tell me, "I don't know," perfunctorily as though he didn't even hear me and hurry back to speaking about his girlfriend. I was astounded each time. It became poignantly clear as I watched this keep happening that the barrier he was so convinced was protecting him was in fact imprisoning him. Although tempted, I didn't press him hard with this because of the chaos in his thinking and his risk of committing suicide. Rather, I wanted the contact between us to be as gentle as possible.

By the end of these chaotic sessions, George's suicidal remarks would become more direct. He would say things like, "I don't belong in this world," or, "I don't know what's going to happen to me." After he did this a few times (giving me once again that nearly uncontainable feeling of helplessness), I was able to shift my perspective and let him know that whatever he was communicating to me had registered. I was fully aware of my client's sense of helplessness and hopelessness, manifested by the suicidal threats beneath his words, and wanted him to know it. What I did was to matter-of-factly predict the feelings that led to his suicidal thoughts, trying to convey to him that although I was concerned, I was not rattled by his painful, angry, helpless feelings. In the middle of the session, when George's feelings of helplessness would begin to intensify, I would interject that I expected him to sound more seriously suicidal in the closing moments of the session. And when this happened and I interrupted his suicide threats to point out the fulfillment of my prediction (saying in effect, "See what I know about you now?"), I could see by his fleeting smile, which was different from the one a couple of weeks before, that he was surprised by my accuracy and perhaps by my dispassion, but also touched by them as well. Our work was from moment to moment; there was no feeling of progress in treatment. Meanwhile the rest of his life continued to come apart.

George's girlfriend was no longer living with him. He heard about her liaisons with various men from acquaintances at local bars. In therapy sessions he would wallow in his loneliness for her, his inadequacy at being unable to keep her, and his guilt over having driven her away.

Although it took a great deal of my concentration and will power, I tried to keep myself focused on the idea that if I kept my anxiety to a manageable level, I could help George tap into his power—the ingenuity he possessed for living his life—which was locked up inside him. What I told him, in the face of the agony he presented to me, was how clever I thought he had been in the way he went about telling his girlfriend to leave. It was clear, I said, that he did not really want her to be with him while she was in such bad shape. It was brilliant, I told him, that he was able to conceal his assertiveness in his self-hatred and self-criticism and that he was so effective in both respects at the same time. The self-hatred is what he was conditioned by his father to project to the world while the assertiveness, among his other talents, derived from his underlying strength. While telling these things to George, I tried very hard to keep my feelings under control as waves of helplessness threatened to pour over me. Beyond a hint of a smile, George did not show that this registered at all and clung ferociously and desperately to shooting stinging reproaches and accusations at himself. Even after my interventions, his feelings of failure seemed to intensify into more frequent suicidal innuendoes.

George's suicidal references led to the final surge in my own feelings of helplessness. There was a distinct moment when this surge occurred, a few sessions later, when I felt myself losing all hope, giving up on him and feeling very sad. I said to him at the end of the session, "You might really need to kill yourself, George. I wouldn't want you to do it, but I know I have no control over it. That's a very personal decision. I mean, I could point you in the direction that I think you could move in to feel better, but I can't move you in that direction. That's why nobody could be held responsible for your suicide if it happens. It's a very personal decision. You're the only one who can make it. It would be a real loss to the world if you do, though. I think the world could use more people with your values and talents. And I have to tell you, unfortunately, that the world will forget about you very quickly if you kill yourself—it's an unfortunate thing about the world, but it would happen that way."

Next came the moments of transformation. George seemed at a complete loss after I said this. His face was blank for the longest moment we had spent together. The session was over.

The next three months of sessions were filled with George's uncontrollable crying, something he had never done before in therapy. George expressed rage toward both his girlfriend and his father for their abuse and because they made him feel responsible for their alcoholism and their unhappiness. I had to repeat that I did not want him to commit suicide, but that I had no control over it nearly a dozen times. Each time, for some reason, it seemed to be healing to him. He actually seemed to be in mourning, weeping poignantly from the beginning to the end of every session. It's not clear to me yet whether it was my basic respect for his life and power to make decisions or the firm declaration of the limits of my power and feelings of responsibility for him, or the two of these combined, that started to help.

George's physical appearance and his emotional condition continued to improve steadily. He was lonely and wanted his girlfriend to come back, but eventually overcame the feeling of needing her so desperately. When he disconnected his telephone and obtained a new unlisted number, she immediately returned. Eight months later, they are living together in his home. He says they do not drink, that she does not use cocaine, and that there has been no violence between them. More recently George has started his own business.

Although the suicidal phase of George's life appears to be over and some new moments have managed to break through to him, his thinking is still more influenced by his wounding past, and by the barriers he built then, than by the more promising present.

Endless Funeral:
The Alzheimer's Experience

Alzheimer's disease is found in all types of families and among all kinds of people—mothers, brothers, husbands, wives and grandparents. The stories told at support group meetings are always similar. In the group, the caregivers talk about stress, the loss of friends, the resentments they feel and the pain they experience. A son once told the group that he still felt guilty about placing his mother in a nursing home. Another couple's dream of enjoying retirement was shattered when the husband was diagnosed with dementia. His daughter described the anger she felt.

Support group members receive help by sharing their concerns and problems with each other. Everyone gains a great deal from the experience of others. Every person has a story to tell. At one meeting, a young man suggested creating a group for people who know that they have Alzheimer's disease. The man added, "It's got to be a terrible thing to realize your brain is dying a little each day. It's like an endless funeral." The stories below were contributed by support group members.

Still Struggling: A Son's Story

The difficulty started about 18 months ago. My mother had lived alone in a rural area since my father's death, but at that time it became obvious that she could no longer take care of herself. She stopped taking her heart medication. She kept going to the store for "a gallon of milk and a loaf of bread" when the refrigerator was chock-full of bread and milk. Neighbors informed me that she had driven through red lights. My first struggle with her occurred when I took her car away. She called me a no-good son and a bad ogre. To this day, I feel like an ogre. She told me that she was going to get a job so that she could buy another car, then she glared at me.

A little over a year ago, my brother, my sister and I made an arrangement

141

whereby my mother would spend a month at each of our houses. I dreaded it when it was my turn to have my mother. She would always want to go home and arguments would occur. I know this stress affected both my home life and my job. I also know it adversely affected my wife. On the one hand we were taking care of my mother because she is my mother, and on the other hand we were wishing that she could stay by herself again.

Finally, the day came when it was necessary to place my mother in a nursing home. She had gone through a series of tests and the results indicated that she had suffered brain damage because of small strokes. There was no hope that she would recover, and we were told that her condition would progressively deteriorate. Her symptoms and prognosis were similar to that of an Alzheimer's victim.

The day we took my mother to the nursing home was an extremely stressful day. No one wants to put a loved one in a nursing home, and the loved one does not usually want to go. For a short time after we placed my mother in the home, I found it necessary to have a stiff drink before going to bed; otherwise, I would be unable to sleep. I have given up this crutch now, but that period of time wasn't easy. I felt guilt, anxiety and severe stress. But it really doesn't get any easier. Every time we visit my mother, she always tells us that she wants to go home with us.

My personal observation is that the family of a dementia patient has a worse time than even the families of cancer or heart patients. If there is a cancer or a heart patient in the family, at least you can communicate with that person. The family makes suggestions, but decisions are still the patient's. The families of dementia patients must make decisions for their loved ones—medical, economic and social. At times they must make decisions that contradict the wishes of the patient. This is extremely hard and painful.

During this period I'm not really sure whether I felt grief; I had too much on my mind. I had to take care of Medicare and other financial problems. Perhaps it's all the emotions rolled into one that creates stress.

At times my burden seems too heavy to endure, but I try to persevere. I have begun to realize that I don't cope with this type of stress very well.

The two support groups that I have attended have been helpful in explaining many things relating to dementia, such as care in the home and nursing home care. Even after this period of time I am struggling to keep everything on an even keel. My wife has been extremely helpful and understanding. If it were not for her support, I really don't think I could have handled the problems, the pain and the hurt that come from having a dementia-stricken mother.

My Loss: A Daughter's Story

As Dad started to decline due to Alzheimer's, Mom just automatically took control. I watched closely as she suffered various losses. She lost the companionship of my father and her close friends too. For my mother, life had always revolved completely around Dad; now their golden years could not be shared. Mom dressed, fed and saw to it that Dad exercised every day. She did all the housework, shopping, foster child care and yard work. All of the things they had done together joyfully were now a burden for her. My own immaturity at that time surely didn't help matters. I was now learning about life from half of a parent team. A lifestyle I couldn't understand was forced upon us. Then came the last straw. In April, 10 years ago, Dad was finally institutionalized.

Mom went to see Dad daily; she became a fixture at the nursing home. She would dress, feed and walk or wheel Dad around. Her love for him grew stronger. The nurses said she brought a sparkle to his eyes.

Now it's Mom's turn for the disaster: she, too, has Alzheimer's and my family (Cindy, Chris and I) care for her. One of her wishes was never to be put in a nursing home, so I gathered my siblings together to ask for their help with Mom. To my utter amazement, they refused, giving all types of excuses. It was up to me to keep my promise to Mom and take her into my family.

Now my family is unable to do even the simplest things away from home without making arrangements for Mom, which sometimes cannot be done. Still, we attempt to make our home safe, bright and happy. That's why when asked about my loss, I say that it is a loss of a family that I thought I knew, but never did. In other words, that my siblings betrayed me and my parents in a time of need hurt more than the fact that my parents became so ill. After all the years of love that our parents gave to their children, it's hard for me to understand how my sisters could turn their backs on people who were always there for them.

Over the years, I've yearned so many times for a "normal" family life. Not having a complete family during my growing years was tough to deal with. Many times I felt that God swindled me and my parents, but then I was never promised a rose garden, as the saying goes.

But we'll get through. Why? How? Because our little family has something that is often missing in the world today—love, all types of love. And most important, I still have a family, unlike my sisters. They don't know what they're missing.

Andy's Circle:
A Lesson in Care

He was lying on his back when I first met him. I said, "Hello." He said, "Go away," but in a faint voice because he had not yet learned to coordinate his voice with the movement of the respirator. His name was Andy. I was to be his intensive care unit nurse.

Just days before Andy had been a healthy three year old, able to run and tumble with his seven-year-old brother, Brian. Then a car accident left him paralyzed from the neck down and unable to breathe without a ventilator. The events of that day had shattered his family's security. The accident that placed Andy in one hospital put his mother in another one, and left his dad and his brother Brian miles away at home. Andy's parents felt that they had failed to protect him and their dreams for his future were now flooded with uncertainty.

The disabling of a normal three year old elicits grieving from everyone. Many of the nurses in our unit were hesitant or reluctant to care for Andy because his story was so tragic. A few of us were comfortable enough to visit Andy's room, but most of the other nurses would stay away because it was so painful to see him. And it was with a certain reluctance that I volunteered to be his nurse.

I made a point of approaching Andy as I would any other three year old and soon we became comfortable with each other. When Andy said, "I can't get up; I keep trying," I decided that perhaps music and motion needed to be introduced into his care plan. I brought him a cassette tape of songs. Andy's respiratory therapist and I reserved mornings for the sole purpose of singing to Andy. More than once I looked up to see other staff members standing at Andy's door watching our performances.

After a while the hospital took over Andy's parents' role of determining Andy's schedule. His father didn't approve of this and firmly indicated that he wanted to re-establish his role as parent. He thought it was time for Andy's

144

life in the hospital to be more like it was at home. Among other things, this included a daily afternoon nap and the viewing of only parent-approved TV programs. I asked Andy's father to write down for me the times that Andy had engaged in activities before the accident. To this list I added all of the care and therapy sessions that now were part of Andy's life. Andy's father gave me a list of TV programs that he approved of, which we then posted at Andy's bedside. Soon "Sesame Street" and "Mr. Rogers" were again a daily part of Andy's life. As the gap between hospital and home was narrowed, both father and son seemed to cope better with the situation.

It was entirely understandable that the dynamics in Andy's family would be tense. Usually I tried to learn as much as I could about each family's situation from the family members of my patients, but it was not always easy. In this case, I found that I had to adapt to Andy's family's world instead of asking them to adapt to my world—the ICU. The traumatic events that had caused Andy's and his mother's hospitalizations had a domino effect on all the family relationships. Their bonds of security were gone. Even though Andy's parents did not give consistent feedback to the nursing staff, I believe that they responded positively to our efforts to help. Andy's dad was doing all he could to stabilize the family, but his mother's physical wounds would heal long before she could face her emotional pain. I still think of Andy's brother and hope that his life has returned to normal.

Andy's father traveled back and forth between his home and two hospitals. Although he fully understood the ramifications of his son's injuries, he did not express his grief outwardly. When I asked him about his family or how he was doing, he always responded positively. He reacted to information about Andy's care in a matter-of-fact way. He and Andy had always been very close, and he worked to keep it this way. Sometimes Andy's smiles would turn to frowns when his dad entered the room. Although a three-year-old's anger is understandable when his parents leave him in the care of strange babysitters, Andy's anger stung and hurt the father; it was not something he had any control over. So that they might heal their relationship, I tried to provide opportunities for Andy's father to feed and bathe his son. He was eager to do this, but he could not always be there because his family members were in three different places and he had responsibilities to all of them.

After her release from the hospital, Andy's mother continued to experience medical problems, making her visits with Andy sporadic. Like Andy, she had sustained a neck injury in the car accident; however, unlike Andy, she did not suffer any permanent disabilities. She said she felt guilty about this, and as a result her interactions with her son were very controlled. She often had a shell-shocked look on her face, which was accentuated by the pale tone of her skin. Her appearance was disheveled, and her hands would shake as she approached him. Andy was always delighted to see her, but tearful. Each time Andy's mother would visit, she would call me to administer Tylenol to Andy for an earache. This may have been her way of trying to do something for Andy that would make them both feel better. Andy had been prone to earaches at home, but had never complained about them to the nursing staff. Usually if he was unhappy he could be easily distracted from tears to smiles; however, I always complied with his mother's requests. When his mother was present, Andy always agreed with her that he had an earache. Both of them always seemed more comfortable after the Tylenol was given.

The only way I was able to help his mother with her grief was by the care I gave Andy. She did not seek or accept support from the staff. Her emotions seemed to be in turmoil; she seemed to view her sorrow as a personal matter, and would not even share it with the psychiatrist whom the staff had contacted. She disclosed the most to me when I visited her in the hospital after she had been readmitted. When we had talked before, we shared stories about Andy's playfulness and smiles, but when she was outside of the intensive care unit, she talked of paralysis and ventilators. It was during these discussions that I learned of her respect for Andy's nurses. We were relieving some of her burden because she trusted us with her son's care.

Brian's visits with his brother were limited to weekends. During these visits it seemed he spent more time with his parents and Andy was left in the background. The visits were stiff, with both boys following their parents' behavior. Although the boys read stories and played games with their dad, they did not have the one-on-one time with each other that they used to have before Andy's injury. I encouraged Andy's dad to permit Brian to sit on Andy's bed, but Brian never did so. My heart went out to this seven year old. He missed his mother, his brother, and the family life they had shared. The staff was in an awkward position. We wanted to help Brian, but his parents' ability to be with Andy was so restricted that their needs had to be met first. Brian's adjustment to the family loss was an issue that would not be resolved during Andy's stay in the ICU. I felt it could be more effectively addressed once Andy's condition had stabilized, when Brian and his parents could be involved in Andy's rehabilitation program.

Andy stayed in the ICU for four weeks before being transferred to the Rehabilitation Unit. He was discharged six months later. Rachel, the respiratory therapist, told me that she felt that she had experienced a real loss; she missed Andy when the time came for him to move on to the Rehabilitation Unit. I experienced the same feelings. During the month he was with us, Andy became very secure in his surroundings. We found that both Andy and his parents would become ill-at-ease if his schedule or care changed. Therefore, the ICU staff made an effort to maintain consistency, thereby providing the stability he needed.

During this time there was no resolution to the family's grief; Andy's condition was a constant reminder of their loss. It was easy to imagine Andy as his father described him: independent, even-tempered, adept at learning new tasks, able to recite his ABCs, learning to comb his hair and dress himself. I could not dwell on his past because it really didn't matter anymore. Andy and his family had an entirely new set of issues to deal with, and I was able to help them in this difficult endeavor. I was grateful that I ignored my initial hesitation about caring for him. As heartbreaking as it was to see this small boy paralyzed, I had been able to help him and his family, and that made all the pain I felt worthwhile.

EMPOWERED BY LOSS

Donating Life

One day a sudden tragedy occurred. John Smith was a 30-year-old, single man who sustained a head injury after falling down the basement stairs in his parents' home. He was found unresponsive by his father, and a paramedic unit was called. He received prompt and aggressive medical management upon his arrival in the emergency room. The CT scan demonstrated a large intracerebral bleed. John was placed on respiratory support, his vital signs were stabilized and he was transferred to the surgical neurointensive care unit.

John's parents were in the emergency room family waiting area notifying his seven brothers and sisters of his accident. The neurosurgeon sat down with the Smith family to discuss the extent of John's head injury. John's condition was very serious: he had irreversible brain damage and there was little hope for full recovery.

John's family spent as much time as possible at his bedside. They watched his chest rise and fall as the ventilator delivered breaths of oxygen to his body. They also held John's warm, motionless hand in theirs and tried to understand the severity of his condition. Gradually they reviewed what the physician had said to them and began to see the hopelessness of John's deteriorating condition. After several hours an EEG was performed on him. It confirmed the neurosurgeon's clinical diagnosis of brain death.

As organ recovery coordinator at the hospital, I was notified of John's condition by the neurosurgeon. We discussed the possibility of John being an organ donor and a family conference was scheduled. The physician reviewed the protocol for the determination of brain death with the Smith family and explained that in terms of technology, nothing more could be done for John. The physician then suggested the option of organ donation. Our experiences had shown that donating a loved one's organs can give meaning to what might otherwise seem a senseless death. Sometimes, families feel comforted by making such a generous gift. Even though they have experienced a terrible loss, if they are able to give someone a second chance to live, at least some good has come from it. However, we assured John's family that we would support them in whatever decision they made. Later, with the help of clergy, the family decided to donate John's organs.

The Smith family said their tearful goodbyes to John as he was taken to the operating room. The critical care nurses hugged family members, comforting them with the thought that John's abrupt and tragic death would soon give life to others.

All personnel involved in John's care were affected by the irreversibility of this young man's condition. As health care professionals, they were dedicated to saving John's life and felt helpless when they could no longer prevent his death. I provided support to the medical and nursing staff so they could express their feelings about caring for a brain-dead patient. I emphasized to all of them—those who cared for John in the emergency room, the intensive care unit and in the operating room—that at least something good was resulting from John's death. I tried to replace the caregivers' feelings of loss with feelings of hope. It was a very difficult time for everyone involved in this case.

John's family also received information about the transplant recipients. I wanted to convey to them how thankful the transplant recipients were to have received the opportunity to lead new lives because of the Smiths' generous donation. This appreciation has helped ease the family's pain in losing John. They view their gift as the one positive aspect of John's tragic death. Their feelings of helplessness and loss have been replaced with the knowledge that their action gave others a second chance for life.

Discussion

My experiences as an organ recovery coordinator have affirmed the great value of organ donation to a grieving family at the time of their loved one's death. When a family decides, in the midst of their pain, to donate an organ to give someone else a second chance at life, they are truly helped with their loss. It is very important for care providers to see the outcome of their efforts in organ donation cases and as a recovery coordinator, it is my responsibility to communicate the positive aspects of the donation.

My reward is the comfort brought to the donor's family. After the medical staff receives news about the transplant recipients, they too can share in this comfort. Finally, I have the joy of knowing that through the cooperative efforts of everyone involved, several people will reexperience the gift of life.

He's Still My Son

Sometimes when I am driving down a busy street, I see a young man purposefully striding along the sidewalk. From the back he is tall and lanky, with slightly longish, brown curly hair. He's wearing a brightly colored ski jacket. For a moment my heart stops and then for the hundredth time I realize it isn't Jeff.

Five years ago, my son Jeff collapsed in a parking lot early in the morning. He was rushed by ambulance to the nearest hospital. He was suffering from hypothermia and his heart had stopped. Though the doctors worked feverishly and were able to restore Jeff's heartbeat, he had been deprived of oxygen so long that he suffered severe brain damage. His brain was so damaged that he did not regain consciousness. Today, he is still in a coma.

I remember that first year beside Jeff's bed. I kept having flashbacks about that awful first day. It seems like I can still hear the phone ringing and the strange voice on the other end of the line telling me to hurry to the hospital, that my son was in critical condition and not expected to live. I relive the utter panic I felt rushing to the hospital, and I still hear the crazy voice in my head saying "This can't be. It's a mistake. It's not Jeff." I still remember arriving at the hospital, half-walking and half-running down the corridor, terribly frightened. Then the doctors and nurses surrounded me. They were all talking, but I didn't hear what they were saying. I stepped into the room and remember the shock of seeing him lying there. He was so still. The only noise in the room was the air rushing through the respirator. What now, I thought. What now?

I decided to pray even though I was not comfortable doing it. Praying had always been what I would do when I wanted something, like an in-ground swimming pool, or more money or more happiness. Occasionally I would throw in a few crumbs for my fellow man and ask for world peace or an end to hunger. I'm certainly not what people would call devout. I believe in God and I really believe in family. However, I had never experienced a daily relationship with God. But Jeff's situation was so serious and I was terrified. What if God wouldn't listen to me? What if he turned down my request? Why had I been such a schmuck in the past? Why hadn't I prayed for something of consequence? Again I asked, Why? Why?

The irony of the situation is that six months later I was still praying for my son's life to be restored to what it had been. He was alive (that part of the prayer was answered), but he would never wake up. He would never stand up, or talk to me, or be a part of the world of the living. He would live in his bed, deteriorate, vegetate and die.

How cruel God had been. Didn't he care? Where was all of the love and justice I had heard about? Was he punishing me for my past sins? I didn't think that he was punishing my son, so that left me. What had I done that was so terrible that I deserved this? Isn't it strange that I was unable to understand these circumstances except in terms of guilt and punishment? Somehow I felt guilt deep inside of me. Yet intellectually I knew I wasn't responsible for Jeff's accident. My mind and body would not agree.

I felt self-recrimination. All of a sudden, I felt I should have been the perfect mother. I told myself I could have done this and that differently. I was doing a number on myself and causing myself more suffering. As a result, I became so emotionally drained that I forgot to have compassion for other members of our family. Then I felt guilty about that, too. When I recognized the deep sadness they were experiencing, I reached a point where I wanted to die in order to stop thinking. There is actually nothing more wasteful than speculative thinking. It threw me into a past place and time and it kept me there. Painful, painful.

Time passed and the pain subsided somewhat. I returned gradually to the world around me. Still, I had many unanswered questions. I could not believe God would allow Jeff to remain in a coma. There is no greater power, is there? Angrily, I told myself that God was slow-witted; he obviously wasn't getting my request. At this point, I felt more betrayed than guilty. I argued with God daily. I knew without a doubt that I was right and God was wrong. Even He could make a mistake. If I waited long enough, prayed enough, He would surely fix all the painful matters in my life.

I was finding it increasingly difficult to visit Jeff. He began to look sunken and hollow. I couldn't walk into his room without crying. His body was positively grotesque; he was so emaciated that he looked like a German concentration camp victim. When I looked at him, I felt sick to my stomach. Finally, I stopped going to see him. I couldn't...no, it was that I wouldn't. I didn't visit him for over two years, and during that time I felt bitterness and frustration. I didn't want to see him, but I couldn't forget him. I hated God and the people who asked about Jeff. Most of all I wanted him to let go and die.

I lived my life angry most of the time. When I wasn't angry, I was tired. The energy drain was incredible. I would not let people support me (although I was unaware of that behavior until later). I had this idea of being like Good Mother Earth. I thrived on people saying how wonderfully I was handling the situation. God forbid. Certainly I had been far less than the perfect mother, but now I had found an opportunity to appear like a shining light. How paradoxical. All this, while inside I was being eroded by anger, just like soil that's left unprotected from the wind and rain.

What interests me now is how I perceived the whole situation of my son's accident. As I relived it, I could not separate past from present, so later on I often felt as bad as I did when the accident first happened. For a while, I relived the first day of the accident over and over. Finally I became aware of this thinking pattern, and then my struggle was considerably lessened.

It was still unacceptable to me that Jeff was in a coma, and I did not resume my visits. I wanted so much more for him. I wanted more for me. Nevertheless, I would not see him.

Finally, I felt that I just had to see him, but I was afraid to go alone and my husband would not go with me. Thankfully, a very good friend said she would go with me. It had been two and a half years since I had seen Jeff. I couldn't imagine what he would look like.

When I stepped into his room and looked the tears spilled down my cheeks. He was thinner than I had remembered. Oh God. Then my friend spoke to me in a soft, gentle voice: "Talk to him, Mother." It was difficult; I was choking on my words, but I began. I told him how much I loved him, how truly sorry I was that this had happened. I apologized for not visiting him and explained to him why I had not been there for two years. He just lay there listening to me. I remember thinking that he was hearing me even if he didn't understand the words. I felt suspended in time. I've no idea how long I was there. But I felt lighter that day, a weight was taken off my shoulders and I was actually looking forward to my next visit.

The following week, I went to see him alone. I touched him and he was so warm. I told stories and shared my dreams and ambitions with him. It was so wonderful. Then, when I looked at his poor shrunken body, I didn't see it, I just saw Jeff. I suddenly realized that his body didn't matter, I loved him the way he was. No expectations, no conditions. Just love.

It has since become clear to me that for most of my adult life, I had loved people within the realm of certain conditions and expectations. I wasn't necessarily unkind in the way I loved, it was simply that the love I gave was not unconditional love. Jeff changed that for me. My relationship with him gave me insight. I learned to create a different space and found a different way that I could be with the people who are part of my life. Now they can be just what and who they are, whatever way they are—loving, kind, supportive, sensitive, cranky, crabby—it's all OK, marvelously OK.

I have a peacefulness and sense of love that was not available to me before. I also feel empowered, that I will be able to get through anything, whatever it may be. What an extraordinary gift I have received from this son of mine. What a difference he's made in my life. If Jeff could hear me, he would hear me say, "Thank you, thank you so very much. I love you."

The End of Camelot:
Facing a Physical Disability

My "Camelot" came to an abrupt halt as my physical limitations from multiple sclerosis increased. I thought this couldn't be happening to me; I was only 28 years old! My life had finally become what I always dreamed it would be; I had a job that I loved, a wonderful home, sports and friends galore. But most of these joys slowly slipped away from me as my losses accumulated over a period of years.

The first symptom I had from this progressive illness was sciatica in my right leg. It developed from weakness to paralysis that lasted for nine weeks. This initial complication eventually subsided, but the weakness and pain in my right leg became constant companions. Next I discovered a progressive weakness in my left arm and then relentless muscle spasms in my back and neck followed. I was working as a nurse anesthetist at the time and needed considerable strength in my arms to intubate my patients. It became clear that I would have to begin looking for an alternative occupation.

So, while I kept my job, I returned to school to work on a degree in mass media communications. I thought that public relations work would be possible for someone with my limitations. Although I enjoyed school, I became more and more depressed as I grieved for the loss of my previous lifestyle. I had to stop working as an anesthetist and then sell my house because the small pension I received, only a small percentage of what I made before, wasn't enough to pay the rent.

Because I could no longer engage in competitive sports, many of the "friends" with whom I had skied and played tennis were no longer interested in me now that I wasn't able to move around like before. I didn't blame them for withdrawing from me because I did not even enjoy being with myself. My world was collapsing.

I finished my course work and internships in mass media and graduated with honors. But finding a job in public relations was difficult. After five months of intensive searching, I found a public relations job with a small corporation. However, working a 40-hour week proved disastrous to my health. The muscle spasms became unbearable and the pain medications I was taking made me ineffective in my job. Additionally, I was having recurrent optic neuritis and some difficulty with urinary incontinence. It was obvious that I couldn't cope with the situation any longer.

Always believing that I was the captain of my own ship made my ability to accept these losses even more difficult. I felt that I was no longer in control of my present situation or of my future. Before my illness I had always been able to overcome adversity by working hard. With multiple sclerosis, I had an adversary that hard work only made worse. I grieved for the loss of my past life and became more depressed.

At this time I thought about having to become increasingly dependent on others. Torturing myself with these images only further depleted my coping resources. I even tried to commit suicide by drug overdose, but I did not die. I awoke from a drug-induced coma in the intensive care unit of a local hospital with a ventilator breathing for me. Talk about the ultimate failure; I couldn't even succeed at suicide!

It is often darkest before the dawn. I had no residual brain damage from the foolish attempt to end my suffering permanently. I thought that perhaps I had been saved for some purpose. But I wondered what kind of a future I had to look forward to as I became progressively more disabled and increasingly dependent.

Fortunately, at that time I met an excellent psychologist who helped me to see that I still had alternatives in life. I also had a very supportive family and some true friends. Most helpful was a friend who made me aware of the fallacy of thinking that dependence and independence were opposites. She pointed out that we are all dependent on each other for different things.

I learned that I needed to pace my life and daily activities so that I could put the little energy I had to the best use and so that I would have enough time to rest. I also started attending a pain control clinic to learn to control the muscle spasms without medication. Thankfully, this was successful; I found that I can moderate my response to pain by using a transcutaneous electroneural stimulator (TENS) unit and therefore I no longer need to take addictive pain medications.

Once again, I felt that I was in control of my life. The multiple sclerosis was no longer controlling me; rather, I was in control of it. What a wonderful feeling to be in control again. I felt absolutely empowered. The energy that had previously been consumed by depression and disability slowly began to return. For the next year, I sorted out my future goals while I did volunteer work for various community organizations.

I decided to commit my life to helping others learn how to adjust to life with a chronic physical disability. I didn't want to see anyone else go through the needless despair that I had experienced. I decided that the best way to reach my goal was to return to nursing. I completed my master's work in family health nursing and my doctoral studies in nursing with a focus on rehabilitation psychology. Now, as a professor of nursing, I work with others who have chronic physical disabilities, teach student nurses how to work with these individuals and their families and conduct research in the area of adjustment to chronic physical disability.

In a sense I was reborn when I learned how to regain control of my life. I discovered long-term solutions to life after loss. I now know that when grief abates, no matter how miserable one may feel at the time, it is entirely possible to resume a happy and productive life. I may not change the world all that much, but I can help to make it a better place for those facing the loss that accompanies a chronic physical disability.

A Contemporary Miracle

I first saw him in the main hospital corridor. He was walking swiftly away from where I stood toward a door that led to an enclosed garden. He wore a dark blue suit and black shoes. I noticed that he was almost bald and I remember thinking he was probably a hospital administrator because he walked as if he had authority. I also remember having a very strange feeling that the moment was important for me.

That hospital was situated in an affluent suburb of The Hague in the Netherlands. I had gone there for a visit and to collect data about Dutch health care practices while I worked at the hospital. Later I learned that the man I had seen had come from Belgium and that he was not a hospital administrator. His life was in jeopardy; he had only one kidney that was becoming obstructed by a particular kind of kidney stone, a staghorn calculus, that was threatening the kidney function on which his life depended. A famous surgeon who worked at the Dutch hospital had agreed to remove the stone in the hope that it would save his life. The man I saw that day was 37 years old.

Involved in the excitement of a new country and culture, I forgot about him for several weeks. Then one day the Director of Nursing asked me if I would be willing to serve as special nurse for a seriously ill patient. I protested because I spoke very little Dutch, but she assured me that the patient was too ill to communicate much and that his mother, who was constantly beside him, spoke English well. I wanted to show my gratitude for the privileges the hospital was providing me, so I agreed that I would try.

Coincidence?

On the first day of my special duty I was surprised to find that my patient was the same man I had seen in the hallway that very first day. By this time he was critically ill. He never stopped bleeding after his surgery, which had been

160

long and complicated. The bleeding was related to some chemical imbalance that had occurred as a result of previous lengthy treatments with medication. The surgeon ordered liters of blood for the poor man, but he was bleeding at a rate equal to or greater than the rate of the intravenous blood drip. It looked as if he would not survive. Sometimes I tried to console his mother who sat by his bed constantly praying. I also noticed that a prayer book of some kind was on the patient's bedside table. Once I had to move it and the patient became agitated, indicating to me exactly where he wanted the book to be. I concluded that he understood the seriousness of his condition and that he was a man of faith.

One day in the second week, though he appeared no better, I had to tell him that I was going away for a few days to visit Belgium. He asked where in Belgium I was going and I explained to him (with help from his mother) that I planned to visit Bruges to attend the historic "Holy Blood Play." The procession and play take place every fifth year in this exquisite medieval city and friends told me that I should not miss it. During this pageant, the townspeople take part in ceremonies of great religious significance. According to legend, a vial of Christ's blood was brought back to Bruges by the Crusaders and it is believed to protect the city and its inhabitants. It is said that the blood liquefies whenever the city is threatened. For example, it was said to liquefy during World War II when Belgium capitulated to the Germans. Because the Holy Blood has deep significance for Catholics, many believers make religious pilgrimages to Bruges to pray for miracles. These miracles are said to happen particularly to those who have blood disorders. When I told my patient that I was going to Bruges, he asked me if I would visit the basilica that houses the miraculous shrine. When I replied that I would, he promptly asked me to take along a small scapular he was wearing, touch the cloth to the reliquary that holds the Holy Blood and pray for his recovery.

My first reaction was embarrassment, but compassion took over and I told him that of course I would do it. At the time I recall thinking that it would not work, that nothing could help him because he was so quickly losing ground. I wondered how long the physicians would agree to pump blood into his poor body before they decided it was a hopeless effort. I said goodbye and went to prepare for my trip.

Bruges

The Holy Blood Play was very impressive. The city is very beautiful, in fact it is often called the Venice of the North, and it made me feel like I was in a past century. My skeptical ideas about the relic of the Holy Blood soon began to change. On the day I went to see the famous shrine to fulfill my promise to my patient, I tried to be open-minded. "Why not?" I thought as I touched the scapular to the reliquary, "This can do no harm and maybe it will bring him some psychological and religious support." I dropped to my knees and concluded my visit with the promised prayer.

After I returned to Holland, I entered the hospital and I encountered the charge nurse of my patient's floor. After greeting her, I inquired about my patient. She said that he appeared to be somewhat better. When I entered the room, I knew that things had changed. He was propped up in bed in a semi-reclining position. This time there was no sign of the intravenous blood drip that before had seemed permanently attached to his body. He smiled shyly as I approached and stretched out his hand in greeting. I offered him the scapular and the small gift. He sat staring at the scapular and then, with tears in his eyes, he asked me, "When did you go to the Basilica?"

I replied, "It must have been on Thursday."

"Do you remember what time you went?"

A little curious, I said, "Yes. Around three in the afternoon."

He remained silent for a short time. Then he looked up at me, "That is exactly when the bleeding stopped."

I drew in a deep breath, went cold and felt the hairs rising on the back of my neck.

Although I had been brought up with religious beliefs, it was not the sort of faith that could prepare me for an experience of this kind. I believed the days of miracles were long gone. Not in my wildest dreams had I ever imagined that I would ever be a part of one. Returning to my room after my visit with my patient, I closed the door and sat down to ponder the whole strange affair. I knew that this experience was one I would never forget. It was difficult to believe that a miracle had been granted in response to my prayer and equally difficult to believe that what had happened could have been coincidental. When I returned to care for my patient in subsequent days, it was with a growing sense of curiosity and wonder. What kind of person could this be who believed with such energy that he could change heaven's mind? It seemed unbelievable to me and to many others. We did not talk about the miracle—it was too strange and too private.

Aftermath

The days went by and I prepared to return to my own country. As the departure date drew near, I felt a growing sadness. Something truly momentous had connected me to this special person and now it seemed possible that I would never see him again. I spent as much of my free time visiting him as I could and when it came time for me to leave, we said we would write.

It is not within the scope of this story to relate the details of the years that followed, but it is appropriate to add that the man became my husband. We spent 10 and a half extraordinary years together before his health broke down completely. It has now been 24 years since he died, but every detail of those first days is still clearly etched in my memory.

Me and My Body:
Learning from Loss

The memories will linger forever. There are days when I am able to share even though my tears will still flow. The times that I am able to share without crying, I feel I have accomplished one more day of healing. Sometimes all of the many memories blend together and my body tightens at their recall.

All of this started when I was 17 years old and was diagnosed with a kidney disease. Having such a serious problem as a teenager was a lonely experience. The only other person I heard of with a life-threatening problem was a childhood friend who had had polio. When I became ill, there was no one to talk to about my confusion and my family was as poorly informed as I was. For many years I lived with kidney pain every single day and thought that was a normal condition. Due to my medication, I lacked the high level of energy my peers had. I learned that others did not know how to relate to me, and that in order to maintain my relationships, I could not discuss my illness. This fact only increased my feelings of isolation.

Yet I remained true to the times. I interrupted my college education, married young and gave birth to two children. I was active in many community organizations. I even played golf and tennis. I was determined to be like everyone else. However, I became very sick and was hospitalized four times in nine months with kidney infections and complications. My absences took a toll on my family. My husband wanted me home before I was ready. All my very young children knew about those hospitalizations was that I was gone. My in-laws made cutting remarks about my illness that made me feel as if there was something "bad" about me because I had a kidney disease. They believed that I had a less-than-acceptable body.

During the next 10 years I had several kidney infections but was still able to function like most young wives and mothers. Then, during a check-up, my physician found that my good kidney was also being damaged by disease. Surgery was scheduled to remove my left kidney 48 hours later. I was informed that if I did not do this, I would be dead in a year. However, my deepest sense told me that I was not terminally ill. I was 27 years old and knew I had to get another opinion. I was referred to a competent, caring urologist who performed surgery and saved my kidney.

My husband responded to the stress of my surgery with an acute episode of colitis that lasted for two weeks. As a result, I received little emotional support from him the entire time I was hospitalized. But I was too weak to deal with my feelings. My hair fell out in bunches, and I was in a great deal of pain. My physical condition made it so that I could no longer care for myself, and I therefore became dependent on others. When the staff didn't answer my call light in time, I became incontinent, then felt angry and ashamed. It was a huge relief to finally come home, even though my hospital room had been filled with flowers and cards. Full recuperation took about six months. Twelve months later my husband left me, leaving me alone with two young children and no career skills.

Divorce carried a huge social stigma at that time. Many people avoided me and I quickly found out who my true friends were. My early reactions were hurt, sadness, betrayal, helplessness, embarrassment and anger. After many hours of talking and many months of starting to work it through, I evolved into a more caring and insightful person. The emotional growth has been more difficult, but more rewarding, than all of my physical pain.

For the next five years I was free of symptoms and was happy and productive. I had enough energy to pursue a baccalaureate degree in nursing, returning to school as an adult student in 1973. Then suddenly I experienced sharp, persistent pain in my right kidney. I went to see the urologist who had operated on me in 1968, even though he lived 500 miles from my home.

I entered the hospital in the spring of 1975, fully expecting to return home in two weeks. After 10 weeks, three major surgeries and multiple complications, I was able to do that. During one of the surgeries I had a "near death experience" and something very deep inside of me changed for the better. To this day I do not understand how it was that I found the courage to go through procedure after procedure with few visits from family or friends.

Four weeks after coming home, I returned to school. For six months I was euphoric because I had lived, and then suddenly I began to have nightmares about my experiences. For the first time I began to realize how sick I had been and how close to death I had come. I was 35 years old at that time and the youngest patient on the hospital unit. I had lived while others less sick had not.

I had been told that within a year I would feel OK again, but I did not.

Instead, I started to experience violent episodes of acute pain at the surgery site. The problem was diagnosed as torn nerves from the third kidney operation. After a year of painful nerve block injection therapy, I was advised to undergo surgery to sever these nerves at the spinal cord. My anxiety at having to go through another operation surfaced in a terrible argument with the resident physician. Maybe I could have handled the situation differently if I had been less anxious.

Spending a week in one of Dr. Elisabeth Kübler-Ross' workshops taught me that if you are going to get over negative feelings, you must share your experiences, thoughts and feelings. I also learned a great deal about the limitations of others and how to find my creative options so that I could begin to heal. That week-long workshop gave me a new emotional lease on life and I was even able to write at length to the physician who had caused my initial problems. To my surprise I received a beautiful letter in response.

Now remarried, I have found a new challenge for growth in my career and in my relationships. I've learned how to share and how to ask for what I want and need. I continue to be pain-ridden, but I have learned to set up the support that I need and that it is all right to ask for help. I know that I have a depth of understanding most others do not. My illness has taught me. I've learned how important it is to resolve the issues that hold me back from reaching my goals. It has been my experience that no one survives the emotional impact of serious illness alone. Help from family, friends, clergy, support groups or counseling is essential to enable victims of illness to integrate their many physical and emotional losses.

No Regrets: The Life and Death of My Mother

As a nurse I had seen this scene many times before. An elderly woman lying in bed, pale, with labored breathing, oxygen tubing in her nose and an IV running into her arm. But this time it was different. This was my mom.

I stood beside the bed a few moments before she awakened.

"What is it you want?" she asked, thinking I was her nurse.

"I want a hug," I said.

It was then that she realized that her daughter was standing there.

"Mary! I should have known you would be here," she said. "Now I'll be fine."

The day before, Mom had been admitted to the hospital with pneumonia. At that time she was one month shy of her 84th birthday. Before this she had had severe hearing loss and a moderate case of unstable angina, but nothing seemed to slow her down. She had always been on the move: driving her friends on errands, taking little treats to friends in the nursing home, entertaining her church group or meeting monthly with her bridge club of old high school friends. She had paid for an Alaskan cruise that was coming up in June and had bought a red suit to wear on the trip.

I drove four hours that morning to be with her. The evening before, her doctor had told me that there was no immediate need for me to make the trip, that she was doing very well. He told me that it was really only because of her age that she was hospitalized. Until she recovered from the pneumonia, he felt, she should be where others could take care of her.

During the drive I had time to think about what life would be like without her. And I thought that when she did die, I wanted it to be a "good death." As an oncology nurse I had seen many people die. I tended to classify these deaths as "good" and "bad." My definition of a bad death was one that came so suddenly that there was no time for goodbyes, where the patient was unable to complete the necessary communications with loved ones or to accept the completion of life. Probably he or she was experiencing pain or trauma. On the other hand, a good death, in my view, came to patients with completed communications, a calm acceptance of death, and the permission to die with dignity. Also, they would have a family member at their bedside when they died.

Before Mom came to the hospital, I had been fearful that she might fall down the basement stairs or have a heart attack while she was alone and if that happened she might be unable to reach a phone. I didn't want her to die without having someone with her. I had worked so hard to help achieve "good" deaths for my patients and their families and I certainly wanted my own mother's to be good.

At the time of that last hospitalization I hadn't seen her for two months. Phone calls had not been possible because of Mom's severe hearing loss, so we resorted to a lot of letter writing. But somehow it just wasn't the same as talking to each other.

When I entered her room that day, she sat up in her bed, and I got my hug. As usual we both had a lot to say, but after just a sentence or two, she became very short of breath. Because it was difficult for her to be content just listening to me (she was a participant in life and needed to respond or ask questions), I just sat with her as she dozed intermittently. After dinner, I tucked her into bed. Then I got the keys to her house and headed for my own dinner and a night's sleep.

The next day she was feeling much better. Her shortness of breath was minimal and her appetite was much improved. We took short walks in the hall and we talked and talked and talked. It was a good day for both of us. She got herself ready for bed; I gave her a back rub, a hug and a kiss goodnight. It was 8 o'clock.

That same night around 9:15, I received a call from her nurse. Mom had awakened from a nightmare; she was very anxious and she wanted me there. She was not having chest pain, but I asked the nurse not to leave her.

In less than 10 minutes I was at the hospital. I walked into Mom's room and suddenly became two people: Mary, the daughter, and Mary, the nurse. Mom was sitting at the edge of her bed, her nurse's arm around her shoulders. I kneeled down in front of her so she could read my lips and I could look into her eyes. I detected relief when she saw me. I saw that she was not frightened.

Then Mary, the daughter, stepped back and Mary, the nurse, moved forward. I asked Mom if she was in any pain. "Not too much," she told me. I felt for her pulse and found that it was rapid. She was also diaphoretic.

"Please get an EKG stat," I said. "She needs some oxygen. What were her vital signs and when did you last take them?"

Then I switched back to the daughter hearing her mother say: "You have been such a wonderful daughter. You're always there when I need you. I love you. I'm so proud of all my children and all of my grandchildren." Then she sat a little straighter and said: "I even have a great-grandchild. I've had a wonderful full life. I've been fortunate to have seen a lot of this country. I've had a lot of friends. I have no regrets."

She was getting short of breath from talking. "Mom, you're not dying. Just stop talking so you can breathe better."

She paid no attention to me. "Do you think one of the grandchildren would say something at my funeral? That would mean so much to me."

"Mom, you're not dying. Please stop talking so you can breathe easier." Tears streamed down the daughter's face.

Then the doctor and the EKG technician hurried into the room. Past experiences flashed before my eyes. Too often as a nurse I had seen frail elderly patients put through the degradation and humiliation of having CPR and intubation imposed upon them when their hearts stopped or they stopped breathing. Too often I had seen them denied the dignity in death they had had in life.

"I don't want a code on this lady," I said, meaning that if she died the staff should take no heroic measures to intervene.

"Thanks for the input but I doubt very much if that will be necessary," the doctor said. As he took command, the nurse in me once again retreated and the daughter returned.

Mom's EKG showed some changes occurring "but nothing major at this point," the doctor said. "Let's take her to Cardiac Care so we can watch her closely and treat as necessary."

It was difficult getting Mom to understand where we were taking her because of her hearing problems and also because she continued to talk about her wonderful life and family. When she finally seemed to understand, we wheeled her bed down the hall and into the elevator. She held my hand and squeezed it tightly.

"Whatever happens," she said, "I'm not afraid. I'm ready to die. I have no regrets."

Her bed was pushed into one of the CCU rooms. I was asked to leave while they took her vital signs and connected her to a monitor. A few minutes later I came back into the room; she was propped up on pillows in a sitting position. She looked so tired. I took her in my arms.

"I love you," she said, and her head fell back on the pillow. The nurse knew. The daughter knew. "I love you too, Mom."

It was a "good death." What I had worked so hard to give others had been achieved for one I loved so dearly: communications completed, family at bedside, no pain or suffering, no regrets.

But if it was "good," then why do I continue to hurt so much? Why was the second Christmas without Mom harder than the first? Maybe that's just the nature of grief. But I cannot imagine any pain worse than that of natural grief compounded by serious regrets.

Moving Forward with Paralysis

Seven years ago, while vacationing in Florida, I went swimming off the Sarasota Bay. I was jumping off a tree that hung over the bay. The first time, I landed on my feet in shallow water, so when I climbed onto the tree again, I dove out further, toward what I thought was deeper water. But the water was not deeper. I hit a sandbar and fractured my sixth and seventh vertebrae. Unfortunately, my brother who was fishing nearby, didn't see me right away. Luckily, I didn't lose consciousness and was able to hold my breath and lie on my back. The next thing I knew he was pulling me out of the water onto the shore. Then I blacked out. I'm told the paramedics came and quickly took me to the local hospital.

I woke up in intensive care with a severed spinal cord. I was on a turning bed with stabilizing tongs in my head. It's hard to explain my feelings. I was stunned and scared. I was virtually helpless and was told my paralysis would be permanent. I had no movement from the armpits down. The nurses had to do everything for me: brush my teeth, bathe me, take care of all my bodily functions. I had to be turned frequently to avoid bedsores. They did this by strapping me down and literally flipping the bed over. At first that was very scary; I wasn't sure if I'd fall or not. Later I learned to trust the nurses and I felt safe and cared for.

After six weeks, the stabilizing tongs were removed and I was flown by air ambulance to a regional rehabilitation hospital. This staff was much rougher. Right away they gave me the first shower I had had in six weeks. I was rolled naked into the bathroom on a cart that looked like a fishnet and sprayed down like an object. I felt very vulnerable and realized that I had to shape up.

The next day the nurse came in and told me I was going to have to work hard now. I'd always been athletic and considered myself sort of macho. I didn't want to feel like a wimp, but every time I sat up I'd black out. Finally, after a few tries, I was able to sit without fainting—a major accomplishment. Then there was the pain. It came and went. Sometimes I thought I couldn't bear it.

Before this I'd always been a private person and now I had to live with several people in the same room for many months. I felt an acute loss of privacy. I had to take showers with other people around and other people took care of my most intimate needs. There was never a place where I could get away by myself. I lost a sense of who I was. I felt like a piece of meat. It took a long time to get my identity back.

There were counselors available, but I never felt comfortable talking with them. At night, I'd lie in the dark for hours thinking about what was happening to me and what I'd do with my life. I'd cry when no one could see me.

Before the accident, my marriage hadn't been good and afterwards it was too much for both me and my wife. First we separated and later we were divorced.

My rehabilitation program was rigorous and lasted for several months. There were daily physical therapy treatments and instruction on how to care for myself. My family was in another state so I had to rely on people at the hospital for emotional support, relationships that became very important to me. In fact, that's where I met my present wife. Before I was discharged from the hospital, I lived alone in a unit that was attached to the hospital. There I learned to do things for myself and raised my self-confidence, but no matter how well I prepared, finally being on my own was scary.

Leaving the hospital wasn't easy. Even just going outside was hard. It was traumatic. The first time I went out in a wheelchair, I realized that people stared at me. I wanted to stay in the protective environment of the hospital forever. Even after I left the hospital for good, I thought of excuses to go back and visit the staff and other patients. This went on for several weeks. Finally, I felt more comfortable in my new life and I didn't need to go back as much.

Upon discharge, I took an apartment by myself. I needed help with my bowel and bladder regimen, so I had a visiting nurse come to help. It didn't work out too well because each day a different nurse came and I needed to train each of them. It was more of a hassle than it was worth, so I eventually decided to take care of everything on my own.

When I was ready, I was given the opportunity to go back to the company where I'd worked before my injury. The job they offered me, however, was answering phones—for one-third the salary I'd earned previously. Before I had worked as a salesman and I liked getting out and meeting people. I decided that answering phones wasn't for me.

I was very despondent. Before my accident I'd had a marriage, a child, a good car, a home and a job. Afterward, I was sitting in an apartment by myself, reliant on others. In the condition I was in, I knew I would not be able to get satisfying work. So I contemplated suicide, even planned how I would do it. Something stopped me, perhaps that I'd been raised to believe you'd go to hell if you killed yourself. Even though I was afraid to keep living my life as it was now, I decided that I had to go forward and do the best I could.

With the help of my friends and the people at the rehab hospital, I set goals that I believed I could achieve and also a time frame in which to achieve them. Approximately two years after I was hurt, I became involved in a national spinal cord injury association and now I am president of the local chapter. I make visits to newly injured patients in area hospitals. I think it helps people to see that someone like me—someone who was in the same boat they're in—has been able to move on and make it. I'm also chairman of the board of a housing development for individuals who have suffered spine injuries and I'm training to take part in the national marathon for handicapped people. Even though I don't receive pay for these activities, I am now busier than I was when I had a full-time job before the accident.

Socially, I'm much happier today than I was before my accident. Today I'm married to a person who I really love and who loves me. Between us, we have two daughters who we love very much. I try not to ask for help to do certain things, but I know someone is there if I need it. I also have free time to enjoy my family; before I was so caught up in my career that I didn't take time to enjoy life. Now I can take off with the family when I want, yet I am involved in very worthwhile projects that are fulfilling and also help others.

Most of the stress I now feel comes from the inability to do certain physical things that other able-bodied people do without thinking. If I try to pick up something and drop it and I try again with the same results, I get upset. While I may have lost control over many activities, I don't have the stress others have in their jobs. I control my own schedule and have a good family life.

I'm not saying I don't regret being paralyzed. Sure, I'd like to get rid of this chair. But in so many ways I'm much better off today than I was before the accident. Losing my ability to ambulate was a devastating loss. Yet while people may find it hard to believe, in many ways my life is much richer now. I've gained a lot.

What is *Really* Important:
A Nurse's Learning Experience

I am a primary nurse in a busy cardiovascular intensive care unit (CVICU) at a large urban hospital. Because I have shared second chances at life with many open-heart surgery patients, I have been prompted to look at life a little differently. The fact that a patient's life may depend on my assessments is a responsibility that I do not take lightly. These assessments involve more than technical interpretation from diagnostic equipment, they involve people—on a very human level. Some very special patients taught me a great deal about what is *really* important in life, and at the end of a life. In the following case study, I will share what I learned from one such patient.

As I unpacked Rose's personal belongings before admitting her to the unit, I began to see what a strong woman she was. She was in the hospital for a double valve replacement. Several photographs tucked inside her belongings revealed that she had been a very robust woman. One could also see that she was very proud of her large family. She was the wife of a pig farmer from a small rural Wisconsin town, and her children were farmers, too. Dozens of homemade cards encouraged, "Get well for Thanksgiving, Grandma. Dinner is at your house!" In a picture from a previous holiday dinner, I counted 40 chairs around the dinner table. Because Thanksgiving was less than a month away, I expected to see Rose leave the operating room nearly stable, so she could get home quickly to begin her holiday plans. What actually occurred was very different.

After her surgery, Rose's condition was extremely unstable. She was admitted to the CVICU on two support medications and she had a temporary pacemaker operating. She was unconscious for several hours. Prior to their visit, Rose's family was informed of her condition by the surgeon. Nevertheless, when they arrived they immediately began communicating with her in words, caresses and kisses. One daughter became the spokesperson for her father and nine brothers and sisters. She was just like I envisioned Rose was before her illness: stable and realistic, but still optimistic. This daughter would become a rock for her family over the next few weeks.

The early weeks of Rose's recovery were complicated by frequent bouts with congestive heart failure and renal failure and dialysis became a necessary daily treatment for her. Rose was alert during most of those days. Although dependence on the ventilator meant that she could not convey her needs verbally, she was able to let us know what she needed or wanted. You could see the satisfaction in her eyes each time the need she communicated was met. She beamed when we set her hair, gave her a back rub, or readjusted her pillows to a more comfortable position. Often these things had to be done before she allowed us to change her dressings or recalibrate her monitoring equipment.

Rose wanted to look and feel her best, especially for her family. Regardless of how hectic the day had been, she managed to smile at the sight of them. This provided a tremendous lift for her fragile husband who approached the bed apprehensively. After he saw her smile, he would hold her hand and whisper things to her for hours. Her sons and daughters understood their parents' close bond and would allow them time to be alone each day. Also, Rose's children and grandchildren treated her with the utmost respect. They did not want her to feel left out of anything. Every day someone read her their hometown paper or the volumes of cards and letters that arrived daily. This frequent stimulation kept Rose well-oriented. I assisted by making a large calendar for her, which the family kept updated with important events.

When Thanksgiving was less than a week away, more cards arrived with "We're thankful for you, Grandma. We'll make dinner. You must get well." Rose was able to share in the holiday planning through words and the new photographs that rotated through her room weekly. Her family was a strong motivator for Rose to recover. They tried to be optimistic, but their concerns continued to mount. Rose was having a hard time; she still managed to smile for her visitors, but fell asleep soon after their arrival. Sleep was one way she could escape the feeling of being trapped, a feeling she had expressed to me while I was alone with her. Sleep also allowed her to escape her pain. While she slept, her family told me of their fears. It was clear that they were as much my patients as Rose was, and all of them had needs that had to be addressed. As Rose slept more often, the family sought more answers about the situation.

Shortly after Thanksgiving, I set up a care conference with Rose's family, her doctors, a clinical nurse specialist, her associate nurses, and myself. The renal doctor took the lead in this conference because he directed Rose's current treatment. He was very straightforward; Rose was extremely ill. Though she did not seem to be getting drastically worse, she was not getting better. Rose's husband, with tears in his eyes, asked if Rose was suffering. I assured him that we were doing all we could to keep her comfortable. "Good, I couldn't bear to see her suffer," her husband responded. Next, Rose's daughter, the family spokesperson, wanted to know what the medical plan and prognosis were for her mother. The doctor directing the dialysis informed them that everything available was already being utilized to get Rose well. "We can only do so much," he said, "and then it goes beyond our hands." Family members slumped. Their eyes darted desperately around the room and finally focused on the floor. An uneasy silence followed. Slowly, the daughter lifted her head and asked the doctor, "What next?"

The doctor said, "We could let nature run its course and not use any further extraordinary measures to prolong your mother's life." With a terrified look on her face, the daughter told him that her family was not prepared for such a decision on that day. They decided to wait a week with the present treatment and depending on how things were then, they would make a decision. They all agreed with this plan. Before concluding the conference it was also agreed that the family would be given liberal visiting privileges and be kept informed of any changes in the patient's treatment or condition.

After the physicians left, the other nurses and I stayed with the family. Tears and nervous questions filled the conference room. "What should we do?" was repeated by the sons, daughters and Rose's husband over and over again. As the tears began to subside, some answers began to emerge. *Let's tell Mom, she should have a say in this. Let's take her home. I don't want her to suffer. She still may come out of this.* Rose had slept in her room during the conference and continued to sleep when it was over. The family kissed her before they left. They told me they were going home to discuss matters.

Because I had the next two days off, I had no interaction with Rose or her family. Upon my return to work I learned that the family had given Rose all the information from the conference. Rose had told them that she would also be ready to make a decision at the end of the week and that she was not afraid to die. She then thanked her family for giving her such a wonderful life. I was also informed that a verbal "No Code" had been ordered by Rose's renal doctor and written in her file by the surgeon's nurse (this meant that no efforts were to be made to resuscitate Rose if her heart was to fail again). This was a full week before a decision was to have been made! I asked how the family had felt when they were informed of this, but none of the other nurses knew whether or not they had been told. I felt angry that my patients had been betrayed in my absence. Because Rose required intense physical care, it was easy to neglect the emotional support she required. Also, because no one had seen the "No Code" order being written, no one wanted to take responsibility for taking the order off the chart. But I knew that this situation needed to be addressed right away. My initial anger toward the physician broadened to a genuine concern for Rose and her family's emotional well-being.

With that mindset, I approached the doctor as he entered the unit. First, I asked him why he had given the "No Code" order. He looked at me and said that we could not put this responsibility on the family, that we must use our best medical knowledge and make the decision for them. I reiterated the agreement made at the conclusion of the case conference that the family had the right to be informed of the prognosis as well as the available options and to share in the decision-making process. Though my heart was racing, preparing for the inevitable explosion, I kept my voice steady and my eye contact constant. The doctor jumped out of his seat. "It is our duty to make those decisions," he said.

"I disagree," I said. "The family has told us that they are not ready for that. We promised them a week to 10 days before a decision would be made. They need to prepare themselves emotionally." I then told him that I needed to get back to my patient's bedside, but would discuss this matter with him further when he made rounds. As I turned to walk away, my heart was in my throat. I felt unsure about whether I had done the right thing—maybe the doctor had been right. Maybe this was too much for the family to decide. After all, they would have to live with their decision if Rose died. I went to Rose's bedside with the doctor close behind. He ripped open her chart, wrote nothing, swore at me, and said that I should write the orders. Then he stormed off. I was stunned and wondered if I had been out of line.

Soon after the doctor left, nearly all the nurses on duty that day came up to me and expressed their support. *You did the right thing. Patients and families have rights, too. He was just frustrated because he didn't know what to say and because everything you said was right. That's why he left like that.* I was pleased that my co-workers had supported me, and pleased with the way I had presented myself and stood up for what was right. The doubts I had earlier were now gone: I had done the right thing, I had protected the emotional needs of my patient.

Ultimately, the doctor also must have realized that this was the case. Thirty minutes after our confrontation I received a call from him. He informed me that he had just called Rose's family and discussed her condition with them. He said that they had all decided that no major decisions regarding life-sustaining measures would be made for one week. I felt like I had won a battle. I had given some control back to Rose and her family.

The next week passed without any progress in Rose's recovery. At the end of that week Rose said, "I've lived my piece and I'm ready to die." Her family decided that, above all, they did not want Rose to suffer. The "No Code" order was agreed upon. Rose was kept well-medicated to keep her comfortable and she was moved to a floor where visiting was easier. Then, halfway between Thanksgiving and Christmas, Rose died.

Several weeks later we received this note from Rose's family: "We're simple folks—but we value life, family and health. We hurt bad, but you helped. You let us be human to the end. You treated her real special—like she was important. She sure was to us. Thanks." Rose had been special to me and made quite an impact on my life.

I learned a great deal from this experience. From Rose's family I learned that comfort, information, health and the ability to feel in control of a situation are very important. This was emphasized by their questions and comments during the case conference. I also learned that doctors are vulnerable, too, and they can make mistakes. We should challenge them when we disagree with them. I found that a calm approach is very effective. I realized clearly that the patient is not just the person lying in bed, but also the people in that person's life. By giving these people a say in the care of their loved one, they were made to feel less helpless. They were also able to help my patient.

Fourth of July:
Taking Charge of Death

Several winters ago as I was leaving a hospice board meeting I ran into Judy Waggoner, a woman I had gone to high school with 25 years earlier. As our conversation unfolded, I learned that Judy's father was in the hospital and dying of cancer. I told her what kind of work I did and about the services our hospice provided and suggested that perhaps I could arrange to visit her parents as soon as her father returned home.

The day I visited her parents, a touch of spring was in the air. Judy's mother graciously welcomed me into their home. As her mother led me through the house to a back room, I was overwhelmed by the view of the lake through windows that extended from the floor to the ceiling. Many pictures of their children and grandchildren at various ages were clustered on tables in the room. Mr. Waggoner lay on a sofa that faced the lake. When this once-handsome man smiled at me, his love for life and people was instantly apparent. I introduced myself to him and he began to share the story of his illness with me. He told me that he was dying and that he had many things to do before he died. "I need to get all of my finances in order, and I will not die until the Fourth of July."

"Until the Fourth of July?" I remarked, surprised that he had actually set a date.

"Yes, all of my children and grandchildren always come to the lake for the Fourth of July. I *will* live until then!"

I left their home thinking that there was no way Mr. Waggoner would live until the Fourth of July. It was then April, and the medical and radiology reports confirmed a very aggressive and fast-growing tumor.

Each week that I visited him, Mr. Waggoner appeared thinner and weaker. Each week he told me about what he was planning for the Fourth of July and exactly how the day would be. As April turned into May, Mr. Waggoner became frailer and his pain became more intense. On one visit, I explained

179

to him that we could do something about the pain. He remarked, "Yes, we could, but that would not be living, would it?"

By June, Mr. Waggoner was so debilitated he could no longer get out of bed. During the times I visited him, I learned about every picture on every table: his beloved granddaughter Amy, who had Down's syndrome and had won the Special Olympics in gymnastics; Jennifer, Amy's mother, who had become an activist for handicapped children; his daughter, Judy, who was recently divorced. We looked at pictures from all the previous Fourth of July family gatherings. We cried that this would be his last Fourth of July.

Finally the weekend of the Fourth came. It was a beautiful day. Mr. Waggoner now lay on a hospital bed in a room that had no view of the lake. When I came to see him, he said, "It is the Fourth of July. All my family is here. I need to see the fireworks display over the lake. Could you move this bed?" He could no longer walk and his pain was too severe for us to move him to the sofa in the other room. Furthermore, the bed was too large to fit through the door. I didn't know what to do.

I met with Mr. Waggoner's children and we puzzled about how we could meet his request. Then his son-in-law said, "All we have to do is take a crowbar and remove the door frame. Then we could move the bed." Each one of us helped with this task. As the first boom of the fireworks sounded over the lake, we got the bed through the doorway. We positioned the bed so that Mr. Waggoner could see the spectacular display. And while we were absorbed in watching the fireworks, Mr. Waggoner died. He died surrounded by the people he loved. He died viewing the magnificent lake that reflected each flash of light from above. He died at the time he said he would.

Discussion

Caring for Mr. Waggoner taught me a lesson that I shall never forget: people can indeed have control over their own life and death. It is not for us professionals to predict when and how a death will occur. I also learned from Mr. Waggoner that dying people will endure pain in order to feel alive and that their wishes must be respected.

For me, caring for a dying person is a privilege. I value the fact that I get to share special moments with my patients.

Of Hope and Memories:
Coping with Our Child's Death

Two years ago, early in the evening on Father's Day, our 12-year-old son Tim was crossing the road behind our house when he was struck by a car. My husband and I arrived at the scene of the accident moments apart and we saw our son lying face down in the street with blood pouring out of his mouth and ears. He had a gaping wound in the back of his head and he was breathing irregularly. But he was alive and there was still hope that he would be OK. But that hope was short-lived. Despite herculean efforts by the ER staff, Tim died within the hour. We were in shock for weeks. We never thought we would see the death of our child because children, we thought, are supposed to outlive their parents.

Through this terrible tragedy, the fragility of life became a stark reality for us. Keeping a human being alive (especially for a parent) is an amazingly difficult task – a thought that neither of us had considered before. It is so easy to die; to be full of life, with an entire future to experience and the next minute it is gone, extinguished in a moment. Even still, so many of us take growing old for granted. We never thought this would happen to us. I guess no parent does...

Fifteen years have passed since we first became parents. When Tim was born, we reveled in the experience of my pregnancy and the development of a new human being. We were ecstatic at the miracle of birth and the product of our co-creation. As the years went by we enjoyed and anguished over the positive and negative aspects of our four children's development. Parenting was hard work, but we loved our children and had high hopes for them, so it was always rewarding. As parents, we often tried to look into our children's future. What would they be like as adults? What jobs would they hold? How would they look? What kind of relationships would they have with us once we were no longer their caretakers? We never asked the question, How will we survive if they do not? Most of us never even consider the possibility that our children may die before us. It is too frightening and too painful. Now that Tim had died, we had to face a hard fact that this had really happened. We had no idea how we were going to cope.

On that Father's Day, we touched Tim's still warm but unresponsive body and had to begin to say goodbye forever. That was two years ago and we are still in the process of saying goodbye. It has been frightening, panic-inducing and painful. We have learned that coping with the death of a child is truly a lonely journey, one unique to each parent (even for the parents of the same child). So much of the grief process is dependent on each parent's previous life experience and what that child meant to him or her. Saying goodbye to one's child is a devastating experience. Sometimes a parent simply never recovers from it.

Our relationship as husband and wife has been severely tested under these difficult circumstances. Even though we were both in great pain, we could not lean on each other for support. Our lives, our faith and our values were shattered. It isn't easy for either of us to give support or comfort to each other because we both feel so empty, we've both lost part of our own lives. At first we both had gaping wounds and exposed nerves, we were shattered and lost. Even though we have tried to resume a "normal" life, the hurt and sadness is never far away.

When Tim died, both of us felt as if a part of us died. We didn't know if we could live without him. Both of us were completely nonfunctional in our most central roles. For my husband, Ron, going to the office and attempting to continue as the breadwinner was excruciatingly difficult. Ron would lock his office door so no one could come in and see him crying. By staying at home, I was able to do the same thing. Trying to be a mother to my other children only served to remind me of Tim and that he was gone.

Because Tim died suddenly and unexpectedly, we were totally taken off guard. One day life was normal and happy and the next day, we found ourselves immersed in agony. We were so completely unprepared. The state of shock both of us were in seemed to be our only future. The grieving "process" that we heard about with it's timetables for various stages of grief didn't seem to apply to us. From the moment our son died, a process began that we now realize will probably never end. While that may sound pessimistic, it is, in actuality, realistic and optimistic. We are now aware that a year is a very short period in this very painful process. Even two years is still a small amount of time.

While it may be depressing to think about how long it takes to accept death and to go through that initial grief over the loss of a child, it is comforting to note that we are not abnormal. Though there are times when we still feel the searing pain of our son's death as if it had just occurred, these times are less frequent than they were at first. There are even times when we feel almost normal and can enjoy life. We have learned to accept that the bad times will come and that sometimes we will sink into sadness and depression. While those times will still come, we know that the pain will not be continuous. It does pass. The grief comes in waves that must be ridden, felt, experienced and then released. To deny such feelings or to place them in a time frame would be a mistake. Unless expressed, these feelings will always be lurking, ready to attack us at some unknown time. To try to deny them will only make this dreadful event tougher to live with.

Giving in to a period of mourning is not an easy task. People sometimes try to help us return to "normalcy", hoping to make life easier for us. But a normal life as we know it is over. We must find a new level on which to function. Those of us who have family and friends that offer companionship and let us ride through our pain at our own pace are lucky (if such a word can ever be applied in such cases).

Our families were not there when our son was killed. Friends were, but even with their support, we knew it would be a long time before we felt better. We needed to find others to walk with us on our journey toward acceptance, others to listen to us talk when we needed to. We found this in support groups for parents who had lost children and from professionals and friends who were not afraid to be there.

That something in us died when Tim was killed will never change; it is a horrible fact. Though we can see nothing good about his death itself, we may have gained something positive from the experience of losing him. Living in a hell of pain and suffering has caused us to change and to grow and with growth there is always loss. Sometimes growth requires extreme events, extreme experiences, extreme circumstances. But that's how people become better. That's how life can increase in value: by living, caring, sharing and losing.

We have read in books that living involves losses; such losses are a normal part of the human process. These "normal" losses are necessary, but they are not necessarily easy to adjust to. They require flexibility, adaptability and the restructuring of thoughts, lifestyles and goals. But we must experience them and hopefully grow because of them. Our mental health and happiness will be reflected in how well we are able to cope. We know that life rests on nothing more than a thread and it can break at any moment.

In her writings on death and dying, Elisabeth Kübler-Ross states that pain is sometimes necessary for growth. Human life, she says, might even be stagnant without significant emotional events, without tragedy, without pain.

Death is a fact of life. We know that everyone who lives will in time die, but it is our hope that love will keep us alive, even after death. We hope that the love we have for our child will keep us joined with him and that when we die we will be reunited with him. Then our family will be together again. Until then, we have our memories of him and we have hope. We are different people because of what has happened. We wish it had not happened, but it did. So we have changed and we have grown accordingly. Now our priorities and values are different. Life is more sacred and has more meaning. One day we may understand the mystery of life. Until then, we cherish memories of the past and look to the future with hope. This way of thinking makes death not so frightening anymore.

Death of a Family Star

Like many children of my generation and ethnicity, both of my parents emigrated from Europe. My father and the other men of the family left Greece during the first quarter of the century. In America they found the opportunities and gained the ability to do better financially and culturally.

Because my brother, my cousins and I grew up in the aftermath of the Depression and during the terror of the Second World War, we felt privileged to have opportunities that were not available to our forefathers. Of special importance was education because no one in our family had received more than a grade school education. All of us prized our new educational opportunities because they could open doors to a higher standard of living. More importantly, education could provide the "calling card" to a higher social position.

In many families there is someone who surfaces as "the star." Family stars are owned by the family: their achievements are a reflection of the family. Our family star was my cousin, Peter. Peter had the strong good looks of his Mediterranean ancestors and the charm and wit of his Irish ancestors. Peter had a keen mind and he embodied the fulfillment of the family's dream for opportunity and success.

From early youth Peter used his attributes wisely. He married a lovely and talented woman who also promoted his career. He pursued law and later became a judge. Peter had a special charisma that attracted young people; he was their role model and counselor. The other adults in the family both envied and adored him. He was, in essence, their alter ego. When they spoke of "The Judge" they were full of pride. One of them had "made it."

For the elders in the family, Peter represented the culmination of their dreams. He was proof that their sacrifices had not been in vain. And they enjoyed his successes and the public accolades as though they were theirs.

Then one sultry August night, death crept in and stole our star in his sleep. There was no preparation, no lingering illness—he was just gone. Peter's

185

funeral was a tribute to the family. The scores of dignitaries that attended and the throngs of the bereaved were evidence that our Peter was truly a star.

It has now been over four years since our star left us, but our grief is still not assuaged. There is an undeclared feeling of emptiness at our family get-togethers. In fact, it was several years before we all felt comfortable enough to even get together because it was too painful for us to acknowledge our loss. The mourning was for the loved one, but also for the loss of our family's future. No longer could we count on Peter's success as a mark of our family's worthiness.

After Peter's death family members grew closer together. Through our grieving we became painfully aware that waiting for tomorrow can be a mistake; tomorrow may never materialize. We also learned that we must be our own persons, that it is unfair and unrealistic to gain recognition through another. So we no longer look for one star, but rather try to foster star qualities in everyone, including ourselves.

The Final Gift

For many people, overcoming tragedy means dealing with grief so that one can hopefully carry on with daily life as it was before. For me, it was an opportunity to face my life stronger than I've ever been.

When Peter, my best friend and brother, fell into a coma after a motorcycle accident in Taiwan last year, I felt a brief surge of violent feelings followed by a deep sadness. We were as close as two brothers could be. For the previous 29 years we had shared rooms, debts, books, jobs, friends, ID cards, social and family responsibilities, dreams and underwear. There wasn't anything we would not or did not ask of each other. This meant we depended on each other greatly, a fact that I became acutely aware of when I realized that he was no longer there and I couldn't ask him for advice on how to handle his accident. My parents and I flew to Taiwan to do what we could for Peter and his Taiwanese wife, Julie.

For several days I fluctuated between wanting Peter to live with a damaged brain and wishing he would die. The thought of him living only partially recovered is, to this day, an incredibly horrible thought. After several days I decided that I must accept the outcome, whatever it would be. Nothing in life had prepared me for anything like this.

I did not cry much when I first heard about the accident. Somehow the horror of Peter's injury hit head-on against my usual optimism and made me feel numb inside. All I could do was react to whatever happened. Normally a deliberate person, this was unnatural for me, but it was the only way I could function.

In retrospect, it is amazing how similarly our family and Julie's family reacted to the crisis. Julie's family was constantly taking her to temples to pray and burn incense. Every day her family summoned a Buddhist monk to heal my brother. The presence of a Buddhist monk performing healing rites on my brother was not something my mother's Roman Catholic upbringing had prepared her for. Biting her lip, she acknowledged that anything that might help her son should be tolerated. I believe she compensated by bringing in at least five priests and ministers on her own. However, complete respect was always shown by both families in an extremely tense environment. Religion was, for both families, a guiding force that provided direction and a sense of confidence and pacification.

Culture and language did not seem to be barriers between our families. We exchanged food and comforted each other in the hospital waiting area. Most of the visual barriers common to Asian/Caucasian couples had already been overcome by my brother. He had worked hard at gaining the acceptance of his wife's family. Interestingly, he had developed a close affection for his mother-in-law and she for him. However, I was told that after the accident the mother-in-law expressed anger to her daughter for marrying a foreigner. But perhaps this anger was only an attempt to vent the grief and pain that she and her daughter were feeling.

My father reacted to my brother's accident with a great deal of anger. He voiced his disgust at Peter because he suspected that alcohol might have played a part in this tragedy. Like Peter's mother-in-law, my father experienced great pain and frustration. Both wanted a resolution to the tragedy and the look in their eyes is something still vivid in my mind.

During visiting hours at the hospital, I took care to make sure someone was in Peter's room all the time. When no one else wanted to go in, I gladly sat and talked to him. I recalled many stories we shared together. These moments alone with him were very important to me. I had the opportunity to say things to him for the last time. For this, I will be forever grateful.

Toward the end of the week after the accident, Peter became brain-dead. We needed to make many decisions, but interestingly enough, Peter had explicitly instructed me as to his wishes should a tragedy of this nature befall him. He had told me that he would not want to live on a respirator and that he wanted his organs to be donated. Unfortunately, Julie's religion and beliefs did not allow for the honoring of either of these requests. According to her beliefs, if Peter continued to live on a respirator, she could fulfill her responsibilities to him by visiting the hospital every day for the rest of her life. Because Peter's instructions were contrary to these beliefs, I felt it was my responsibility to convince her to honor Peter's wishes. Persuading Julie was the most difficult task of my life. She was terribly weakened by pain and grief; I have never seen a more vulnerable human being in my life. But she knew how close Peter and I had been, so she did not doubt my words.

I slept outside Julie's room the night before Peter's requests were to be granted. She awoke from a dream upset and ran to tell me that Peter could not see because we had donated his eyes. According to her beliefs, dreams are real and so it was hard for me to comfort her. It was even harder to persuade her to sign the necessary papers carrying out Peter's wishes to have his organs donated. Although only her signature was required, I co-signed to share her responsibility.

Peter died before the respirator was removed. Afterwards, Julie wanted Peter to be shaved and bathed before his cremation. Since the nurse could not assure her that this would be done, we decided to do it ourselves. I shaved Peter's face and then helped turn his body while Julie bathed him. She was so calm, so gentle. She winced in pain when I accidentally made his shoulder crack.

It was at this point that the full weight of what had happened surfaced inside of me. I felt blood rushing to my head and everything turned fuzzy. I wondered if I had gone crazy and just didn't know it. Inside I felt many things for Julie and Peter all at once: love, sadness, pity and respect. Gradually my head began to clear. I had walked up to the edge of an abyss of turmoil and confusion, yet I had been strong enough to walk away. Finally, I felt at peace. More importantly, I knew very deep inside of me that I could handle anything life would throw at me. There was a certain calmness that came with this feeling of internal stability.

I knew my life was changed by his death; it couldn't help but be different. Now Peter is no longer around for me. Still, the fact that I was able to say goodbye to him and carry out his final requests strengthened me. I have lost a great friend and brother, but in many ways dealing with his death is as important as how I dealt with his life. My life was enriched by his and continues to be.

Tears and sadness still find me sometimes. But the experience of saying goodbye prepared me to face a new and different life. I believe it was his final gift to me.

Death with Dignity

Mary Gates was diagnosed with end-stage renal disease, a terminal condition. The physician's notes in the medical records indicated that Mrs. Gates was aware of the fact that she was terminally ill. Mrs. Gates left the nursing home three times each week to have kidney dialysis. The treatments left her feeling weak and nauseous. In an attempt to help her regain her strength, the physician ordered physical therapy. I met Mrs. Gates in her hospital room before her first treatment session to introduce myself to her as her physical therapist.

Mrs. Gates greeted me warmly as I entered her room. She was lying on her bed on top of the bedspread. She appeared to be elderly, pale, frail, very thin and petite and she spoke in a voice that was audible only at close range. She apologized for being in bed and said that she was very anxious to begin therapy. Her dignified determination to improve her strength and endurance was evident not only in her words, but also in her tone of voice and body language. She made good eye contact and seemed extremely alert.

As I glanced around her room, personal possessions emphasized Mrs. Gates' identity—her unique individuality. Furniture that had been brought from her home replaced the traditional institutional dresser and bedside stand. Although her physical ailments made a hospital bed a necessity, her flowered bedspread and silk pillowcase added warmth to the room. Mrs. Gates' favorite chair was positioned near her bed for easy access. There were flowers and plants on the windowsill and pictures on the walls. The room had been transformed into her home.

During the following weeks, Mrs. Gates became a regular participant in physical therapy. Her program consisted of exercises designed to enhance muscle tone and walking to improve her strength and endurance. From there she quickly became involved in the therapy community. She observed other patients' progress and offered them encouragement and compliments. She shared her positive outlook with clients and staff. Her philosophy was to make the most of every day and every situation. When nausea or respiratory problems prevented her from attending a scheduled therapy session, she apologized for canceling her session. She never complained about her discomforts or questioned why she was ill. Rather, she expressed concern and deep admiration for her husband who visited her daily and had assumed the responsibility of running their household.

As the weeks turned into months, Mrs. Gates' attendance in therapy became sporadic due to her various medical complications. Mrs. Gates, her physician and Mr. Gates all agreed that therapy should continue whenever Mrs. Gates could attend. Her strength and endurance varied from day to day, but she was gradually getting weaker. Mrs. Gates required frequent rest periods to complete her already adjusted exercise program. She also began to report discomfort in her right shoulder. This discomfort persisted and increased in intensity. As this discomfort progressed to pain, Mrs. Gates' exterior cheerfulness began to fade. She continued to be pleasant and cooperative, but her usual smile would suddenly be replaced by a grimace of pain. Conversation became an effort for her. She now spent rest periods lying down with her eyes closed. A form of deep heat was prescribed to relieve her shoulder pain. After that, Mrs. Gates was pleased that her pain was being treated and her spirits seemed to improve.

Several days later, Mrs. Gates was transferred to the hospital with severe medical complications. She died before returning to the nursing home.

When I was notified of her death, several feelings and thoughts occurred to me. I felt sadness for Mr. Gates, but also relief that Mrs. Gates was no longer fighting a losing battle. While the physical therapy did not prolong Mrs. Gates' life, I do believe it enhanced the quality of her life. Through physical therapy Mrs. Gates was able to maintain some control over her body and this gave her a real sense of satisfaction. She was able to maintain and express her individuality in a health care system that tends to be impersonal and she maintained a supportive, caring and loving relationship with her spouse. She also earned the respect of an entire therapy department by her ability to remain pleasant, motivated and involved with life while being challenged by pain and impending death every day.

Mrs. Gates lived with dignity. She died with dignity as well.

The Wind:
When AIDS Takes a Friend

I have always told people that suffering from AIDS is not like the romantic drama portrayed in *Love Story*. It isn't poetic and sweet to drift into death; it is painful and miserable. Many people with AIDS have died alone and frightened while they are treated like toxic waste. But people with AIDS have taught me that even AIDS can have a loving ending.

My friend Jim was a robust, bright, immensely caring person who fought AIDS for over two years—a long time to fight AIDS. It is a disease that usually beats its victims in much less time. But Jim had had relatively few opportunistic infections and he was able to work until quite late in his illness. He was active with friends and family and did volunteer work even after his health forced him to quit his job. I couldn't sit next to Jim without wanting to put my arms around him, hold his hand or kiss his cheek, because I could see that he was always concerned about others—under circumstances in which most people would only be able to think of themselves.

I was one of those people he always thought about. For me, Jim served as an anchor. When my crazy job in nursing administration upset me, I would call Jim and say, "What am I doing this for? All I can see is budgets and grants and statistics and deadlines. I'm so tired and frustrated. Please, remind me why I'm really here." Jim always knew what to say to remind me of what mattered in life. His view of the world and our place in it always gave me the courage to forget petty frustrations and continue.

From Jim I learned about the power of spirituality. I never thought much about it before I spent time with someone dying from AIDS. Before my relationship with Jim, I believed that there was more to human beings than meets the eye, but that all this "spirit" stuff was hocus pocus. I still cannot define what it is I learned from him. Maybe I have just discovered what many have known forever: that life doesn't end with death. Although I miss Jim, I don't feel as far away from him as I thought I would. I don't hear his voice or see him in visions, but I do feel every bit as close to him as if he was sitting here with me now.

Before he died, we talked about what the worst part of his AIDS experience was for each of us. For him, it was not knowing what to expect. For me, it would be saying goodbye, losing him and the ongoing pain of missing him. So we made up scenarios of what the afterlife might be like. Some of these scenarios were philosophical masterpieces; others were hilarious.

Jim told me not to worry about missing him, because he would always be around me. I told him that when I die I want to be a shaft of sunlight brightly shining through a cloud and down to earth. Jim said that he wanted to be like the wind, always moving around us—sometimes gently and sometimes ferociously. And that is the way I experience him now. I can feel a subtle connection with him that tells me what he would have said to me about why I'm here. It isn't ghostly or creepy, it is comforting like a cool breeze on a summer day. It assuages my fears about his death. And I have a feeling that Jim's questions about the unknown no longer scare him.

In the last stages of his illness, Jim checked out of the hospital and into a hospice. When he chose to do this instead of coming home, many of us were shocked. "But he's not that sick yet," we told ourselves. "He can't be dying! He doesn't look like he's dying." I talked to him in the hospital on the day he left. I told him what people were saying about his choice and asked him, "Have you given up?" "No," he said with one of those wise Jim smiles, "I've just decided." We agreed through many tears and some laughter that we would not say goodbye. Goodbye seemed like a sentiment that didn't really apply to what we were experiencing.

Since Jim died, I have had to learn to grieve over what we have lost, and to rejoice over what we still have. This isn't as easy as we thought it would be. Jim used his time in life well. He wanted to accomplish three things before he died. He wanted to leave funds for his nephew's college education and to finish earning his own degree. Finally, he wanted to be baptized.

Before he died, friends and volunteers helped him to get all of his bills paid and to prepare his will. A bequest for his nephew was also set up to his satisfaction. Friends even helped him to complete his last school project. His nurse delivered his diploma to him when he was in the hospice.

His final wish was also fulfilled. A clergy friend baptized him in the hospice and he died quietly a half hour later. When I look back at those days when we wanted so much for him to "finish business," I remember pain. But now I can also see the silver lining. How many of us will actually have the opportunity to complete all of the things we want to do before we die? I'm sure that Jim had more dreams for his life. But he focused on the things that were most important to him and then set about achieving them.

Discussion

Retaining control in life is a major issue for a person with AIDS because the disease can strip a person and his loved ones of all security and independence quickly. The body deteriorates rapidly. In the space of a few weeks the simplest tasks often became major hurdles. The disease bankrupts a victim. A person who is self-sufficient one day is left wondering how he will pay for tomorrow's medication and how he might live for another year. Thoughts of death are constant.

The stigma of AIDS puts limitations on a person's trust in others. He wonders, Who can I tell? Who will understand? Who will turn me into a public pariah? Some persons with AIDS are so bound by these limitations that their final days are spent in anger and hostility. Others, like my friend Jim, have the wisdom to move beyond these.

Back on My Feet

"My feet are killing me," I said to my wife. "I've got to get a different pair of shoes." Looking concerned, she said, "You have at least a dozen pairs that are hardly worn. Why not see a foot doctor instead?" Realizing she was right, I made an appointment with a foot specialist downtown.

I was a 45-year-old general foreman of maintenance at a large cast steel foundry. Because I had an enormous amount of energy, working seven days a week, 12 hours a day was just fine with me. As a rule, after work I would eat a quick meal, mow the lawn, work on something in the garage, or repair various problems with my wife or six children. If I did not have anything to do, I would go back to the plant for another four or five hours. I had done this type of work and kept this schedule all of my working life and never had any problems. So why now?

My appointment with the foot doctor was anything but enjoyable. He told me that I had arthritis. I wasn't sure why he asked me if I was afraid of shots until the nurse strapped my feet and legs to the chair and proceeded to hold my shoulders back; it was incredibly painful. Two days passed before I could walk without pain, and then, almost like a miracle, it went away.

Within a month the pain returned. At first I tried to ignore it and as long as I kept moving, by the afternoon, the pain and stiffness would usually let up. Eventually, however, a cane became my constant companion. I felt like everyone was staring at me, and I knew I was right when my supervisor suggested I go to a doctor to take care of the problem. This was the first time that I felt my job might be in jeopardy.

"The tests are positive. You have rheumatoid arthritis," my family doctor said after he had evaluated blood samples and x-rays and given me a good examination. He prescribed medications and instructed me to take a couple weeks off so I could rest up.

The words "rheumatoid arthritis" didn't mean anything to me and I continued working as usual. I tried to ignore the pain with work as I had always done in the past when I was sick, but the arthritis pain was increasing in my knees, ankles, hands, elbows and shoulders, making it harder and harder to ignore.

My doctor told me to try to take 30 days off from work and he increased my medication. By now I was on crutches. When I went back to work, I sensed that my boss was watching me and I worried that at any time he might replace me with someone who was healthy. This anxiety and tension greatly exacerbated my condition. Where would I go if I lost my job? What would I do?

The day finally came when the pain was too great to go on and I knew I had to go to the doctor. As soon as he saw me, he knew I had been working and said I had to face up to the fact that I had a problem. Because I worked so hard and would not take time off, the doctor would not sign the release that would let me go back to work. I realized that there was no doubt about the rheumatoid arthritis. The words finally set in and I really knew I had a serious problem.

After notifying my employer that I could not work until further notice on doctor's orders, I went home to try to sort everything out. I was sure that taking 30 days off would cure whatever ailed me, so what a surprise when even after doing nothing but rest and take it easy, the pain and stiffness got worse. The thought resurfaced that I might never work again and it hit me like a locomotive. We had bought a new home two years earlier and a new car seven months ago. I wondered how I was to provide for my wife and kids. What was I to do now?

As these things grew larger in my mind, I became very depressed and withdrawn. I could not seem to make any decisions or think for myself.

"Let's go for an ice cream cone," one of my daughters suggested.

"Does Dad want one?" another asked.

Then I heard, "No, he's fine. Let's go."

This is how far down I was in my own self-pity; I was not being asked and couldn't even make a simple choice. If I'd raise my voice in agitation I would hear, "Pay no attention, that's just the arthritis talking."

This always made me mad as hell. I could no longer assert myself like a normal person. It progressed to the point where I was becoming a vegetable and everything was being done for me. My family really cared, but had no training in the treatment of depression. The highlight of my day was waiting for the mailman to arrive, as if he might be bringing some magical cure. To say I was depressed was not the half of it; I wished I were dead. I regretted that more of my time had not been spent with the kids when they were younger and I was healthy. Nothing was important anymore, yet everything was. I felt my mind would be the next thing to go.

Even though I was now on Social Security disability and receiving a small disability pension from my employer, my income was nowhere near what we had been accustomed to. Somehow we were managing, but my depression would not ease up.

One day, after a very sleepless night, I was sitting in the special highback chair that was prescribed by my doctor when, from somewhere in my head, I heard a voice say, "Jack, if you want to die, you are going at it full speed. If you don't start to help yourself, nobody will." Hearing this, my thoughts started to clear up and I wondered if I could find something to do. Certainly, it would have to be something I could do whenever my body felt good enough, maybe for just an hour or two a week. Knowing that no company could hire me without a doctor's release, and that it would be very hard to find a job for only a couple hours a week, I thought about the possibility of volunteer work. Maybe it would take my mind off some of my problems.

Several days passed before I came up with a decision. I had belonged to a professional organization for maintenance managers and had attended some of the general meetings. I wondered if they could use me for anything. As I stood there on my crutches at an open board meeting, they looked at me in obvious pity and suggested that maybe I could sign up a member or two. I think this was purely to pacify me, but I was excited because here at last was a challenge of sorts. This was the first time in a long while that I felt anyone needed me for anything.

I read all the literature I had on the group and made my first phone call. Much to my surprise, the maintenance manager on the other end said he would like more information. I made three phone calls that day and, to my delight, two people were interested. I continued to make phone calls at a rate of two or three a day, noticing that they got easier each time.

By the time of the next board meeting, 33 new members had been enrolled due to my efforts. I was given a round of applause that made me think, "Hey, I am needed." I felt like a person who belonged again. This gave me a renewed sense of purpose that is hard to describe. During the next year, 164 new members were referred by me and I was well on the road to recovery. My handicap became nothing more than an inconvenience; I was able to stand, to walk and to talk with dignity again.

During this same time period, my wife and I attended a self-help class. I was taught how to pace myself, what exercises to do, how to rest and how to take my medication. In addition, I heard the issues that my peers were experiencing. My wife learned how she could help me and I was able to get a look into what she was going through because of me. I was learning.

Together with the program and what I was doing for my organization, the positive attitude I developed was incomparable to anything I'd ever felt before. No longer do I race to get things done. Asking for help has become easier. I even found time to do volunteer work for the Arthritis Foundation.

It's a far cry from "never working again." Granted, I'm not keeping anywhere near the pace I had set for so many years, but it is so satisfying to have something to do besides waiting for the mailman. Now I wait only to see when I am scheduled to speak at the next self-help class.

Don't Forget He Lived!

When June called our office and asked if there was someone she could talk to about her son's death, I told her that perhaps I could help. When I asked when he had died, she said "Six months ago. He was only four months old when he died. I found your number in the telephone book and would like to make an appointment." We arranged a time for her to come in later that week. I looked forward to meeting with her.

When June walked in, I noted that her appearance was neat and tidy. She was wearing black slacks and a black shirt. Her manner was calm, yet she was anxious to get to the topic that had brought her in. I quickly learned that June was a 23-year-old single parent and that her deceased son Jeff had been her only child. Jeff had been a healthy baby until he suddenly became ill with a terrible infection that caused his unanticipated and sudden death.

The reason June contacted me was to discuss a problem she was experiencing with her co-workers. June indicated that her peers at work had been very supportive at the time of Jeff's death, but their recent behavior toward her made her angry and she did not know how to handle the situation.

One of June's co-workers and friends had recently had a baby and another was in her second trimester of pregnancy. During coffee breaks their conversation often revolved around these two pregnancies. Her co-workers shared their experiences of pregnancy, labor and delivery. They talked constantly of diapers, sleepless nights with a newborn and feeding dilemmas. When June offered comments about her experiences during her pregnancy and when Jeff was still a newborn baby, the others would quickly change the subject of the conversation. Also, if she entered the coffee room during a similar conversation, the subject of pregnancy and children would be dropped.

"I just want to yell at them and tell them not to act as if Jeff had never lived! Just because he died doesn't make the fact that I was pregnant and had experiences just like they did any less real." She also felt shut out when family pictures were shared among the group. June wanted to show Jeff's picture as well, but felt that would not be acceptable to these women. The new mother in the group also had become uncomfortable when June offered her some of Jeff's clothes and other infant items. It seemed to June that Jeff's death had negated both her pregnancy and Jeff's short life, at least in the eyes of her co-workers.

We talked about what she would like to happen when discussions regarding children and pregnancy occurred at work. I pointed out that most likely her friends did not know how to respond to her loss. If asked, I suggested, they would probably indicate that they were doing what they thought was in June's best interest. I told her that other parents who had lost babies experienced similar problems and that many of them found that they had to take the initiative to let other people know what was helpful to them and what was not. I also pointed out that she may have to learn to live with the fact that some people probably would not change their behavior toward her, even with an increased awareness of her wishes.

We discussed some strategies about how she could let people know that she would like to be included in these discussions and would appreciate the opportunity to share her experiences. I encouraged her to approach one or two of her friends individually, talk about how she felt in these situations, and ask if they would help to get others to include her in the coffee break chats. June felt this approach might be helpful and was willing to try it.

In this session we reached an agreement about strategies that would help her to deal with her first concern, but I sensed that she had something else she wanted to talk about. I initiated a general conversation with her about issues expressed by other bereaved parents about six months or so after the death of their infant. I commented that often, as parents find themselves moving on in the grief process, they realize that not every waking moment includes thoughts of their child. This is often a cause of great concern for them because it makes them feel both guilty and fearful that they may forget their child.

June drew in a deep breath. There was a look of surprise on her face. Then she began to cry. "That is exactly what is happening. I have to tell myself: 'Don't forget he lived.' I started wearing black to remind myself that I should be grieving and that I should not forget him. I feel guilty because I don't think about him all the time—like I did just after he died." She mentioned that she didn't cry as often now and that this reinforced her fear that she would forget Jeff. She said that she was relieved to find that others experienced similar feelings.

I discussed the importance of memories, but explained that part of the grieving process was finding a balance between the past and the present. We talked about how hard it is to work through not only the loss of Jeff, but the loss of her dreams for their future—dreams about what life would be like for Jeff and her.

Our conversation ended with June expressing relief and a feeling of peace of mind. She asked for some literature that might help her deal with her child's death and asked permission to call me again. I encouraged her to let me know how her plan to deal with her friends at work turned out.

About 10 days after June's initial visit to the Center, she stopped by unannounced. She was dressed in a red skirt and a brightly colored blouse with flowers on it. She brought a picture of Jeff to show me and told me that the plan to improve her work situation had been a success. June's friends were relieved when she initiated a discussion about how the coffee break conversations affected her. After that things improved. Still, she was aware that there would be ups and downs along the way. She told me that she knew she would learn to accept the reality of Jeff's death without forgetting that he had lived.

Discussion

The death of an infant or young child, whether sudden or anticipated, has a profound impact on the family. Grieving actually never ends and parents have often commented that a "normal" life never returns. Often parents say that although they can never accept the idea that their child had to die, they have learned to accept the reality while remembering that the child did live. Memories are a vital part of this process.

June's story is not uncommon. Often parents will call the Sudden Infant Death Syndrome Center about three to six months after losing a child and express concern about their progress with grieving. They don't understand why they don't feel bad all the time and why they don't cry whenever they think of the child. At the same time, they wonder why "the grief" hasn't gone away yet.

An effective plan of health care for a family following a sudden infant death from any cause should include ongoing contact with care professionals for approximately one year or longer after the death. Because it is often difficult for parents to reach out for support, periodic contact initiated by the health care provider may be useful to help them identify their concerns. Giving parents "permission" to feel the way they do and to be where they are in the grieving process is an important part of this support. "It's OK not to be OK" is a phrase that many parents have found healing.

Anniversaries and holiday remembrances are also an important part of comprehensive support. However, a counselor must recognize the importance of unusual or personal holidays when setting up an individualized plan of care. For example, one mother had more difficulty dealing with Easter than other religious holidays. She had always dreamed of dressing her daughter in a frilly dress with lace and ribbons for Easter, but her only daughter had died at eight months of age, three months before her dream was to become a reality.

It is common for many persons to need assistance from time to time while going through the healing process of grieving. As June's story illustrates, one such time often occurs between three and six months after the death. A contact at this time from a knowledgeable and supportive health care provider can help clients move toward learning to live with the death and realizing that they will never forget the child who lived.

OTHER KINDS OF LOSS

The Contagion of Hopelessness

This story illustrates the need for caregivers to take a proactive approach when a patient is experiencing multiple losses. As the following case will show, caregivers' personal attitudes toward a patient's losses can negatively influence that patient in a very serious way. Caregivers must learn to recognize how the nature of their caregiving affects their patients.

I became involved with Julie's case at the time of her initial diagnosis and continued to see her throughout the course of her illness. Julie was 43 years old, had experienced difficulty swallowing and had recently lost 15 pounds. She had undergone a laryngoscopy and had been diagnosed with squamous cell carcinoma of the pharynx and right tonsilar region.

Since her tumor was large, it was necessary to give chemotherapy in order to shrink the tumor prior to surgery. The chemotherapy was successful in shrinking the tumor, but it also produced severe nausea, vomiting and mouth ulcers. Julie could not eat enough to maintain her weight, so a feeding tube was placed through her nose to her stomach. Since she was suffering from severe exhaustion, surgery was postponed until she regained her strength.

Her surgery took place six weeks after chemotherapy. Julie's tonsils and pharynx were removed, as well as the tissue from the right side of her neck. This resulted in an obvious facial disfigurement. Her postoperative complications were numerous. In addition, her original swallowing problem was no better, and she now required a permanent feeding tube. She was also depressed because she felt that nothing had been accomplished by her surgery. Because the feeding tube now had to be inserted through the abdominal wall to the stomach, yet another surgery was necessary. She had also sustained wound infections in her neck and abdomen, which required that she undergo vigorous skin care rituals. Furthermore, her respiratory problems finally led to a tracheostomy and profuse bleeding began in her lungs. Julie's dream of "getting better, going home and being normal" seemed to be out of reach.

Julie's anxiety was very visible. She would frequently say, "I don't know exactly how I'm going to manage," and laugh at the end of the sentence. If there was a silence she would find something to say. She would often pace the floor as she talked. When she was confined to her bed, she would move up and down in the bed and comment, "I can't sit still."

Julie had a limited network of family and friends. Her home was very far from the hospital, and her husband, who was self-employed, found it almost impossible to visit during the week. Telephone conversations with him had been one of her major sources of support, but after the tracheostomy she rarely used the telephone because speaking was difficult.

As her condition grew worse, Julie became fatigued, lacked a sense of motivation, was depressed and did not communicate. Soon it was too much of an effort to write legibly, and she stopped attempting to mouth words. When questioned, she rarely even moved her head to indicate yes or no. It was becoming increasingly apparent that Julie's hopes of "getting better, going home and being normal" were not going to be realized. Her involvement in her treatments and daily care became sporadic, and the nursing staff, having given up on Julie, stopped encouraging her participation.

The physicians involved in Julie's care saw her behavior as "adolescent." They thought she wouldn't listen to them unless they told her what she wanted to hear. Other staff members said that they were overwhelmed with Julie's complications and problems. I listened to the other health care providers and became overwhelmed myself. I was beginning to wonder what would go wrong next. I, too, began to think of Julie as a sad, hopeless patient.

Once I was able to recognize my own feelings of hopelessness and could see that we had all given up on Julie, I attempted a proactive approach. I assessed the situation and decided that Julie was suffering from a lack of coordinated nursing and medical efforts. A care conference was initiated, and pertinent problems relating to Julie's nutrition, skin, respiratory status, communication patterns, pain management and anxiety were identified and addressed. The conference allowed the caregivers to identify their own feelings and see past the immediate problems to offer possible solutions. A plan was developed.

First, Julie was invited to take an active role in her care. She was allowed to decide how often and for how long her treatments would take place. We also called on family members to spend more time with Julie. They were encouraged to call her even though her tracheostomy made speaking difficult. A system of tapping was developed to enable Julie to have some sort of telephone contact with family and friends. Staff members also increased the time they spent with Julie. They deliberately spent time with her when treatments were not scheduled. Attentive care to her appearance helped increase Julie's self-esteem. Also, consistent physical and occupational therapy helped to increase her energy and activity levels. The staff made an effort to improve Julie's knowledge about her treatments and disease. This appeared to reduce her anxiety. It was this coordinated effort among staff, patient and physicians that provided an organized approach to Julie's recovery and a sense of hopefulness.

Julie's physical complications gradually decreased. She participated in treatments and care as planned. Communication with her improved and her wish to be able to go home became more of a possibility. After Julie's tracheostomy was removed, she was able to say that it was when everyone began working toward *her* goals that she had started to feel hopeful. The goals set for and with Julie were achieved, allowing her finally to return home.

Discussion

The staff and I found that it was much easier to recognize Julie's sense of hopelessness and loss than it was to confront our own similar feelings. It was clear to see the problems Julie had developed both physically and psychologically, but what took time was to recognize and admit my own sense of loss. Because of this, I focused on Julie's complications instead of setting an overall goal for her care, and as a result, her condition worsened. I had introduced myself to Julie as one who might dispel her anxieties about unknown procedures and outcomes. Yet when I was faced with her multiple complications (and my own inability to understand their causes or control them), I must have been giving Julie the message that I did not support her. The inconsistent care and lack of encouragement from all of Julie's health care providers allowed her to feel that it was pointless for her to put any effort into her recovery. It must have seemed to her that we thought her recovery was not possible. In order to change that message, active care planning with her participation was initiated. This technique conveyed the message that something wasn't right, something needed to be done and this is what it was going to be. Our new attitude gave Julie the sense of hope she needed to recover.

Active care planning included setting goals that addressed each physical complication. Julie participated in setting some of these goals, as well as planning the means to achieve them. For a person who is extremely anxious about unknown procedures and outcomes, this plan gave Julie a sense of direction (a goal that was set to reduce anxiety). A structured plan offered patient and staff a measure of control in a situation that had uncontrollable complications. As a result of our planning, Julie felt confident and assured that she had support from her caregivers; she saw that we were actively planning for her return home.

I now realize that identifying short- and long-term outcomes added some perspective to Julie's treatment process—for her as well as for me.

Jimmy's Accident:
A Family Learns to Adjust

We have 10 rooms and 20 beds in our burn unit. Rarely are they all filled at once—thank goodness. If they were, it would be hard for everyone—parents, children and staff alike. All of the children who come through these doors are different, but in many ways they are very much alike. Each child and family that comes here embarks on a similar journey that is always filled with many intense emotions. More than anything else it is a journey of loss and rediscovery.

It had been an unfortunate accident—a gasoline explosion, and Jimmy had suffered severe burns over his face, torso, arms and hands. When I first met Jimmy's family I was impressed with how close and supportive they were to each other. As with many parents, Jimmy's folks wanted and needed to talk about their son. The father showed me a picture of Jimmy before the accident and with that, he and his wife began the process of grieving. They shared the story of their life with their son: his birth, joys, strengths and struggles. They were always very proud of him.

As the days and weeks went by, the family gradually came to understand the reality of what they and their son had to face. His pain became their pain. At first Jimmy's mother was determined to participate in his treatment. She helped with his baths, debriding and bandaging. But as her identification with his pain increased, she got to the point where she could no longer help with this part of her child's care. Jimmy's father found it equally difficult. As the days passed, the father's absence from Jimmy's room became more and more obvious. Jimmy's mother saw her husband's behavior as a withdrawal of support. Nevertheless she always defended his behavior to others. She became consumed by Jimmy's past accomplishments. She tried to wipe away the reality of Jimmy's accident and tried to make the past become the future—perhaps as a way of putting Jimmy back together and so that others would see the child she had known in the past, the child she knew he was inside. She was frightened by the way her son looked now that he was disfigured by the burn.

Once Jimmy's mother got over the initial shock she found that she needed to get some emotional distance so that she could help herself. As a result of this withdrawal, she made the initial phases of treatment proceed easily. At this point, Jimmy's curiosity took over and he began to engage and cooperate in his own treatment. His rage subsided and the anger he felt became focused. He developed outlets for his emotions and channeled his energies. He began to participate in the more painful procedures and would bite a washcloth to deal with the pain as he helped pull burned skin off.

Jimmy underwent multiple surgeries and his spirits began to brighten as his skin healed. But that was before he caught a glimpse of himself in a mirror; seeing his scarred face was traumatic for him. It was as if he had been detached from his body and seeing his face again forced him to identify with his pain. Another stormy period of grieving followed.

Gradually, Jimmy began to heal emotionally. He became aware of the other children on the unit, most of whom were younger, and he watched their progress and encouraged them. As Jimmy's focus began to move outside of himself, he first got pleasure from the other patients' progress and then took pride in his own. His attitude became more positive and future-oriented.

While Jimmy was discovering himself and healing physically and emotionally, his family was also going through a period of tremendous change. His mother's response to the chaos was to retreat, and she decided to move the family to an isolated farm. She made this decision with little or no consultation with Jimmy or his father. The father did not openly disagree with her plans, but supported her silently, as if to say, "She needs these plans now, and if it is best, then we will move when the time comes." Jimmy's mother spoke of the move for weeks, until one day Jimmy exploded. His friends had been visiting him. They tried to talk about school, but the mother kept refocusing the conversation on the move. Suddenly Jimmy yelled so loud that the entire unit could hear him. He asked her why she was forcing him to leave his friends. Was she ashamed of him? He said he would leave the family before moving. His mother was extremely upset and she left the room sobbing. It was as if all her pent-up grief was finally being released. After this, his mother no longer felt the need to retreat. She stopped talking about moving to the country.

At that time Jimmy was in the last phases of inpatient treatment. He was given the freedom to move about the unit and, just prior to his discharge, he was allowed to leave the unit. Often I saw him in the lounge talking with his folks and other families. Each time I held a session with his family, they were more relaxed and comfortable with each other. In these sessions, Jimmy began talking about his plans for school and the activities he wished to participate in. His mother began making plans to accommodate the new routines that would be necessary to complete his treatment. Jimmy's father spoke of the things they would do together as a family. As Jimmy's discharge approached, I found the family together more and more often. They began to look more like the close, supportive family I saw when Jimmy was admitted.

One always feels mixed emotions when a patient returns home: joy at his discharge, but sadness at saying goodbye after so many months. In Jimmy's case, I knew he and his family were on their way to real recovery when, at a subsequent clinic visit, his father pulled out a recent family photo and began sharing family activities, Jimmy's accomplishments and his own hopes for their future.

The process of grieving for hopes and dreams allowed Jimmy and his family to face the many internal and external changes ahead of them. Only when they had grieved for their losses could they look at Jimmy and accept him. Grieving those losses and integrating the past with a new future allowed Jimmy and his family to move forward with their lives.

Discussion

My role as the social worker on the burn unit took many forms. In this case, it was to provide a supportive environment in which each family member could test reality in order to make a personal adjustment to Jimmy's condition. The members of the family needed to find their own particular methods of grieving. Jimmy's father, faced with his own helplessness to restore his son, needed to be allowed to withdraw and immerse himself in something he could control—his work. Eventually, he was able to move beyond his helplessness. Jimmy's mother grieved by building an entire new life for the family in her fantasies. She needed these fantasies to hang onto until she was ready to face the changes that had to be made. Jimmy had changed; therefore they all must change. Jimmy confronted his mother's avoidance behavior. He felt it was a rejection of himself and a confirmation of his limitations. He saw it for what it was—running away—something he had refused to do.

When the family realized that Jimmy was going to "make it" psychologically, socially and physically, they were able to see that they would too. They realized that his physical alterations were only as limiting as they made them. They also began to value Jimmy's newly developed strengths; he was certainly more mature and complex than prior to the accident. This family was strong enough to allow each member to do the grieving each needed in order to cope. The outcome was a stronger, healthier family.

Incest: Why Me?

23 Years Ago

Daddy, why does Grandpa put his hand under my skirt while we're watching TV? Why do you and Mommy pretend it's not happening? I feel funny. I feel dirty. I don't like what he's doing. Maybe it's my fault. Maybe if I wasn't so cuddly, or pretty, or funny he wouldn't do that. Am I different from everyone else? I feel very silly wondering about this when no one else wonders about it. I love to sit on Grandpa's lap, but I don't want him to keep touching me. Please stop, Grandpa! I want to tell him, "Stop right now." But he's not listening. He's not stopping and Mom and Dad aren't doing anything. Get away from me, Grandpa! You're creepy! Why are they letting him do this to me? Why does he do this? Why can't he stop? Doesn't he love me?

Today

I hate what my grandfather did to me. I was robbed of a child's innocence and right to learn how to love and trust other people. I was robbed of a child's spontaneous playfulness and natural curiosity. I was robbed of the ability to feel secure with my family, with myself, with men and other people who enter my life.

I feel sad that I have to carry the secret that my grandfather abused me. I will never be able to make up the years of my childhood that he spoiled. Even now, it's hard for me to see other grandparents treating their grandchildren gently and kindly. I ask myself why I couldn't have had a safe, meaningful relationship with Grandpa. I sometimes sit and cry over what I missed. Why me? I ask myself.

I want to feel whole and I don't want to feel different from everyone else. I want to take those trusting baby steps I missed. Now, as an adult, I hope I can protect myself so I won't be violated like that again, but I need to test

212

the world and myself. I need to remind myself that Grandpa was a sick, confused and weak man. What happened was not my fault. He was selfish and didn't respect my rights. I am still so angry! For over 20 years I have been worrying about this. And I resent the fact that I must spend energy undoing what my sick grandfather did to me with seemingly no conscience.

At times I feel helpless and powerless to change things in my life. I have difficulty telling my boss I want different hours, telling a co-worker that she is taking advantage of me, reaching out to a friend for a hug, or seeking someone to talk to. I ask myself, Who am I? Where do I go from here? I want to move forward and leave the past behind, but I don't know which path to take. I want to believe that I deserve trusting men and supportive friends. I also deserve to feel and look sexy, and feel free to act on my sexual feelings when I want to. I deserve to say no to the people that take from me emotionally and expect me to take care of their needs instead of my own, but my early sexual abuse makes all these things (that should have come naturally) very difficult.

Trust men. I wonder what that means? I will have to meet many different men and experiment. I will have to learn to listen to the little voice inside me that says, *he's neat, he cares, he seems fake,* or *he seems like he's after something.* I want a new life and I know that with patience I can let go of the garbage in my abusive past and move on.

So now I'm starting over, erasing the damage of what happened by talking about it. Working through the pain of my memories takes a lot of time; I feel like a little girl wearing different glasses. The feelings are new and unfamiliar. I'm learning how to be gentle with myself. I am nurturing myself to help myself heal. Through it all, I will believe in me. I will believe in life. I will trust again. I will.

Solving a Patient-Practitioner Problem

At the time I worked with her, Mrs. Milton was 34 years old and had been diagnosed with chronic leukemia. She had little formal education and only limited life experiences. She was married and had a 14-year-old daughter. Her husband, a high school graduate, was extremely obese and seemed quite shy. The family was of the Quaker faith and religion played an important role in their daily activities.

Part of Mrs. Milton's continuing treatment was conducted on an outpatient basis. She received chemotherapy on a "one day admission" unit at a local community hospital. During the period of her treatment, she and her husband (and frequently her daughter) would travel together to the hospital. Mrs. Milton was referred to the counseling department in which I worked to learn about her illness, treatment and support services. Because I generally worked with leukemia patients, I accepted the referral.

From the beginning, I found it difficult to establish a rapport with Mrs. Milton. She was withdrawn and uncommunicative, something that wasn't noted by her physician or the nurses on the unit. I saw her when she came to her appointments, but because her husband was always with her, I rarely saw her alone. This was acceptable to me because I preferred working with the entire family. Also the husband and daughter were slightly more communicative than Mrs. Milton.

The family definitely needed to be educated about Mrs. Milton's illness. At one session, Mrs. Milton angrily said that they had looked up leukemia in an encyclopedia, and it said that patients with leukemia rarely lived longer than six months. I realized that this was a testing statement; she did not quite believe the prognosis her doctors had given her about living longer. I explained the differences between acute and chronic leukemia and asked them to check the date of their reference book (it turned out to be almost 20 years old). I felt that the two sessions in which these issues were discussed had gone well and that we were finally making some progress.

214

On the day of the next treatment there was a bad storm. The family had to travel about 35 miles to get to the hospital and roads were hazardous. Things were running behind on the unit. I stopped to see Mrs. Milton early in the day and when I arrived, Mr. Milton seemed extremely uncomfortable and excused himself immediately to go to the coffee shop. This was a most unusual thing for him to do, as he rarely left his wife's side. Mrs. Milton said she didn't feel like talking right then, and I said I would return later.

I stopped by again that afternoon. Mrs. Milton's chemotherapy had started late and she was still receiving it intravenously when I got there. Her husband was sitting near the foot of the bed and again he seemed very uneasy when I entered the room. I stayed only a short time and encouraged them to contact me if they had any problems. As I went to leave, I touched Mr. Milton's shoulder briefly and cautioned him to drive carefully going home in the bad weather.

Quite unexpectedly, Mrs. Milton became agitated and began shouting loudly, accusing me of trying to "steal her husband." She claimed I was just waiting for her to die so I could "have him for myself." She shouted that she was leaving the hospital and not returning, and pulled the IV from her arm. She put on her coat and shoes, and yelling profanities, ran down the hall and left the unit.

Her husband was extremely embarrassed, mumbled apologies and hastily went after her. The nurses who had come to the door when the shouting began were stunned. I had been unable to calm Mrs. Milton or to prevent her from leaving, probably because her behavior was so sudden and extreme. I think we were all particularly stunned by her extensive use of profanity, which was so out of character with her usual quiet and religious demeanor.

Discussion

Personally and professionally, I was surprised by Mrs. Milton's accusation. I had obviously missed some important cues in our interactions: our continuing difficulty in establishing a rapport, her lack of trust about the prognosis, and her husband's recent uneasiness when I walked into the room. At the time I worked with Mrs. Milton, we were both about the same age and both of us were mothers of 14-year-old daughters. I do not believe I had touched her husband before except to shake his hand when we met, but my touching his shoulder as I left was perceived by Mrs. Milton as the final evidence that I was trying to take her place. I realized that Mrs. Milton's anger was misplaced and that it was a product of her fear of dying and losing her husband and daughter. She was angry at me for several reasons, one of which was the fact that we were the same age and I was healthy.

After the incident, I alerted Mrs. Milton's physician and we met to decide what action to take. We decided that the doctor would call Mrs. Milton and ask her to return early the following week to continue her treatment. When he spoke to her, he emphasized that I was sorry she had misinterpreted my behavior, and that if it were her wish, someone else from the counseling staff would work with her in my place. She consented to return only on the condition that I no longer be involved. The following week another carefully chosen social worker, who was 25 years older than Mrs. Milton, was assigned to work with her. When the new case worker was introduced to Mrs. Milton, she was accompanied by the physician. No mention was made of me or the problem of the previous week. While Mrs. Milton still remained guarded and reserved, she did eventually relate better to the new social worker and was able to accept support from her.

I feel that the decision to remove myself from this case was correct. The temptation was great to try to vindicate myself in Mrs. Milton's eyes and to respond to the attack on my professional competence. However, to do so might have been at the patient's expense. The most important factor was getting her to continue her treatment and she certainly needed a good deal of emotional support. She was unable to accept this help from me and neither the situation nor the time seemed appropriate for trying to rectify our patient-practitioner relationship.

The Things I Lost
Because of Divorce

Two years ago, after 22 years of marriage, my husband and I decided to divorce. It was a decision made with appropriate consideration and discussion by two adults who had shared both good and bad times and two very special children. It was made with relief. We both knew what we needed to do to optimize our remaining years. There was no rancor, no name-calling, no accusing. Maybe we anticipated some adjustment or loneliness, but ultimately we expected peace and calm.

Yet what I really experienced in the past two years can only be compared to a roller coaster ride of emotions: constant changes and challenges. I certainly was not prepared for the number of painful changes associated with the divorce or how unsettled the next two years would be. Among these changes were the sale of my home of 15 years (the home where I had raised our children), two relocations in 13 months, the death of the family pet, the distress and anger of my two children and the loss of about one-half of my social network. Some of the couples who had been my friends during the marriage drifted away following the divorce. Though I gradually formed new friendships, I was saddened by the loss of my old friends. During this time I also lost my church community.

The first weeks after my husband moved out were blessedly wonderful. I experienced a euphoria that was a combination of relief and anticipation of a more positive lifestyle. My teenage daughter and I simplified our lives and reveled in the peace. I would crawl into my bed at night grateful for the solace. I slept better than I had in years. But I knew even then that the euphoria was temporary and would end soon—to be replaced by what, I wasn't sure.

The next six months were quiet, often lonely times. Frequently, Sunday was a day to walk by the lake and shed a few tears. The work week was full, but by Wednesday of each week anxiety about the weekend would begin to build. The weekend represented great expanses of empty, lonely times when I thought the entire world was made up of couples. I felt like I was a child out in the cold looking in through a window at a fun-filled party. Somehow I actually filled each weekend and was always surprised at how quickly they passed. However, the following Wednesday brought the same anxiety; I never seemed to remember that the weekends weren't actually as bad as I anticipated.

Out of financial necessity I sold the house seven months after the divorce. I moved to a rental property that had room for both children, but none for our beloved family dog. Because of his age, I was unable to find a home for him. The only thing I could do was hold him as the vet put him to sleep. That same fall that I moved out of my home, both of my children entered universities far from home. I then had a quiet, organized household for the first time in 22 years. Initially, I had actually looked forward to it. But when it happened I often found myself anxious and fearful. Usually I kept myself so busy that I didn't have time for reflection. I hungered for peace, but I feared being alone.

My work, as always, was demanding, but I lacked organization and generally felt overwhelmed. I often felt like I was in a fog—vague and disorganized. As a clinical nurse specialist, I found myself doing less direct patient care and focusing on less demanding activities. I occasionally missed appointments and meetings (this had never happened before the divorce). I felt that my life was totally out of control. Fortunately, my supervisor was aware of my situation and was understanding. The simplest problem seemed overwhelming to me. My recertification in cardiopulmonary resuscitation class seemed impossible and a misplaced chart sent me into hysterics.

Friends and colleagues tell me now that they were amazed at my calmness throughout those two years. I know that the calm was external. Internally, chaos reigned. Even close friends that I confided in thought I was keeping my head above water; I knew I was close to drowning.

One week after moving out of my house, I was hospitalized for a bleeding ulcer. I took a leave from work to recuperate and to re-evaluate my priorities. I slowed down the pace of my life. I also set more realistic goals in terms of work. My pace was better, but my confusion and uncertainty continued. One moment I would be very cheerful, almost silly. The next I would be depressed. My thinking continued to be disorganized. It was during this time that I developed a very strong anger toward my ex-husband.

Finally I was able to acknowledge that my 22 years of marriage contained many disappointments and broken promises. My anger surfaced because I believed that I had worked hard at the marriage and my husband had failed to keep his part of the bargain. As a result of this anger, I wanted no contact with him and would go out of my way to avoid him.

I then entered into a relationship with another man, but my uncertainty and mood swings badly affected the relationship. I considered psychotherapy, but the timing didn't seem right. I thought I would know when the time was right to see a therapist. I knew all along that eventually a support group would be beneficial, but it wasn't until eight months after the divorce that it felt right to join.

The divorce support groups that I was involved in were very helpful. They helped to normalize my experience for me. It was fun to be with people who were at the same transition point in life. Also helpful was the fact that my close friend was also divorced. We shared many conversations and tears.

At the same time I was struggling to find myself, my children were also struggling. When the three of us got together on holidays, we were uneasy. All of us tried to integrate the old and new into our reshaped family of three. We had many positive experiences the first year, but many negative ones during the second. By the second year, I had changed significantly, and this change, along with my children's need to adjust to my relationship with a man other than their father, made for discomfort and conflict. My need to change and my commitment to grow and improve was strong, but their distress still deeply affected me.

The "lifting of the fog" and the need for psychotherapy occurred almost simultaneously, about 18 months after the divorce. I was finally willing to trust a therapist and put energy into the therapy process. Once I did, I very quickly felt myself regain control over many elements of my life. I also regained perspective about what was really important. Therapy played an important role by validating my emerging self, challenging some skewed thinking and helping me clarify changes that still needed to occur.

My entire healing process was intensified by my purchase of a new home. It has been extremely important for me to have a place of my own where I can continue to grow without worrying about another physical move. When I purchased the house I once again felt euphoric, but this time it progressed into a contentment that I suspect will continue.

In the course of my divorce, I leaned heavily on my support systems of good friends and family. I also developed new support (divorce support groups, new friends and a therapist). These people were really the key to my adaptation.

One major thing that I learned is to be more tolerant of my own need to grieve. I learned to allow myself to be inefficient, to hurt, to regroup. I had been totally unprepared for the extent of the change and loss that the divorce would bring and was unwilling to allow myself to fully express my grief. Nevertheless, I experienced these changes, kicking and resisting most of the way. Next time I hope I will be kinder to myself and more patient too.

Different Loss, Same Story:
A Nurse Loses Her Job

Two Years Ago: Day One, Morning

I am a clinical nurse specialist. I have been a registered nurse for over 10 years and a CNS for a little over a year. I love my career and my job as an advanced practitioner. I am challenged, stimulated, function autonomously, and am able to practice nursing in a setting that utilizes many of the advanced nursing concepts I learned during my graduate studies. Yet I cannot believe the rumors I am hearing. The hospital is rampant with rumors of cutbacks and layoffs. The fact that I have the second-lowest seniority means I could lose my job or be laid off. What would I do if I lost my job? I cannot think of that now. I have to counsel a patient who is having difficulty accepting the diagnosis of acute myocardial infarction. Isn't it ironic that this patient and I may both have to cope with a loss? How will we manage?

My encounter with this patient is somewhat difficult. Mr. Schmidt states he does not believe that he has had a heart attack: "those doctors mixed up my test results...it can't happen to me...I'm 42 years old...I have young children...a wonderful job as a bank executive...." Throughout our discussion, he constantly moves back and forth from the bed to the chair. He scowls and in a tense, staccato voice he angrily states that he feels fine. "Heart attacks only happen to really old people," he tells me.

By the end of the session we have developed several strategies that will assist him in coping with his medical diagnosis. But I'm not sure that I have helped him. I tell the staff nurse what occurred during my meeting with Mr. Schmidt. She reassures me that my treatment plan is appropriate. The nursing interventions I developed for him will be implemented during her shift. (How I love working here. There is an excellent nursing staff that is open to suggestions that will enhance patient care.)

When I sit down to update the nursing care plan, I cannot concentrate.

My mind is wandering. I am so tired. As I reflect on the interaction with Mr. Schmidt, I focus on his mechanisms for coping: denial and anger. He has so much energy; I wish I could have some of his energy so I could finish my work for the day.

Day One, Afternoon

After updating the care plan I return to the office. There more rumors are flying. Layoffs are certain. CNSs will be laid off; no one is sure who or how many. I leave work thinking, will it be me? No, it can't be. I work in critical care and these units always have a full patient census. They need me. I decide to go to my health club and take an aerobic dance class to work out my frustrations. Halfway to the health club, I realize that I am too tired to exercise. I pick up food at a fast-food restaurant and go home.

It is another evening of sitting at home. Maybe tonight, I hope, I will sleep more than four hours. I wish I knew about my future. I cannot be laid off, the voice in my head continues, I am a nurse and there is always a need for nurses. As I ponder my future, I think of Mr. Schmidt. We are very similar. We are both denying possible losses.

Day Two

Mr. Schmidt's medical diagnosis has been confirmed. The cardiac catheterization results show he has severe coronary artery disease and will require open-heart surgery. When I see him, he is depressed; his lifestyle has to be changed. He lies in bed and does not want to talk to me or participate in his care. He is just going through the motions, and so am I. My condition has also been determined. I have been laid off.

After receiving the news of my layoff, my immediate urge is to leave the hospital. I need to cry and be alone. The news of my layoff spreads rapidly. By early evening several of my colleagues have phoned me or dropped by for a visit. This helps. We eat, we drink and we cry together. Again sleep is difficult and by morning I feel drained. I do not want to go to work, but I must. As I get ready to leave for work, I think of Mr. Schmidt. I realize that he had open-heart surgery yesterday. I wonder who is experiencing more pain—him with all his physical aches and stiffness, or me with my hopeless and depressed attitude?

Being at work is difficult. Most of the people I work with on a daily basis have heard the news. We just look at each other and cry. I am glad to be at work today. I feel so sad and it feels so good to share my sadness with friends who care and truly understand. No work is accomplished today. I sneak in a quick visit to Mr. Schmidt. He is progressing very well. No complications. This is good news—the only good news.

After work I decide to go to my health club. Tonight I am able to exercise and feel invigorated afterwards. I return home totally exhausted and for the first time in weeks, I have a restful night.

Day Three

Another day of work, but this time I feel better physically. I am eager to get to work and begin terminating my present and planning my future. My boss comes over to my desk. She wants to counsel and comfort me. I do not want her near, nor do I want her help. I feel intense rage and anger well up within me. I am so angry at this person who has terminated my employment from the best job I ever had. I suddenly lose my temper and allow the anger to pour out.

She is the target of my rage. After my outburst, she asks if there is anything she can do for me. I tell her to drop dead and to leave me alone. I have never spoken to a boss in this manner. I do feel slightly guilty for losing my temper, but I am also very energized. Can anger be energizing? Am I beginning to accept my loss?

Today I am able to observe my colleagues. We are a very nonproductive group, each grieving and each at her own stage of grief. Not many job activities will be accomplished today—another day to grieve, share feelings and be supportive.

During my last days of employment, I begin to accept the layoff and plan my future. I call colleagues throughout the city to learn of potential job opportunities. I make appointments to have final meetings with supervisors and nursing administrators. I feel that I am taking charge and am in control of my future. I am hopeful.

Mr. Schmidt and I are now very similar. We have accepted our loss and are hopeful about our futures. We are energized and logically planning lifestyle changes. Although we experience different losses and use different coping mechanisms at different times, we ultimately achieved the same end result: healthy coping in response to loss.

Reflection

Two years have elapsed since this experience occurred. When I reflect upon it, I remember the factors that helped me resolve my initial depression and ultimately accept my layoff and job loss.

First and foremost, I realized that the hospital's decision to terminate me was a logical move. It made sense to lay off someone with low seniority. Also, there were several colleagues with similar areas of expertise who could easily assume my job responsibilities. If, as a supervisor, I was confronted with the same factors, I would have made a similar decision. Second, hearing from colleagues that I would be missed helped me feel good about myself. This helped maintain my ego strength. Lastly, the presence of family, friends and colleagues was vital to my coping. It was so helpful to be surrounded by people who were open, honest and supportive. These people facilitated the grieving process by providing avenues and mechanisms that allowed me to frankly express the various emotions that I had as I was grieving.

I have grown because of this loss and become more resilient. But most importantly, I am more sensitive to patients when they experience losses and have to grieve.

My Experience with
Breast Cancer

On an otherwise unremarkable morning, I discovered a lump in my breast while I was taking a shower. I call that day D-Day (Discovery Day).

I didn't consider the possibility that it was anything serious, much less cancer. I am a nurse and in my 56 years I had never had a health problem that was serious. I decided to wait to see if the lump would go away. Besides, my internist had given me a complete physical a month before and he had not noticed any problems. Two weeks later, the lump was still there and palpable. I immediately scheduled a mammogram at the breast diagnostic clinic (BDC) and went in very shortly after work one evening. They did a mammogram, an ultrasound and a thermal test. The nice thing about the BDC is that you can schedule an appointment yourself without having to go through your family doctor as many of the hospital radiology departments require.

The physician at the clinic informed me on the spot that the tumor was probably carcinogenic. At my request he also gave me the names of several surgeons who specialized in breast cancer. I was in shock and turmoil that night, angry at my regular physician for missing the lump in his examination and also angry at myself for not doing regular breast self-exams or getting mammograms. I felt very much alone. The shock of the diagnosis of cancer is devastating to anyone, but I believe it is harder for those who do not have a family (I was unmarried and had no children). Up to this point in my life, I had been feeling physically fine and had simply gone merrily on my way. I had never given a thought to the possibility of breast cancer. In retrospect, I was a prime candidate. I was postmenopausal and I had a marked tendency toward obesity.

There was never a question in my mind about what course of action I should take. The day after the mammogram, I selected a surgeon and called for an appointment, but because he was out of town, I had to wait several weeks. It was a time of high anxiety. When I finally got in to see him, he was very helpful and carefully outlined my options. I decided to have a biopsy, to be followed by a modified radical mastectomy if necessary. He discussed reconstructive surgery, but I wouldn't even consider it. I only wanted the cancer to be removed as soon as possible. I liked the surgeon and immediately had confidence in him. My appointment was scheduled for the first week in May and, at that point, I was still hopeful that the tumor would be benign. At that time I told a few friends and some relatives what had happened. On the day of surgery the doctor examined me and found I had an infected finger on the same side as the tumor. He immediately canceled surgery and put me on soaks and antibiotics. Because that meant another two-week wait, I went back to work. I tried to keep busy and not think about it, but I really don't know how I made it through those weeks.

Finally the day of surgery arrived. I woke up in the recovery room with excruciating pain in my right arm, knowing immediately that they had removed my right breast. The two weeks I spent in the hospital were very busy ones. I had many visitors and my friends and the staff were of great support.

When the postoperative report came back, I learned that the cancer had extended to my lymph nodes, which meant the chances for reoccurrence elsewhere were increased. The clinical nurse specialist associated with the surgeon and the oncologist spent a lot of time with me and she was very supportive. I obtained material from the library and gave myself a crash course on treatment. The doctors were very careful to let me make my own decisions, and I appreciated this, but I really needed some direct advice about which was the best course of action to take. I was concerned about having standard chemotherapy. My physician wanted me to go on a research protocol, but if I did, the decision as to what treatment I'd get would be a random selection by the computer. The three different protocols were: Tamoxifen only; two other drugs for a limited time period; and other drugs for an extended period. The idea of going on one of the protocols is to determine which regimen is the most effective in terms of the extension of a disease-free life.

I had done a lot of reading about Tamoxifen, a relatively new treatment given to postmenopausal women who had estrogen receptor-positive tumors and extension to the lymph nodes. (This treatment has recently been advocated as a preventive measure for women whose cancer is confined to the breast.) I fit the criteria for using Tamoxifen. Random selection placed me in the "Tamoxifen only" course of therapy, but I had mixed feelings about this. I was happy I didn't need to suffer the side effects of conventional chemotherapy, but at the same time I was worried that the Tamoxifen alone wouldn't be enough—that I should have the "double whammy." Despite my misgivings and reluctance, I elected to go ahead with treatment, or adjuvant therapy as it is called. Following the hospitalization, I stayed off work for four weeks and then resumed my busy schedule. I was fitted for a prosthesis after the sensitivity lessened. My emotional state in the months following surgery was very fragile. I cried easily, had no tolerance for the fatigue and was irritable and short-fused. I had not regained my high energy level, it was hard for me to concentrate and I was very forgetful.

I have blood work, x-rays and scans every three months. I have had some abnormal liver function tests, but so far no evidence of disease. The biggest problems I encounter are intense fatigue and the persistent pain and discomfort in my arm. I am wondering in retrospect if the fatigue may have been associated with unresolved depression. And I cannot forget my constant companion—the fear of metastases. Every physical ailment I have is colored with the specter of cancer. A common cold for me becomes lung cancer. My fatigue or a headache becomes a brain tumor. The fact that my liver function tests are abnormal tells me I have liver cancer. Thankfully, this fear seems to be letting up as time goes on.

It has taken me about two years to get back to my normal self. I still get easily fatigued, but some of this is due to the drug I take. I marvel at the women who are able to bounce back without any problems. I have not gone to any support groups because I feel that I can manage by myself. Everyone who has these experiences needs to decide for themselves what will best help them. Self-help groups are very popular and do provide a framework for relating with people who have similar problems. The reason I did not participate is that I have friends who also have had mastectomies and who provide me with a great deal of psychological support. Many women experience feelings of the loss of femininity or sexual attractiveness or of being less than a whole woman. I have not had these feelings of loss. My concern centers on recurrence and the dreaded thought of getting brain, liver or bone cancer. I now have mammograms every year and I preach the gospel of doing breast self-examinations to my staff and friends.

I am concerned about the stress that I encounter in my job. I am always trying to figure out a way to reduce it because there is some indication that increased stress can cause breast cancer. I plan on retiring earlier than I originally anticipated so I can have some time for relaxation and leisure activities.

I must admit that the demands and structure of my position have held everything together for me and have not allowed me the time to feel sorry for myself. I want to emphasize that I could not have made it without the support and encouragement from friends, staff and family. Since my surgery, two very good friends have had mastectomies and we joke about our "exclusive club."

Of course, I would rather not have had this happen, but it did and hopefully it has given me insights into life that I otherwise would not have explored.

No More Miracles:
The Heartbreak of Dementia

I recognize how limited our language really is when I try to describe my loss. To experience a loss is to be overwhelmed by the realization that someone or something that gave you deep satisfaction and immeasurable joy will never exist or happen again. The only thing that remains are the memories that echo the pain and cause an overwhelming sadness.

As I went along, I learned to fold losses into my life experience. I lost my dad, my pets, my soulmate friends, my aunts and a nephew. I lost my youth and transient experiences like breastfeeding. I even lost a part of my body—my ovaries. But the loss that I can't seem to fold in is the loss of my mother or rather loss of the way she used to be. My mother is still alive but she is suffering from dementia resulting from a series of transient ischemic attacks (TIAs), which are forerunners of a stroke. She lives in a nursing home a thousand miles away from me.

When I separated from Mother in late adolescence, I was highly critical of her self-centeredness, her materialism and her failure to love me in the way a daughter is supposed to be loved by a mother. It took more years than I like to admit to come to terms with these things and to love her as a mother is supposed to be loved by a daughter.

Ironically, by the time I finally realized the degree to which our hearts were entwined, Mother was experiencing her last years of being a beautiful, charming and competent woman.

As the number of her TIAs increased, my mother became slovenly. Her impeccable grooming was a thing of the past. And she grew stubborn: her strong will would tolerate no interference. She overturned her drawers onto an empty bed and the contents would still be there weeks later. The woman who had effortlessly spun out feather-light angel food cakes and mouth-watering pies could no longer plug in the coffee pot. In conversations, her previously sweet reminiscences and little jokes were replaced by repetitive

229

stereotyped phrases and, occasionally, unexplained whinnies. The worst moment came one evening when I called her to the phone. As she struggled past me with her walker, she mumbled, "It's probably Jill." That is my name. When your own mother doesn't recognize you, you lose something immense.

A sort of miracle occurred after an especially severe TIA that left her curled up in bed in a fetal position for hours. Maybe the blood circulation to her brain improved as a result of the TIA, I don't know. But in the following weeks as she recovered, her memory, humor and affect came back. It was like she had come back from the dead. I loved to be with her during that time. My life was peaceful again.

In the last few years, nursing home care and good nutrition have slowed her mental deterioration. Bit by bit, however, her personality has faded again. For a moment, she smiles and knows I am her daughter, then her fickle mind goes elsewhere. Disheveled, frail and vacant, she slumps in her wheelchair, oblivious to the caresses I give her.

Now there are no more miracles for us. I have a mother, but my loss is a fact so painful that I am torn between sitting with her forever or never going back to the nursing home again. I leave her each time with tears in my eyes.

"Becoming Real":
Recovery from an Eating Disorder

Nora is 34 years old, married and the mother of a toddler. She is five feet four inches tall with a medium frame. One year ago Nora weighed 95 pounds (her normal weight is approximately 118 pounds). She was consuming 500 calories and walking two hours daily. Her anorexia had been a secret for 18 years. Nora's false sense of self evolved from a childhood belief that she was inherently "bad." Nora had tried to be a good daughter, sister, friend and student, but she never believed she could be good enough.

Four years prior to our meeting, Nora got married, had a child, relocated and obtained a new job. These changes affected the balance between getting her own needs met and meeting the needs of others, so her eating disorder became more powerful. Establishing and maintaining intimate relationships with her husband and child required emotional skills she did not have. Simply "being good" was no longer working for Nora.

To maintain control over the resurfaced belief that she was inherently "bad," she regressed to doing what she knew best: losing weight. As Nora's weight dropped dangerously, her thinking became distorted and she focused on food as a system of reward and punishment. As her physical and psychic energy waned, her fear of losing control of her secret "badness" intensified. She could only eat eight ounces of yogurt if all her work was done by three o'clock. If she didn't, she was bad and could have nothing to eat.

Nora was eventually hospitalized for anorexia. During that time, she continued to deny the fact that her eating disorder controlled her. She was eating three meals a day and as her weight began to increase, she tried to think of ways to lose it—exercising, leaving the hospital and vomiting. Nora became very anxious, irritable and crabby. After three weeks, Nora began to cry with frustration because she couldn't take her obsession with food, weight and how bad she was.

After eight weeks in the hospital Nora gained eight pounds. She started to feel hungry, to experience energy after eating, and realized that there were now actually periods of time between meals when food wasn't the main focus of her thinking. She began to believe that she was capable of learning new ways to live.

In the following nine months of outpatient psychotherapy, Nora's determination and energy were channeled into emotional growth. She no longer automatically thought of food restriction when she experienced a frightening emotion. She no longer felt terrified that she would be abandoned because she wasn't perfect.

The possibility that she is not inherently bad, a new idea for her, is finally becoming real for Nora. She is building a positive self-image by drawing on her achievements in the past year. Nora is like the Velveteen Rabbit in the children's story who takes a long time to "become" and she is not afraid of "being real."

Discussion

I have worked in the area of psychiatric nursing for the past 20 years, and for the last two years I have worked exclusively with people who have eating disorders. I have been dramatically affected by the devastation of this illness and humbled by the courage of its victims as they recover from this disease and reclaim their lives and mental health.

Recovery from an eating disorder is based on the death of a false sense of self. This identity uses the simplified premise that control of oneself is based on control of one's food. Through the grief process the new identity—the "real self"—is born.

Eating disorders affect both sexes; however, the incidence of anorexia and bulimia in women has risen dramatically in the past 15 years. An eating disorder may be present with a concrete thinking style: black vs. white, good vs. bad, right vs. wrong. To patients with such disorders, food is no longer viewed as fuel to sustain life; rather, its control becomes the means to judge oneself. An eating disorder is also a paradoxical, symbolic disease that separates the body and the mind. When the individual becomes preoccupied with food, she is unable to identify, experience and express her needs, thoughts, feelings and physical sensations. As a result of this process the patient's body image is distorted as well.

Living with a Disability

I met Lori about two years ago. She was 32 and had spina bifida. Since then I have been Lori's primary outpatient nurse as well as her counselor and friend. She has come through many tough times; she is strong and yet vulnerable. I suspected that she had suffered many losses in her life and I asked her to tell me about them. Here is Lori's story in her words.

The biggest loss I suffered during my childhood was losing my healthy body. I remember being put into a special education school for children with disabilities. Believing I was stupid, I never talked much at school or at home. I remember feeling lonesome and friendless.

My family was not the greatest. I felt my dad treated me like an outsider. He could not accept me the way I was. I cannot remember my father ever saying he loved me or touching me in an affectionate way. He never helped me with my braces and crutches. I felt he was ashamed of me. When we walked somewhere, he would always walk ahead of me.

My brother is a little older than I am and he seemed to like me. He would playfully throw me in the snow and pretend to steal my crutches. He paid attention to me and I don't remember ever having any serious fights. When he had friends over, he would always introduce me to them before they went to his room to play.

My mom was always at home and took me to all my doctor appointments. I felt I could never do anything right for her. She yelled a lot. I do not remember her hugging or kissing me. She always wanted me to wear slacks to hide my braces. When the family was together, I never talked. I remember my folks arguing about medical bills. I wanted so much to be able to have a conversation with them, but never did.

I was expected to dress myself, straighten my room and not do much more. As far as feelings go, my parents and I never discussed them. I believed I was not supposed to have feelings and if I did, I certainly was not expected to express them.

Basically, I grew up alone and had to learn things for myself. When I was a baby, the doctors told my parents I would be a "vegetable" and that they should institutionalize me. They never thought I could become anything and did not push me to do anything. We did not go to church and I was not involved in any afterschool activities. The only "able-bodied" friend I had was a cousin who would come and play on weekends. Sometimes I stayed at her house. I enjoyed her company. When we could not get together, I spent boring weekends in front of the TV. The lack of a healthy body continued to be the loss I felt most in my teen years. I attended special education classes in a regular high school and became increasingly aware of the difference between able-bodied and disabled people. I realized I would always be accepted by the disabled, but not by the able-bodied population. I did not have the opportunity to meet able-bodied teens as friends, with the exception of a neighbor girl. We got close and did a lot of things together. My folks wanted me to meet able-bodied kids because my father could not stand having "crippled children" in his home. Dating was not even an option for me.

As I grew older I continued to feel uncomfortable with my dad. I became increasingly aware of the friction between us. We could never just sit down and have a conversation. Throughout high school, my mom still insisted that I wear slacks. She expected little from me. I never helped prepare meals or did the laundry. And I was never really taught to be of service to others.

During my high school years, my brother worked a lot, and we seemed to go our separate ways. I remember missing him and wishing I could talk to him. I was very lonely without him. Throughout high school, I was assigned two rehabilitation counselors who really helped me. They were there when I needed them and they treated me very well. I could talk with them any time. I felt valued. Then I would go home where I continued to feel stupid. Because I did not think I could learn to do things, I believed I would live at home forever. I was not steered toward gaining any vocational skills and never thought I could live independently. Toward the end of high school, some of that changed, and thanks to the counselor at the rehabilitation center, I was able to learn several independent living skills. They helped me get set up in the city and find accessible housing and job training.

As an adult, my major loss continues to be the lack of a healthy body. My parents live in California and I usually fly there at their expense once a year. Things are much better with my mom now. We can have conversations. She will listen and try to understand me. I now feel some closeness between us.

When we end our phone conversations, we both say, "I love you." Although things are still awkward with my dad, they are improving. I realize that he does not blame me for being disabled. At the end of a phone conversation this past Christmas, he said, "I love you, sweetheart." And I said, "I love you, too." It was a beginning. My brother lives far away, but we have a closer relationship nowadays. His wife is supportive and I know we could get along. They even visited me at Christmas.

I have cut myself off from most of my able-bodied friends. I feel they cannot really understand what I am going through. They expect me to listen to their problems but do not want to listen to mine. I prefer to have a few disabled friends to whom I can pour my heart out.

I have had intimate relationships with men. I was even married for a short time after I moved to the city. My husband was able-bodied. I do not consider the divorce a loss; the marriage was a mistake. Able-bodied men look at disabled women as a "new experience" and little more. I want from a man what any able-bodied woman wants, but I refuse to be with a man just because he wants to have a new experience.

To block out my fear and disappointment, I got involved in booze and drugs for a while. Because the losses often seem too great to bear, there is a very high incidence of this behavior among the disabled. I do not abuse myself like that anymore.

Today I feel several losses: not being a part of society; not having energy; not being able to be employed; not knowing if I will ever have a husband; not having a good education or adequate educational opportunities; not being able to escape low-income housing; and not having a good chance for a normal lifespan. The greatest fear I have is loneliness.

I also have a lot of good things going for me. I have a good sense of self-esteem, a good personality and I have supportive friends who listen to me. Also, my involvement in the Spina Bifida Adult Support Group is very important to me. All these things help.

Discussion

Care professionals can help clients like Lori by listening attentively. When people are encouraged to pour out their hearts, the hurt can be released and replaced by healthy coping. Counselors must understand the client's need for repeated support and encouragement. It is also important for counselors to encourage clients to pursue community service activities.

Extended involvement with a client such as Lori can lead to "burnout." In order to protect oneself from this it is imperative to include in the client's care plan "significant other" professionals, such as a clergyperson and a social worker. This creates an accessible, supportive network of trusted resource people for the client. It also helps each professional to maintain the energy necessary to provide the high level of support demanded in complex situations like Lori's.

When We Were One:
A Mother's Letter to Her Child

Dear Angela,

My love affair with you began the moment I heard that I was pregnant. I became aware of our oneness, our bond that was so intense and new. I knew our bond would grow and deepen and at times I felt overwhelmed knowing I would eventually have to let you go to be the person you were destined to be.

On the day of your birth you were a tiny, fresh, innocent baby. I said, "Welcome, I know you." Your big beautiful eyes, alert stares and tiny toes formed the all-perfect being I embraced. As I nursed and cuddled you, I knew I was starting a lifelong commitment. What an overwhelming thing it was.

Throughout our first year I could hardly leave your side. I felt your dependency and savored it. A mother-daughter love affair I can hardly describe deeply touched my inner being. Sometimes I was frightened by the responsibility of raising and caring for you. I so wanted to do everything right. I tried to protect you from any physical pain and from negative comments from others. I wanted you only to know and feel the deep love and commitment I and my close family members and friends felt for you.

Your world and mine changed as you began to crawl. I saw the excitement in your eyes as you discovered new things in your world. Eating, touching, biting and grabbing at everything you could, you displayed your intense eagerness to explore, learn and experiment. Your sense of discovery was limitless and the world was yours. I so enjoyed your energy. Yet, at the same time, I also began to see the physical things that threatened you. Pointed corners on coffee tables, plunging stairs and unchildproofed homes presented perils. I knew I could not prevent every fall or bump. That was hard for me.

Then you became even more mobile—you took your first step. I enjoyed seeing your face light up with your newfound freedom. Off you went walking and running. You reached out with eager and curious arms. A precious dependent baby had been transformed into a toddler. You were becoming your own person.

I suddenly realized that I was angry and sad. You were moving away from me physically with your walking and crawling, but in another way too. I wanted to hold and cuddle; you wanted to explore. Deep down I wanted you to spread your wings, but I was torn thinking that you didn't need me in the same way anymore.

At 14 months you seemed to decide that nursing from my breasts took too much time away from having fun. I knew I needed to say goodbye to nursing you, but I didn't want to. Stopping nursing meant accepting that you were moving on, separating from me. I felt torn, excited for you and sad for me. The intense closeness I experienced with you as a baby was changing. I needed to let go of this part of our history and relationship.

Looking back, I think I first began to let go when you were born and I pushed you into the world. With the pangs of childbirth, I said goodbye to nine months of physical communion. Then I continued to say goodbye to your dependency as you crawled, walked and developed beyond the intimacy of nursing. It hurt, but it was also exhilarating. With every goodbye, there was a hello to something new.

It is still difficult to say goodbye to those days of oneness. You're off becoming you as you learn and grow. So am I. But I will always remember and treasure that special period of time when you were one with me.

Living with the Loss of Sight

I had been a diabetic since I was 11. Then, when I was 27, I developed diabetic retinopathy. I was driving down a busy thoroughfare during rush hour when I suffered a retinal hemorrhage. It was frightening because I was driving and didn't know what was happening. Very soon after that it was confirmed that I had a complication of diabetes that would change my life drastically.

I was terrified. My life was falling apart around me, and I didn't know how I was going to hold it together. At the time I said I would not allow my illness to make me give up certain things. My work in a pediatric intensive care unit was the most important thing to me. In my mind I felt that my job wasn't negotiable. Little did I realize that illness does not negotiate; there is no compromise. You aren't in control.

The hardest part of living with this disability was my uncertainty about the future. I didn't know what was going to happen. I didn't know how bad my vision would become. I wanted desperately to hold onto the sight I had, but I knew that that wouldn't be possible. I felt that my sight was central to my life, my identity and my career, and that everything was slipping away. What was ahead seemed to be nothingness. I could not imagine anything that would fulfill me as much as intensive care nursing. I wanted to help sick children. I would have been willing to do things that were difficult or demanding just to maintain my career, but it seemed increasingly probable that I would have to give it up.

I am a person who values independence, making my own choices and having control over my own life. I continued to fight for that independence, but despite my efforts to do what the doctors advised, and the care of a very fine, dedicated ophthalmologist, my eye disease progressed. I realized that if I lost my job I would have no way of supporting myself, and would most likely lose my home. My vision soon became so poor that I had to give up driving.

Within approximately six months my independence, my autonomy (the

239

cornerstone of my identity) and my nursing career were all gone. I no longer saw myself as a healthy, normal person. I had known that my diabetes would be a chronic problem, but up until this time it had not changed my life. I guess I had assumed that if I took care of my body it would take care of me, and I would be guaranteed a reasonably healthy lifestyle. I know now that this is not the case.

So I moved back with my parents. This was extremely difficult. For years I'd been an adult able to care for myself. I felt like I was regressing. It was like I needed to start my life over again without knowing where it was going. I didn't know if I could do that, if I could find something that would be as fulfilling or as rewarding as my previous career. I felt very much adrift. I was truly in a crisis for the first time in my life.

I didn't work for almost two years. As is common for people with my type of retinopathy, I experienced further hemorrhages periodically. Then, six months after the retinopathy occurred, I developed glaucoma. I became very ill very suddenly and had to have emergency surgery to relieve the pressure and (I hoped) save my sight. Again I felt out of control.

Some friends and clergy suggested I just give up my career and sit at home. Initially, I was frightened that they were right. Because I was losing my sight, I felt I was losing my identity and all my individual uniqueness. Because I saw my career as an indicator of my accomplishment as a person, when I began to lose it, I began to lose faith in myself.

Some of my closest friends no longer came around. I was surprised and hurt. Many were professional health care providers and should have understood. Now I see that they were probably very frightened themselves. Somehow, professionals in health care seem to think they are immune to disease and disaster. I think they may have thought that if it could happen to me, it could happen to them. I understand them now, but I was terribly disappointed at the time. Perhaps it was self-protective, but I felt that if these people in my life couldn't support me, I'd move on and find people who could. And that's what I did.

I began to conjure up a mental image of life as a parade. For a long time I just sat back and watched. Though I was invited by people to join in, they were actually too busy to bother with me. In some ways, it was easier to just sit back. Then I realized that it was up to me alone to join or be a bystander. Once I realized that I still had choices and options, my life became easier. I became aware that I was responsible for what happened to me, whether I had vision or not. It was I who had to deal with my loss so I could get on with my life. So I got busy and spent a lot of time in rehabilitation. I had to learn how to function without sight in daily living. I learned braille, and how to maneuver with a cane. I began to investigate what career options were there for me.

I knew I wanted to continue working with children in some capacity. Therefore, I enrolled in a graduate program in social work on the advice of several professionals who told me that, without vision, nursing was no longer an option.

While I enjoyed the challenge of graduate school, I realized that I was getting restless. I felt I could contribute in the field of social work, but that it might not meet my emotional needs. After asking myself the question, "Is this something you will regret the rest of your life?" and answering "Yes," I realized I had to get back into nursing. I had no idea whether I'd be successful, but I knew I had to try.

After I finished my master's in social work, I entered a graduate program in child psychiatric nursing with the intent of working with sick children and their families, helping them with the emotional issues of illness. I felt that this course of study would be the best way to use my experience both professionally and personally. Doing this work would help to fill the gap caused by leaving my original career. I did not view changing my specialty as a compromise, but rather as a way of applying what I knew best.

After completing graduate school, I went into private practice. That was OK for a while, but I missed having colleagues. I decided to apply around the country for a different position. I recall a job interview in which the interviewer unknowingly stripped me of my identity. She surveyed my resume and said, "You really *had* a very impressive career," but she didn't offer me the job. I felt like shouting, "I didn't lose those skills when I lost my sight. I am a composite of all my experiences." Other interviewers rejected me without the pretense of a compliment.

Finally, I made a call to inquire about another position and was told, "You're just what we're looking for." They hired me and I love the job. My skills are used and appreciated. Returning to nursing has not only reaffirmed my identity but it has helped me grow and keep going. I know that I can live with this loss.

Living with the loss of my sight has forced me to deal with having to give up things that were very important to me. It was a very maturing experience and made me push myself to take responsibility for my life in a way I'd never done before. It forced me to identify what was truly important to me and what I could and could not live without. Though I experienced situations that were extremely disheartening, I was able to find strength that I never knew I had. This strength continuously reassures me that I can endure almost anything and keep going.

Requiescat in Not So Pace:
Life After Job Loss

Suddenly, for the first time in my life, I didn't have a job and no prospects of getting one. The factory I used to manage was about to close. The closing of a large factory is like a funeral, only worse. It affects so many people.

As with many funerals, this one was predicted well in advance. We all knew about the closing seven months before the final date and we all knew we would be terminated. I am over 55, so my dismissal was classified as "early retirement." As a manager I was chosen to be one of the leaders in charge of the employees' unhappiness and this put me in the position of being the funeral director and one of the bereaved at the same time.

I had done some personal accounting prior to the announcement of the closing. My family's financial affairs seemed to be in reasonable order, but I was not physically or emotionally ready for retirement, "early" or otherwise. So I made inquiries with several headhunters about job openings. They replied that my age would be a fatal flaw in the eyes of prospective employers. They told me that these employers could not legally discriminate because of age but that they would give some other reason for not hiring me.

The final day of work came. Like many bad things associated with American industry and its fiscal timetables, it happened close to Christmas. Two weeks later my wife Mary and I took a vacation. We had a lot of time to think on the long ride to Philadelphia. I began to feel the reality of what had happened: a chapter in our lives was over. My realization was gradual at first, then accelerated like a gut-tearing roller coaster, a wild ride going nowhere. I felt a sudden and terrible loss. During the time I had worked over the past 25 years, I had known pleasures reserved for only a few. I had been secure—with status and prestige. These things, along with the respect I had earned, were now gone. I would no longer experience the thrill of being involved in making major decisions.

Throughout the entire trip, these truths washed over me, drowning me in a sea of fear. I did not want to accept my situation as it was, but I was not sure what to do. As the reality of what happened hit me, I got very good at self-pity.

After the trip I knew I had to do something, for Mary's sake as much as mine. But what? I had spent my life working in a profession that was now closed to me. Other than a few technical and social organization member- ships and a few very minor hobbies, my life had been my family and my job. When I had needed work in the past, I had found jobs through executive recruiters. I was now as welcome in their offices as a seasick mother-in-law on a honeymoon cruise, but I wasn't sure I wanted to go on a full-scale, and possibly fruitless, job search on my own either. What other alternatives were there?

I read and talked to many human resource "experts" about making the adjustment to not having a job. I also talked with the state employment service people. That day was a sobering trip to the real world. Most of the counselors I was referred to only restated the obvious to me. They were not really attuned to my problem. Their financial planning counsel was the same that could be found on the business pages of any newspaper. They offered great retirement planning programs, provided the candidate was not over 38 years old. They had no career advice beyond the cerebral blockbuster to "find something you've always wanted to do." I told one of them that Loni Anderson was already married. He did not smile.

Cynicism and melancholy were turning me negative about everything and I became difficult to live with. About this time, I remembered something one of the "experts" had said that had made sense: "Your best source of help in locating another job is your friends." I had one close friend who knew me well. We had many long talks and began to sort out my problems and options.

I don't want to sound like I have all the answers to what, unfortunately, is becoming a much more widespread problem than many people realize, because I don't. What I did might not work for everyone, but it did help me over one of the highest hurdles in my life. It's not really very complicated: my friend and I approached the replacement of my job like a business problem.

The first step was to redefine my situation. I needed to realize that what had happened was not a plot against me by the rest of the human race. When I changed my thinking I felt less angry and stopped feeling sorry for myself. Secondly, I listed my options and looked at the facets of my problem. Because my wife and I were solvent and likely to stay that way and because we had moved a lot in the past and did not relish doing it again, we decided not to investigate jobs that would require moving again. Initially we eliminated any kind of job-hunting as an option, though we knew that might be a plan for later. Instead, I made a list of other options and tried a few.

First I tried doing private consulting work. I did not enjoy that, however, because it felt like being a coach instead of a player. Then I tried teaching. That was OK, but an awful lot of work for someone who wasn't interested in adding to his resume. I also became involved with SCORE (the Service Corps of Retired Executives). It is beneficial to the community, but it didn't take up enough of my time. Lastly, I became involved with technical societies. This experience was a keeper! I had always belonged to such groups but had never been very active in them. After the factory closing, I was elected to an office and gave it a lot of time. I became involved with the things I enjoyed, people I liked, and I was doing something useful.

Even though I had these activities, I still needed something I could do on my own schedule that would demand attention, require effort, pose a challenge, require lots of work, and include discipline and rejection. I found a new occupation: writing.

I still remember that first conversation with my wife about it. "You've tried consulting and teaching and don't care for that. You've always enjoyed writing and have had a few things published. You always said you'd do it if you had the time. Now you've got the time."

"The idea of writing bothers me."

"Why?"

"I keep thinking that to get published, I'll have to get past some 22-year-old university graduate who is polishing her nails and 'editing' my work. She'll know about as much about its content as a tomcat does about virtue, but I'll have to kiss her butt to get the work by her."

"Unless you try it, you'll never know whether or not you'll like it."

"You sound like my mother trying to get me to eat vegetables."

So I decided to try it. I haven't written a sequel to *War and Peace,* but I've had a few things accepted for publication. It's frustrating to see inferior work published and it's challenging to read your work to other writers. It's damn annoying to hear your work criticized and more annoying to know the criticisms are right. Writing is like my job used to be, except I am only responsible for me and that I like.

My solutions to losing my job are not panaceas. They may not work for a lot of people. Even so, my story may make a contribution. The displaced, over-55-year-old middle manager is a growing species, and he (for this is still largely a male problem) has to find a useful outlet for his experience, energy and talent. The solutions I found worked, at least they did for me.

Betrayal of a Dream:
The Loss of Trust

Most people think of loss in terms of people or things we value. Seldom do we consider that the loss of ideas and dreams can be just as devastating as other losses. The loss of a dream together with the loss of trust in others can evoke intense grief responses such as mourning, anger, self-recrimination and self-loathing. Though I had taught others about grief, and had helped others to grieve, I did not anticipate the intensity of my emotions until I experienced the loss of my dream.

My dream was to administer a unique educational program. After some years, this dream was realized when I accepted a position as dean of a baccalaureate program in nursing at a medical college. During my initial days on the job, I was subjected to the usual scrutiny that one bears when entering a new system. There were the usual rumors, doubts and exaggerations about me and my abilities. They quickly faded, however, when people saw I was committed to the program and to making it work.

I felt closer to realizing my dream when, after receiving approval from state and regional boards, the school of nursing entered the second and final stage of the accreditation process. Without outside funding, our program would require financial assistance from the medical college for a lengthy period of time. I asked the administration to assist me in approaching donors to the college to obtain monies to subsidize the program. The administration assured me that there was no need for concern; they would assume the responsibility for supporting the program. The administration even went so far as to publicly proclaim their support and to announce their future intention to develop a doctoral program.

For many reasons I was not entirely comfortable with the president's statements of support, but I thought I needed to trust him if I wanted to continue to work in administration. I tend to be somewhat skeptical, perhaps for good reasons. But taking all things into consideration, my job and the program were going exceptionally well. For the first time in over 30 years I was working in an environment in which faculty were truly committed to their work and the students were enthusiastic and satisfied. Personnel in other health care agencies complimented the program and provided financial support for the initial programs.

The last hurdle in the accreditation process was an on-site visit and review by the professional organization that accredits nursing programs. Preparation for such a visit is very time-consuming and costly. It was necessary to submit a comprehensive report on the finances and curriculum of the program and, just as a precaution, I hired a consultant to review it. Her credentials were excellent. When she reviewed our report, she was extremely complimentary about our curriculum, but informed me that our organizational structure seemed weak. She also said that our full-time faculty complement might be too low to meet accreditation standards.

I shared the consultant's report with the president who agreed to provide additional faculty slots. Any changes in organizational structure were to be postponed until the time of the final report from the accreditors.

I felt the accreditation visit went well. Afterwards, the accreditation visitors read their report to us. In it they listed the strengths of the program as well as their recommendations for change. We were led to believe, however, that these recommendations were not an indication that accreditation might be denied.

But the accreditation panel saw the situation differently. They cited many deficiencies not assessed by the visitors and denied us accreditation. The lack of the college's financial and organizational support was their primary reason for denial. The college decided to appeal the decision and hired one of the best law firms in the city. After the appeal, however, accreditation was still denied.

Soon thereafter, the college administration decided to withhold admissions to the nursing school, pending what they called "an assessment of the situation." I was told that priorities were being reassessed and that there was serious doubt as to whether the college had the financial resources to support the program.

I doubted the college's claim of financial distress. The vice-president of finance was instituting a plan to install a million-dollar computer system to handle the business affairs of the college and a $12 million research facility was about to be built. I could not believe that the nursing program was to be closed for these reasons. Still, the administration withheld admissions.

My first reaction was not shock or disbelief because I had always had doubts about the vows of support from the administration and the physicians. Instead, I was angry at these people for betraying my trust. Yet I turned some of my anger inward. Why hadn't I trusted my intuition? Why hadn't I trusted my peer group of nurses? They had warned me not to join forces with the physician "enemy." The prejudice that nurses sometimes have toward physicians no longer seemed based in fantasy. My peers had been right and I was wrong. The patriarchal institution had not stood behind its largely female nursing program. But, more importantly, I had been unsuccessful in changing the "enemy." In that sense I had been responsible for failing to achieve what I had dreamed. This kept me from being angry only at the physicians.

My anger was also directed toward some of my fellow nurses. There was good evidence that some had given the doctors the ammunition to drop us. I felt betrayed by both groups but refused to admit the loss I felt. I rationalized that although losing the program was bad, at least I had my health. People reinforced my denial by complimenting me on how well I was handling things. My ego would not let me do anything but deny.

I began experiencing a myriad of physical symptoms. I was unable to sleep, gained weight, had little energy and found it a burden to participate in social activities. I had all the symptoms of depression.

I also declined lucrative job offers. Though I realized the finality of the closure decision, I wanted to "hang on to the corpse until it was buried." I stayed with the program until the end, some two years after the announcement of the closure. When the doors of the school finally closed, I lost not only my dream, but my office and secretary as well.

I subsequently took a position as a faculty member in the school of nursing at a state university, but there were several periods in my first week on the job when my feeling of loss was reactivated. One occurred when I first saw the sparse, drab furnishings of my new office and the lack of secretarial support. I became frustrated and angry when I sat in meetings where my new colleagues looked for answers to problems that the staff at my old school had already solved. I became a passive participant rather than the committed, active individual I had been in my previous position.

When I left my dream job, I took with me a few mementoes of my stay at the college. One was the certificate from the state board of nursing. When I was asked to return it, I was immediately incensed. My first reaction was to deny I had it. But I still felt so angry and betrayed that I did neither. Then I decided I'd xerox it, so I could keep a copy. Instead I just waited. I realized clinging to the certificate was a way of denying my loss. Some time later I finally decided I didn't need it anymore and returned it by mail.

Losing my dream job was not the only consequence of my experience with the administration of the medical college. In my professional life, I found that betrayal had altered my ability to trust others and was skewing my judgment. In further contractual agreements I became very cautious, consulting attorneys even about minor matters. I wanted to make sure I wouldn't be "taken" again.

Because I was in my late forties, my unsuccessful experience intensified other crises of this stage in my life. I found myself fixated on my lost job, the betrayal and my sense of helplessness. I felt overwhelmed.

I entered counseling. I looked at why I was stuck and what I wanted to do with the rest of my life. More importantly I looked at the possibilities that now existed for me *because* the school had closed. Some people would call this rationalization; I call it enhancement.

Instead of getting back at those who had hurt me, I learned it was more productive for me to get even. Getting even meant creating opportunities from my loss. I've become involved in several creative projects that will further me personally and professionally.

It's been well over a year since they closed the doors of the school. I still feel fleeting periods of sadness. But now my hope in the possibilities for the future overrides the sadness.

Too Much to Do,
Too Little Time

Mary

I walk into the intensive care unit and immediately see all the tubes, IVs and monitors, devices that are sustaining the lives of infants and young children. I'm here to see Mary and later I will meet her mother. When I look into Mary's crib, she looks weak and fragile. Mary was born with numerous complications including respiratory problems and a serious heart disorder. She is not even three months old and she has already had several surgeries. Her parents, both only 18 years old, are not married. I am a social worker with a large metropolitan social services agency. My job is to arrange the resources and equipment that these young parents will need when they take Mary home.

I leave the ICU and walk to a small, stuffy room where Mary's mother is waiting. She looks younger than her 18 years, yet responds to me as though she is a veteran of the hospital scene. In the last few months she has had to learn about tracheotomy care, ventilators and monitors. We begin by discussing Mary's current physical condition and which services and equipment she will need once she is discharged. The mother is excited about the prospect of Mary coming home, but both of us realize that we have to discuss what they will need to take care of Mary. Can she and her husband find affordable housing with enough electrical outlets to handle Mary's equipment? Will her insurance cover rental or purchase of the equipment? Do they have any friends or relatives who can learn Mary's care routine and give them a break from what will be a round-the-clock job of caring for Mary? How many hours of in-home nursing care will their insurance cover? I noticed that both of us have avoided talking directly about our feelings for Mary.

Mary is not the perfect child her parents were expecting. In fact, they were surprised to be expecting a child at all. But they have no time to cry or wonder what it would have been like if Mary had been born without problems. They are overwhelmed by Mary's immediate needs. These teenage parents suddenly found themselves having to make some major life decisions. Their grief is obvious—I can see it and I can feel it—yet no one, including them, acknowledges it.

The practical issues are worked out. In six weeks, Mary will go home with her parents, but what are we supposed to do with the grief that we both feel? I carry some of it with me as I leave the hospital and Mary's mother carries it with her as she walks into the intensive care unit. We both got through the meeting without facing the pain. It was our first meeting and it seems as if it's too intimate a topic to discuss right now. Besides, the practical issues took up most of the time.

Two months later, Mary is ready to leave the hospital. Her parents are excited to have her come home and all the necessary services are in place. Two weeks later, Mary dies unexpectedly. I talk to her mother on the telephone. This time it is somehow easier to communicate. We talk about Mary's death. Maybe it's easier to talk about death than the loss of the mother's hopes and expectations when Mary was born.

Tony

Later that day, I go to visit Tony, another patient on my caseload. Tony is in his late teens but he looks like he's 12. He is severely disabled by a rare disorder that has already taken the life of one of his brothers, epidermolysis belosa, a disease that causes painful skin lesions and ulcers, anemia and at times—as in Tony's case—congestive heart failure. I've been drawn to Tony ever since I first met him. He has an engaging personality and is friendly and outgoing even in the face of his physical pain. When I first met him, I was shocked by the sight of large sores and raw spots on his body. He cannot walk, dress or bathe himself. In fact, attempting to manage any semblance of a normal life is a continually challenging effort.

I'm visiting Tony and his mother today to discuss the need for additional in-home services. When I arrive at their house, Tony is wrapped in blankets and lying curled up on the couch. He has recently come home from the hospital after developing serious heart problems. His breathing is labored and he is drifting in and out of a semi-sleep state. This sight draws me into a memory of my own painful adolescent years even though it was a different kind of pain that was not deadly and could be diminished. I come back to the moment. Tony's pain is deadly and it cannot be diminished. I discuss with his mom the details of the various services that they can use. She is pleased that further assistance is available.

As I leave, I ask Tony if there is anything else he needs or wants. I feel foolish. He says, "No, there's nothing I can think of." What I have to offer cannot lessen his fear or pain. I'm hoping there's something he wants that I can give. I feel a need to comfort him and also comfort myself. When I leave I tell him I'll see him soon, even though I don't really know if this is true. I don't know how much longer he will live. I get into my car, ready for my next home visit. I'd like a chance to cry just for a few minutes and a moment to remind myself that I cannot control whether Mary, Tony or anyone lives or dies. I move on to the next client without being able to do this.

Mark

This is a new referral. The mother called to seek assistance in caring for her eight-year-old, severely retarded and physically disabled son. I enter their house and am greeted by two young children who are playing and running around the house. A third child, Mark, is lying on a mat in a corner of the room. The TV is blaring two feet from him but he is not paying attention to it. I greet the mother and she points to the corner, looks at me and states that the "little monster" is over there. I bend over, stroke the child's hand and arm and say hello. There is no response, no eye contact.

I sit down, ready to begin gathering information about Mark and determining the assistance that he and his family might need. Mark's mother picks him up and drapes him over her arm. She sits down and continues to hold him as far away from her as possible. She begins the conversation by telling me that she's pregnant again and doesn't want another child. She looks at me for a moment and I wonder if she's waiting for me to express sympathy or outrage. I begin discussing Mark. We talk for a while about varying aspects of his needs, the family's needs and their life together. While we're talking, the two younger children play on the other side of the room. They are smiling and laughing. There is a big contrast between them and Mark; he shows little reaction to anything.

I discuss services that are available to families with disabled children, but the mother resists all of my suggestions; she has an excuse for why each one of them won't work. She continues to express her displeasure that Mark's needs make it impossible for her even to take her other children to the park. I slowly realize that I've not been listening to what she is trying to tell me. She's angry. She doesn't want a "little monster." She doesn't want another child. She doesn't want to hear that there are possibilities for making things a little better. She doesn't want me to help. She wants me to hear her outrage, her disbelief, her sorrow.

Discussion

The program I work with is designed to meet the long-term care needs of severely disabled adults and children in their family homes. Everyone's situations and circumstances and needs are different. Issues of physical and mental disabilities discrimination, poverty, substandard housing, inadequate medical care, lack of insurance, family dysfunction, abuse, neglect and inaccessibility of services all become part of what must be dealt with before we can even begin looking at providing other services. It is sometimes an overwhelming task to meet even the most basic survival needs of clients. Only after these basic needs are met can we begin to help improve the quality of their lives through community services.

It is not easy to face the issues of loss and grief in the midst of what sometimes seems to be total chaos. For clients and nurses alike, there is little time and limited resources for assistance in this area. There is also no conventional outlet for or acknowledgment of the grief and loss we suffer as part of our work. When a client dies, we keep on going without processing our pain, because there is a never-ending list of new clients. Our own thoughts, feelings and needs, along with those of our clients, tend to be neglected in an effort to "get the job done." But is the job ever really done?